psw
26. 2. 08

Social Work
and
Well-being

Bill Jordan

RHP

Russell House Publishing

Published in 2007 by:
Russell House Publishing Ltd.
4 St. George's House
Uplyme Road
Lyme Regis
Dorset DT7 3LS

Tel: 01297-443948
Fax: 01297-442722
e-mail: help@russellhouse.co.uk
www.russellhouse.co.uk

British Library Cataloguing-in-publication Data:

A catalogue record for this book is available from the British Library.

ISBN: 978-1-905541-13-3

Typeset by TW Typesetting, Plymouth, Devon

Printed by HSW Print, Tonypandy, 01443 441100

About Russell House Publishing

Russell House Publishing aims to publish innovative and valuable materials to help managers, practitioners, trainers, educators and students.

Our full catalogue covers: social policy, working with young people, helping children and families, care of older people, social care, combating social exclusion, revitalising communities and working with offenders.

Full details can be found at www.russellhouse.co.uk and we are pleased to send out information to you by post. Our contact details are on this page.

We are always keen to receive feedback on publications and new ideas for future projects.

Contents

About the Author

Bill Jordan worked in the social services for 20 years, as a front-line practitioner, and has since done research and consultancy for several agencies. He has written some 25 books, on social work, social and political theory, migration, social policy and political economy. He has held visiting chairs in Germany, the Netherlands, Denmark, Slovakia, Hungary, the Czech Republic and Australia, and is currently Professor of Social Policy at Plymouth and Huddersfield Universities, and Reader in Social Policy at London Metropolitan University.

Acknowledgements

I would like to thank Nigel Parton for helpful comments on the first draft of this book, and Gordon Jack for stimulating conversations which pointed me towards some of its key themes.

I also appreciated and learned from working with Martyn Rogers, Linus Whitton and other colleagues, and with the members of a focus group on social care, whom I thank for giving their permission to quote from their discussions.

I am especially grateful to Rachel Arnold for typing the manuscript of the book very efficiently and quickly, and for insights about several aspects of the subject.

Introduction: The Value of Social Work

From a high point in the early 1970s, when social work seemed to be the rising star of the human service professions, social workers have experienced a decline in public esteem. Practitioners feel devalued by the media and politicians, even when they are well appreciated by those who use their services. Their expertise and effectiveness are constantly questioned, and they are blamed for notorious scandals, especially over abused children.

This book analyses the largely overlooked value of social work, and shows how it could be increased, and made more evident to sceptics. I shall argue that the profession itself has fallen into many traps in response to criticism, and has underplayed its strengths. This is because it has accepted a false standard by which to measure its value to service users and society.

In professions like medicine, teaching and clinical psychology, the value of practitioners' work is usually measured in terms of the restoration of patients to healthy functioning, the knowledge and skill imparted, and the relief of burdensome symptoms.

This in turn is translated into higher productivity, and hence income, by those who benefit from these services. The outcomes show up in Gross National Product (GNP) – doctors, teachers and psychologists can demonstrate the value realised by their work in hard material terms.

But there is another whole contribution that these services make which is not always recorded or recognised. Good health care, school experiences and therapy make people *feel good*. Even if they are only partially cured, they pass few exams, and are still slightly screwed up, feeling better about themselves and their lives is of real value to them.

This added value, on top of the technical expertise which contributes to material improvement, does not show up in national accounts, but it is real and substantial.

Social work contributes to both these kinds of value. Practitioners do protect children, keep families together, maintain old people in their homes and help in the recovery of those who abuse drugs and alcohol. They also play a part in enabling people with disabilities and mental illnesses to be included in the economy and society.

But, perhaps more than the other human services professions, their work involves a form of practice which aims to get people to feel better about themselves. This is the value of social work which will be emphasised in this book.

Sceptics will, of course, be dismissive of this 'feel-good factor' – social workers as cheerleaders and entertainers – but they should not be. This is because (at last) the value of feeling good about life is being recognised as a fundamental goal of government policies, and of the human services. Politicians now deploy the terms 'well-being' and 'happiness' as buzzwords, and seek advantage for their parties by trying to capture the ground of positive feelings.

Surprisingly, the lead in this re-valuation of emotions and relationships is being taken by economists, notoriously the most hard-nosed of the social scientific community. Modern economics has gained predominance in this community because of its ability to explain and predict from mathematical models, and hence to inform commercial and government decisions. By excluding nebulous human factors such as emotions and relationships from the vast bulk of its analysis, economics is able to construct a working model of how individual choices translate into a global system of production, trade and governance.

The basis for this model is that, whatever people may happen to be feeling about themselves and each other, they will earn and spend in ways which allow them to consume bundles of goods and services that maximise their 'utility'. This means that, however they choose (between income and leisure, spending or saving, Orange or iPods) they will make the best of their resources. So, according to the economic model which now underpins almost all present societies, and the global system of production and trade, we can rely on money and prices as reliable guides to well-being, because people will earn and spend in the ways that make them happiest.

Now leading economists (especially in the USA and UK) are drawing on psychological evidence from all over the world which rebuts this assumption. There is no reliable correlation between a country's national income per head and the average satisfaction of its population with the quality of their lives (Kahneman et al., 1999; Helliwell, 2003; Frey and Stutzer, 2002). Some rather poor countries, such as Ghana, have citizens who assess their overall happiness almost as highly as the inhabitants of affluent countries. Some with middle-ranking levels of national income per head, such as Malta and Uruguay, are also high in league tables of well-being (BBC Radio 4, 2006a). Although rich people in any country tend to be happier than poor ones, the most important components of well-being are health, close relationships, being active in a faith or community, satisfying work and trust in fellow-citizens. Not the latest fashion items or electronic wizardry.

This survey evidence confirms what most social workers see every day in their practice. People's unhappiness is far more connected to their physical and mental health, and their relationships with others, than to their material circumstances. What hurts about being poor is not so much the absence of comforts and luxuries, but the stigma of official surveillance, the contempt of mainstream citizens, the exclusion from civil associations, and the damage to personal relations. Survival strategies are stressful because they have to be pursued against the current of society's complacent assumptions about its own integrity and deservingness.

But social workers never expected these realities to be recognised by economists, of all people. It will come as a surprise to read the soul-searching and self-criticism of leading economic theorists like Richard Layard (2005: i) who calls for a new approach to public policy which promotes the common good, and for 'a shift to a new perspective where people's feelings are paramount'. So will the widespread media acclaim for Avner Offer's (2006) economic history of 'self-control and well-being in Britain and the United States', which laments the decay of commitment and mutuality in the face of affluence and individualism. And these best-selling texts are comple-mented by collections of equally critical reflection on their fundamental assumptions by top economists in edited volumes (Bruni and Porta, 2005; Huppert, Baylis and Keverne, 2005).

So the time is right for a re-assertion of the value of social work, not in terms that echo the demands of accountants, managers and government ministers, but in its own terms. Economists are calling for other social scientists and human service profes-sionals to complement their new insights and shift public policy towards the priorities of well-being and quality of life (Layard, 2005: 145–7). But to do this, social work must first recognise its own potential worth and contribution.

Two objections

Already, I imagine, two objections to my agenda are springing to the reader's mind. First, the return to a justification of social work activity in terms of relationships and feelings seems to throw away hard-won gains in effectiveness, rigour and value-for-money. The past 15 years have seen a major shift towards evidence-based practice in the profession (and in health care too) along with a style of management which demands such evidence before a project or priority is funded.

The advocates for these approaches (Sheldon, 2001; Macdonald and Sheldon, 2000) would argue that, although they are resisted by much of the profession, they have purged it of many of its past illusions and errors. Social work was its own worst enemy during the period of its rapid expansion in the 1970s, because its claims were both vague and grandiose. The social work which has emerged from recent waves of reform and modernisation as well as the redesign of training, is leaner and more competent, street-wise about how to gain political endorsement, and better able to engage with other human service professions.

However, social work is also tied into a particular approach to governance and policy, derived first from Margaret Thatcher's neo-liberal version of public administra-tion, and then Tony Blair's New Labour reformism. Under the latter regime of micro-management, government has set very detailed targets and outcomes, and specified quality in terms of statistical returns. This version of value for taxpayers' money rests on a set of assumptions and principles about the social order which are coming under question. The well-being agenda reflects the beginning of a shift away from individualism, choice, markets and mobility which have driven the transformation of citizenship and public life in the past 25 years (Jordan, 2004, 2006a, Part II).

For social work to be seen to be indissolubly linked with the Third Way agenda might be very damaging in the medium to long term. Already there are strong signs that the consensus of the late 1990s is breaking up, and new political forces are being mobilised. Social work's somewhat contorted and strained efforts to present itself as fully in line with New Labour's modernisation programme will look silly if Tony Blair's project continues to wane.

Above all, the future seems to lie in some new combination of environmental awareness, a revival of respect and mutuality amid ethnic diversity, and a convincing version of our collective quality of life (both globally and nationally). In the face of these challenges, the emphasis on individual consumption and self-expression, and the reliance on big business to deliver personal fulfilment, look dated. In the first sphere, New Labour is beginning to sound like stale news; in the second it seems rather seedy, or even corrupt.

This is where David Cameron has displayed considerable gifts as a politician, capturing the new agendas with a series of eye-catching speeches. Even if the claim to this political ground by a party which pioneered individualism, choice and greed seems implausible, Cameron is shifting the debate to a less explored territory. Above all, he has reintroduced many of the themes in which an older style of social work seems more relevant.

In a speech on 22 May 2006, in Hertfordshire he linked the different aspects of his platform in the following passage:

> It's time we admitted that there's more to life than money, and it's time we focused not on GDP (Gross Domestic Product) but on GWB – General Well-being . . . It is about the beauty of our surroundings, the quality of our culture and above all the strength of our relationships. There is a deep satisfaction which comes from belonging to some one and some place. There comes a point when you can't keep on choosing and have to commit.

(Cameron, 2006)

These themes resonate with social work's concerns about quality of life rather than material consumption or the work ethic. They also contrast with New Labour's emphasis on individual self-responsibility. The government's Green Paper: _Our Vision of the Future of Social Care for Adults in England, Independence, Well-being and Choice_ (DoH, 2005) linked life-quality with self-sufficiency and mobility between options. Cameron cleverly detached well-being from those associations, and challenged the government (and the human service professions) to think again. Even if this was political opportunism, it has moved the debate about society's priorities forward.

Cameron's critics, and those suspicious of any such agenda for social work, will point to the vagueness in his rhetoric. These ideas imply no particular policy agenda or resource allocation. In social work, the drift back into fuzzy concepts like 'relationships' and 'feelings' threatens a loss of intellectual rigour and scientific edge.

In this book, I shall rebut this accusation. The value of social work can never be adequately represented in terms of gains in independence, choice or economic functioning. It will always undersell itself unless it can define and assert its value in the emotional, social and communal spheres of life. But this does not imply cosiness or woolliness. The fact that economists are seeking to analyse these same phenomena indicates a clear opportunity to treat these dimensions of experience with the same clarity of explanation as the material sphere.

This leads to the second objection (also implicit in the adoption of these themes by David Cameron), that the links between nature's beauty, our cultural legacy and the bonds of emotion and belonging, are all inescapably rural, backward-looking and conservative in their ambience. Is this not Old Tory territory – the stuff of writers like Michael Oakeshott, and the One Nation tradition of Disraeli, Churchill and Harold Macmillan (Kettle, 2006)?

Worse still, is not the idea of social work as inducing warm feelings a clear instance of its oiling the wheels of injustice and exploitation, making poor, excluded and oppressed people content with their lot? Is this not a prescription of Prozac or Mogadon for society – social work as tranquiliser or sleeping pill?

Again, I shall seek to argue against this conclusion in this book. What makes people feel good about themselves is complex. People assess their overall happiness in relation to their life-projects, and their situation in society. They are mostly not content with passivity and stagnation, and social work could not induce them to accept this fate if it tried. Individuals may not all want to struggle for Aristotle's 'eudaimonia' (full development, of all their faculties) or Milton's 'strenuous liberty', or to be Wordsworth's 'Happy Warrior' (Nussbaum, 2005) but nor do they willingly embrace injustice and marginalisation.

Indeed, the greater challenge for social workers is how they can shift themselves and service users beyond present-day concerns with material consumption and instrumental outcomes. In a culture of choice and self-expression, well-being demands a balance in the form of emotional closeness, respect and collective solidarity. These are not inherently conservative values, rather the issue should be how to give them a radical new connection with the concepts of justice, inclusion and diversity.

Value and values

In the course of trying to clarify the value of social work, I shall also tackle some of the knotty problems in social work theory. One of the most longstanding is the question of how practitioners reconcile conflicts between the 'subjective' world of their client's experiences, and the 'objective' demands of society (the law, regulations, guidance and procedures).

This issue becomes clearest in relation to protecting children from abuse, and using compulsory power to protect others (or themselves) from people with acute mental illnesses. Whole libraries are filled with books and articles on the ethics and practice principles of these functions. Yet there is always something unfinished and unsatisfactory in the formulae which emerge from such analyses. Whether they favour respecting people's personal experiences and choices or enforcing society's rules, they seem to be missing the process by which good practice can dissolve their apparent contradiction, and help those involved come to a resolution of their conflicts.

At the heart of these disputes in social work theory is the inescapable fact that practitioners have an ethical duty to respect people's individuality, yet also a legal responsibility to enforce society's standards (including the protection of persons and their property). What are called the profession's 'values' feature both the fundamental worth of each person who has contact with a service, and the duty to protect all from avoidable harm. Confusingly, these values co-exist with commitments to fight against oppression and injustice in wider social relations (BASW, 2003).

One of the clearest recent accounts of these dilemmas is in Michael Sheppard's *Social Exclusion and Social Work* (2006). He takes issue with subjectivists, relativists and interpretivists who opt for service users' rights to set their own agendas and assert their own values, where others' vital interests are at stake. Sheppard argues persuasively that there are sometimes objective standards of need and the prevention of harm in practice situations, and that these cannot be suspended or sidelined for the sake of greater understanding, empathy, therapy or creativeness.

But this does not entirely explain how the value of abusers, offenders or mentally ill people is preserved, or their 'values' respected. Sheppard explains that social workers have a duty to negotiate with all parties as rational agents, but to overrule those who cannot recognise or act upon the vital interest of others. The law and regulations define the responsibilities of citizens in terms of rationality, and the harms to be avoided where possible. Social workers should seek to recognise both the external constraints on people, and the limitations of their internal resources, and then engage with them as fully and 'democratically' as these allow (Sheppard, 2006: 116–20).

But it is in the nature of this engagement that something is missing from Sheppard's analysis. While there are crucial decisions to be negotiated and made at the level of rationality and the law, there is another whole dimension of the encounter between persons. This concerns the value of each individual, and how this value is then brought into each human interaction, and either enhanced or diminished.

The value statement that 'each individual is of equal worth' is the fundamental ethical principle, not just of social work, but also of liberal democracy. All the other 'values' of the profession, and of our political system, follow from this first one. But this is not simply a negative liberty, prohibiting social workers or others from encroaching on a service user's freedom and self-ownership. It also asserts that each person adds something to the collective value that makes up a society. How each person does so is through their interactions with others, in various social units, from families to social movements and political parties. These interactions create extra value (though they can also diminish the value experienced by some participants, for example through stigma, disrespect, unfairness or oppression). Each interaction (between two people or a group) is therefore like a small enterprise (a cooperative factory, a shop or service) in which value is produced – but (like these) it may also exploit or cheat some 'workers' or 'customers', or cause 'pollution' to some third parties.

The difference between the material economy producing goods, and the interpersonal economy producing feelings (including morale, team spirit and solidarity) and culture (ideas, images, science, art, music and drama) is that the latter produces something intangible and difficult to measure. But what the interpersonal economy produces is *real*. It determines our emotional state, it shapes our wider engagements with the material economy and the formal systems of government, and it provides us with both the *resources* and the *restraints* for our thoughts and actions. In other words, our social world is shaped and patterned by the interpersonal economy. We use material products and processes in the ways that our emotions and cultures enable. We interpret the formal organised world using the symbols and meanings we derive from the interpersonal one.

So the value of each human being is in their membership of the interpersonal economy, and the fact that (whether we or they like it or not) they share in the giving and receiving of value through these interactions. In this way, they also share in the creation and exchange of emotions and cultural resources. In so far as we are all members of this interpersonal system, our fates are inextricably linked with each other's. We can enhance or damage each other, but we cannot evade our mutual influences, or escape from the web of feelings and ideas that we produce through all our encounters.

The subjectivist, interpretivist and even relativist schools of social work theory are basically asserting this fundamental truth. Service user 'values' enter into their engagements with practitioners, and influence their encounters. They have to be respected, because they are part of the person, and contribute to what is produced in their interactions. I shall discuss this in more detail in relation to 'constructionist' views of practice (Parton and O'Byrne, 2000).

Sheppard is also very critical of others (such as certain feminist theorists) who assert the special validity of a particular standpoint (such as that of disadvantaged women) in negotiations about needs (2006: 126–7). But here the point is that the level of rational-legal discussion between social workers and service users is only one dimension of practice. At the other (interpersonal) level, specific standpoints such as these do have special validity, and can be taken into account in what is constructed by encounters between practitioners and service users.

Sheppard also criticises Marxist theorists for focusing on social structures, arguing that this kind of intervention is inappropriate for social work (2006: 127–31). Again, this is not a fair criticism if what is being claimed is that the culture and institutions of capitalism are often experienced by service users as oppressive, and that ideas and collective action which resist that oppression are of potential value to those experiencing those situations. If group and community work enable service users and members to generate the cultural resources to act together, to mobilise and organise around their collective interests, and to challenge dominant firms' rhetoric, or government agencies' agendas, then this is indeed a valid form of intervention.

The term 'empowerment' (which Sheppard criticises extensively) can stand for just these practices. People such as refugees and asylum seekers, homeless people and the residents of deprived districts are enabled to form movements, to challenge stereotypes, and to debate with power holders. There is no guarantee that they will be able to change structures, achieve redistribution of power, or shift others towards greater equality and justice. But the very act of coming together and pursuing their own purposes allows them to gain new resources (interpersonal cultural goods) to use in other parts of their lives. I shall give examples of this in Part Three of the book.

In the present-day literature of social work, which takes much of its tone from neo-liberal and Third Way political discourse, empowerment is seen primarily as gaining personal capacities, skills and competences, or accumulating 'social capital' in the form of links with other individuals and groups. This is the kind of empowerment appropriate to a society in which individual self-realisation is the main project for citizens, and the focus of positive government interventions.

A psychology of self-improvement pervades our culture (Rose, 1996) encouraged by governments which see independence and self-responsibility as the primary qualities of the good citizen (Ellis and Rogers, 2004). If the interpersonal economy is central to individual well-being, and to good social relations, then individualism, especially in its competitive rivalrous forms, is likely to be self-defeating (Layard, 2005). Only when society's values reflect the value of relationships and a culture of sharing will well-being be reliably increased, and social work play its full part in this process (Jordan, 2006a and b).

Themes and plan of the book

So the main theme of the book is to re-assert those aspects of social work practice which emphasise that relationships between people, and between the practitioner and the service user, are central to professional activity. Although, as I shall show, this defining feature of social work is still implicitly at the heart of theory and practice, and acknowledged as such by those who have contact with practitioners, it has been largely expunged from policy, guidance and management literature.

In Part One of the book, I shall explain the contribution of 'interpersonal goods' to well-being, and how social work practice can help individuals and groups improve their well-being by explicit acknowledgement of this research-based finding (Chapter 1).

I shall then show how the value of social workers came to be defined solely in terms of the ability to deliver services (modelled as marketed products) to individuals whose well-being was taken to lie in a choice of alternative suppliers, or as offering skilled interventions to target and change specific behaviours, or as organisers of voluntary agencies or volunteers, seen as embodying 'community'. Using examples from services for children and adults, I shall illustrate some of the negative consequences of this regime (Chapter 2) and how it overlooks much of the value generated by the 'interpersonal economy'.

Next I shall trace the history of ideas about relationships in social work, and how they have reflected the political context of each successive period in the profession's development. I shall show how ideas of well-being and social justice have been influenced by the political context over time, and social work's understanding of its methods and tasks have changed accordingly. This narrative will be illustrated with examples from the professional literature of each era (Chapter 3) which shows a remarkable continuity in valuing relationships and feelings, and rejecting a purely materialistic notion of equality, justice, membership and well-being.

The second main theme of the book is that practice which focuses on behavioural change, protecting vulnerable individuals and meeting identified needs can be reconciled with the approach to well-being advocated in this book. What is being presented as an adequate analysis of the value of social work is as relevant for statutory practice with disturbed and vulnerable people as it is for counselling or preventive interventions. When David Cameron suggested that mainstream citizens should 'hug a hoodie' (*The Guardian*, 2006a) he was articulating the spirit of a social work which seeks the most marginal, angry and resistant members of society as its clientele, and seeks to advance their inclusion.

This is why 'constructive' approaches to practice are not confined to therapeutic or voluntary services (Parton and O'Byrne, 2000; Gorman, Gregory, Hayles and Parton, 2006). Using examples from child protection work and practice with offenders, I shall illustrate how the objective (harm prevention) and subjective (communicative, creative) aspects of everyday work can be reconciled (Chapter 4).

The goal of enabling service users to be independent and active participants in a market economy is a very narrow interpretation of how to maximise their well-being. It implies that services are one-off experiences, serially consumed, chosen from a menu (much as in a fast food outlet). Using research on older people and people with disabilities, and their perceptions of their needs for services, I shall analyse the shortcomings of this approach, and the need to balance it with provision that enables companionship, sharing, collective experiences and participation (Chapter 5).

The New Labour government has always acknowledged the importance of 'community' and 'cohesion' but seen them as aspects of social relations which are to be separate from the provision of social care and child protection. I shall argue that this is an artificial separation, and that social work and community work share many of the same methods, principles and values in a diverse, multi-ethnic society (Chapter 6). The analysis of well-being in terms of an 'interpersonal economy' is common to both.

The third theme of the book is that relationships produce both interpersonal value (feelings) and cultural goods (ideas, images and meanings). The organisation of the economy, society, and government all feed off these cultural goods, which people use to interpret our social world, and act effectively within it. Social work can contribute to the cultural resources of the most disadvantaged members of our communities.

For this approach to be most effective, services should become more answerable to service users and community members. They should be the people who steer policy and practice; conversely, professionals should be more like coaches or consultants to their clienteles, not agents of surveillance who report to managers, accountants and courts, or impose top-down versions of a government-led social order (Chapter 7).

Professionals cannot evade the possibility of doing harm, and have a responsibility to minimise this risk. This is what is implied by ethical codes and professional competences. But it also involves addressing the risks of members of the community oppressing or excluding others, or doing them direct harm, through bigotry, bullying or exclusion. This will be analysed, with examples from youth and community work (Chapter 8).

Finally, I shall consider the relevance of social work to the kind of society which is emerging in the affluent countries in the new century. This consists of a service economy, with a diverse, mobile population, and many disadvantaged minorities. If the new emphasis of government policy is to be more on well-being, and less on 'independence' and 'security', then social work has a great deal to offer – but only if it is true to its roots in the primacy of social relationships and emotional truth.

The re-emergence of immigration, integration and security as the main themes of government policy threatens the gains in the well-being of disadvantaged groups which policies for inclusion and participation are beginning to promise. Anti-social behaviour and minority disaffection (including extreme violence) signal the non-viability of a mainstream social order based on individual self-responsibility, choice and switching between options. The interpersonal economy provides a more fertile ground for a long-term order in which diversity and freedom are reconciled with respect and belonging (Chapter 9).

Chapter 1

Social Work and the Interpersonal Economy

Introduction

Social work has always described itself in terms of the well-being of those who use its services, and of the societies in which they live. For example, the International Federation of Social Workers (2001: 1) defined it as a profession which:

> . . . promotes social change, problem solving in human relationships and the empowerment and liberation of people to enhance their well-being.

However, it has only been at certain times in its history that social work practitioners and theorists have actively debated the nature of human well-being. For the most part, the profession has adopted whatever the mainstream version of quality of life happened to be.

This book argues that now is a good moment for social workers to re-engage in the debate about well-being, both because this has emerged as a key issue in affluent countries, and because it has something important to offer.

The first reason for this is that the version of well-being which predominates, especially in the USA and the UK, is now under question and scrutiny. As I shall show in this chapter, this version was derived from economics, whose basic assumptions constructed bargain-hunting individuals in markets as the basic units of societies. Influential economists are now queuing up to draw attention to the limitations of this model, and to propose a widening of the influences on political decisions about well-being. This creates a unique opportunity for the other social sciences, and especially for social work.

The second reason is that social work has never fully accepted the economic model, even though it has made pragmatic concessions to it, especially in its organisational structures and accountability frameworks. In a sense, social work has been living a double life under governments of a neo-liberal persuasion (such as those of Margaret Thatcher, Ronald Reagan and George Bush senior) and also under Third Way regimes (such as those of Tony Blair and Bill Clinton).

During this period, the emphasis in social care for adults has been on enabling individual citizens to achieve 'independence' and 'control' over their lives, by allowing them to choose between a range of commercial, charitable and public suppliers of services. As the recent UK government Green Paper, *Independence, Well-being and Choice* puts it, the vision projected for social care is one where:

> . . . *services help maintain the independence of the individual by giving them greater choice and control over the way in which their needs are met.*
>
> (DoH, 2005: 9)

For children and young people, recent policy has had the overall goal of enabling them to reach their full potential, by integrating education, health and social services, to 'promote their well-being' (DfES, 2003: 11). The new organisational framework for child protection, mental health, truancy and delinquency will involve 'targeting' and specialised support (ibid: 9) as well as 'rationalizing performance targets, plans, funding streams, financial accountability and indicators' (p.11). This language points to a structure of children's services in which expertise is measured, contracted for and deployed within an economic paradigm.

Yet the leading texts for social work education project a rather different basis for practice. Rather than emphasising the individual independence of citizens, choice among options, or the quantification of outcomes, they promote a *relational* understanding of service users' needs, and of professional activity. For example, in the highly-regarded US textbook, *The Skills of Helping Individuals, Families, Groups and Communities*, Shulman (1999: 35) states that his model for practice is *interactional*:

> The client in this model is viewed as a self-realising, energy-producing person with certain tasks to perform, and the social worker as having a specific function to carry out. They engage each other as interdependent actors within an organic system that is best described as reciprocal in nature, with each person affecting and being affected by the other on a moment-by-moment basis.'

Shulman makes it clear from the outset that all the other principles for practice, including empowerment, challenging oppression, social justice and the protection of vulnerable individuals, are all best understood within their interactional model, and in terms of relationships. Furthermore, the fundamental method of social work relies on the quality of interactions with service users.

> At the core of the interactional theory of social work practice is a model of the helping process in which the skill of the worker helps to create a positive working relationship.
>
> (Shulman, 1999: 22)

A very similar approach is taken by the leading British guides to practice. In their *Social Work Futures* (2005), Adams, Dominelli and Payne outline a framework for professional work which is 'transformational', which 'seeks to improve social relationships and social work in the future', through 'promoting well-being by changing current configurations of inequality and diswelfare that prevent people from realising their full potential'.

. . . securing these improved relationships in practice requires us as social workers to connect our interpersonal interactions with our political objectives and thereby model and demonstrate increased sociability to remove barriers that cause inequalities and promote social change.

(Adams, Dominelli and Payne, 2005: 2)

This approach is similar to Shulman's, in that it links interactions, both between service users and with practitioners, to 'change . . . that enhances their social relationships and well-being both now and in the future' by 'promoting the bonds that connect social relationships between people', seeking greater equality and enabling improved mutuality (p. 2).

These texts have a different emphasis from the ones which frame law, policy and guidance in the US and UK. The latter are more *individualistic*; they define rights and responsibilities of citizens, and promote a kind of economic competence in a society structured by markets and contracts. The former place far more importance on the interdependence of people, and on their interactions as influencing their well-being. This leads to a different interpretation of equality, oppression, injustice and power in the two sets of documents.

I shall deal in much more detail with the evolution of government policy on social care and children's well-being, and its relation to economics, in Chapter 2. I shall trace the story of relationships as the basis for and focus of social work practice in Chapter 3. Here I shall show how the current orthodoxy on well-being in mainstream affluent cultures – both among official elites and in mainstreams – has come under criticism. This provides the opportunity for the version of well-being still espoused by social work theorists and practitioners to be re-asserted, and to have more widespread influence.

Evidence of stalled well-being

As I mentioned in the Introduction (pp. iv–xiii), there is now a considerable body of evidence to show that citizens in the affluent countries are not experiencing increases in well-being as their incomes rise. Although this evidence is only now being deployed in systematic ways, and conclusions about policy drawn from it, the data all point to a plateau in the well-being of populations in rich countries having been reached about 30 or 40 years ago. Advances in well-being have stalled.

The first step in the accumulation of this evidence was taken by psychologists, who found that people's own assessments of their overall happiness with their lives were remarkably consistent, robust and comparable across countries and over time. These measures of self-assessed happiness were then correlated with other social data, to allow patterns in the distribution of 'Subjective Well-being' (SWB) to be traced (Kahneman et al., 1999).

This research was being conducted in parallel with advances in the neurobiological study of emotions and behaviour (Davidson, 2005) which enabled the development of a 'Science of Well-being', (Huppert et al., 2005). It validated earlier insights by psychologists who had questioned the links between income and happiness (Easterlin, 1974) and demanded an analysis of how people's aspirations and needs in various domains of their lives were attained, and how they related these to each other in an overall assessment (Easterlin, 2005).

What became clear from the evidence of surveys was that, although richer individuals in any one society tended to be happier than poorer ones in that society, there was no reliable correlation between *average* income per head and SWB in comparisons between countries (Diener, 2002). In particular, other social scientists picked up the striking confirmation that the huge recent growth in material prosperity in affluent 'Western' countries (including Japan) had not led to increases in self-assessed happiness (Frey and Stutzer, 2002; Layard, 2005; Helliwell and Putnam, 2005).

Although citizens' SWB was higher in social democratic regimes like Sweden, Denmark and Finland, where incomes are more equal and citizens trust each other more, and in the Netherlands, Switzerland and Canada, where they might feel more involved in democratic processes, neither these nor any other rich states had been able to buck this trend. Conversely, people were far happier in certain much poorer countries than their income-level would have predicted. Among these are Malta in Europe, Ghana and Nigeria in Africa, and several Latin American countries, including Colombia, Mexico, El Salvador and Brazil (Layard 2005: 32–3).

A variation on the analysis of comparative SWB data has been an attempt to combine these statistics with figures on life expectancy and 'environmental footprint' (damage to the environment). The New Economics Foundation has compiled a Happy Planet Index (with Friends of the Earth) giving a league table of the world's nations by these measures. Vanuatu comes top, because of its relatively high SWB, healthy lifestyle and low ecological impact. Out of 178 countries, the UK comes 108th, USA 150th and Russia 172nd. Zimbabwe came last, with civil strife and a short life-span among its citizens (*The Guardian*, 2006b).

So there are two sides to this evidence on well-being. On the one hand, increases in income do not contribute significantly to the overall satisfaction with their lives of the more affluent citizens of economically advanced countries. It may well be that relative gains by poorer people in these societies, making them more equal (as in the Scandinavian states or the Netherlands) would increase SWB more than overall economic growth. This finding, which favours redistribution over growth, applies to states with an average per capita income of about $15,000 or over at 2004 prices.

On the other hand, in poorer countries increases in average incomes are much more likely to bring about rises in SWB, though not by the same extent. This is an argument for *global* redistribution in favour of less developed economies. But even without such shifts, *some* poorer societies are more successful in sustaining SWB than others, and proportionately better at this than rich states.

All this redirects attention from the idea that simple increases in income can be relied upon to improve well-being, towards a study of the other factors in people's lives which increase the overall quality of their experiences. It also casts doubt on the fundamental assumption behind the policies of both neo-liberal and Third Way governments that putting more money in people's pockets, so they can choose the particular bundles of goods and services they prefer, is more important than providing a good overall context for their lives together.

The components of well-being

It is not surprising to discover that the most important factors influencing overall happiness are physical and mental health, work satisfaction and relationships with others. Indeed, because relationships encompass so many aspects of life, they can be regarded as the primary component of well-being. Relationships include close bonds with partner, family and friends, associations with members in organisations, and interactions with fellow citizens.

These findings are far closer to the model of individuals and societies adopted by social work theorists than that used by economists. As we saw at the start of this chapter, writers like Shulman and Adams et al. assume an interactional model, in which relationships are the key to well-being, and their improvement is the focus of practice.

This includes the pursuit of justice, equality and inclusion. Economics assumes that the primary drives of individuals are concerned with consumption and accumulation, following principles of utility-maximisation and rational strategic action.

These findings from a survey of 46 mainly affluent countries show that, if the scale of happiness stretches from 10 points to 100 points, it is possible to chart *losses* in SWB due to various factors in individual's lives. The effect of losing one third of family income is quite small – only two points. But the effect of being separated rather than married is 8 points. The chart below illustrates these changes:

Table 1.1 Components of well-being

	Fall in happiness (points)
Family income down by one third	2
Divorced (rather than married)	5
Separated (rather than married)	8
Widowed (rather than married)	4
Never married	4.5
Cohabiting (rather than married)	2
Unemployed	6
Job insecure	3
General unemployment rate up 10 percentage points	3
Subjective health down 1 point (on 5-point scale)	6

Source: Helliwell, 2003.

These findings confirm the more detailed research on family and close personal relationships conducted by psychologists in many societies (Myers, 1999). But there is also strong evidence of the relevance of wider relationships for SWB. Activists, who participate fully in the community, through formal and informal involvement in the life of groups and organisations, are significantly happier than those who live in passive privatism (Argyle, 1999).

The extent to which people trust others can be shown to influence SWB by 1.5 points on the scale shown above if there is a 50 per cent decline in endorsement of fellow-citizens' trustworthiness – for example, the difference between levels of trust in Sweden and those in France (Helliwell, 2003).

Religious faith is also an important factor, counting for 3.5 points where respondents endorse the statement that 'God is important in my life'. But it is unclear whether this is because such individuals are likely to be active in a faith community, or through the belief itself.

Some analysts have pointed out that bonds with others – what they call 'social capital' – have indirect effects on health of up to 30 per cent (Helliwell and Putnam, 2005: 453). So relationships and community involvement have an impact beyond their direct consequences.

It is clear from these findings that improvements in well-being must rely on the factors addressed by social work more than those by economics, at least in the affluent countries. So why have economists achieved such a dominant position in the counsels of government, and in the organisation of the human services themselves?

The obvious answer is that economics can, by excluding such factors as emotion, loyalty and political affiliation, and creating an abstract model society which can be reduced to a mathematical formula, predict the aggregate effects of government decisions to an impressive extent. Indeed, economists can even claim that their model allows those social factors to be assimilated into their analysis of citizens' choices, since the concept of 'utility' can embrace every element in individuals' preferences, including such 'irrational' ones as a liking for certain kinds of other people or principles.

At a deeper level, progress in civility, trust and prosperity can be traced to the period when rulers began to pay more attention to economics and less to honour, faith or might (Hirschman, 1977). Before the Enlightenment, Europe was consumed in wars of religion, by the dynastic ambitions of kings and emperors, and by patriarchal domestic tyranny. Both personal liberty (of women and slaves as well as citizens) and democracy can therefore be traced to this shift towards a pursuit of economic goals (Jordan, 2004; 2006a and b).

What's more, it can still be contended that the developing countries can best pursue well-being by the same principles. Not only is SWB still fairly reliably linked to economic growth in these contexts; it is also obvious that prosperity requires a more stable political framework than exists in most of the continent of Africa, and in the Middle East.

The take-off of economic growth in South-East Asia, and most recently in China and India, can be attributed to the pursuit of higher incomes, and a turn away from ideology and political strife (most clearly in the case of China after the death of Mao). All this suggests that the Enlightenment arguments for an economic orientation by governments are still valid in those regions.

Perhaps it is characteristic of economies which have reached a stage of post-industrialisation, in which there is a predominance of service employment, and where most citizens are engaged in tasks of 'social reproduction', that the components of well-being become so clearly relational. This will be further discussed in Part 3 of this book.

One of the foremost theorists of well-being, the economic historian Avner Offer (2006), sees affluence as a challenge for US and UK societies. Can we devise and sustain institutions for *quality* of life, rather than simply consuming even more material products, and harming the environment, ourselves and each other in a quest for immediate gratification?

To answer these questions, it is necessary to find a way of analysing the 'interpersonal economy' of relationships.

The interpersonal economy

Some readers may feel repugnance for the idea that there could be an 'economy' of relationships and feelings. But this is a mistake. Economics is simply a way of expressing the value we put on various resources (and beings), and allocating them fairly and rationally. We all 'economise' every moment of our lives, by using our time and energy for the activities and people we value most. This includes altruistic actions, and those dedicated to the celebration of 'higher purposes', such as religion or art.

Our ancestors treated all resources and activities as sacred, and stemming from the organic unity of being. They conserved nature and worshipped their ancestors and the spirit of the tribe, but these principles can all be analysed in terms of economic value (Sahlins, 1974).

In the same way, part of the recognition of the worth of landscapes, the diversity of species and the legacy of history is expressed by protecting them as economic assets, through laws and penalties.

There are at least three reasons why the present moment is a propitious one for a convincing account of the interpersonal economy to be framed, and for social workers to give strong support to this endeavour. The first is that economists are inviting other social scientists and professionals to contribute to the debate about well-being and government policy. The most influential figure in that debate in the UK, Richard (Lord) Layard, has written that:

> . . . the economic model of human nature is far too limited – it has to be combined with knowledge from the other social sciences.
>
> (Layard, 2005: 149)

However, as we have seen, social workers have been asserting the value of relationships for many decades. They will only be listened to if they can argue their corner in a language, and through an analysis, that is compatible with economics. This does *not* mean that they must accept the existing assumptions of market micro-economics, and its attendant public policies. Just as we can translate the beliefs of our ancestors, and the values of art or ecology, into economic terms, so we can do the same for emotions and relationships.

Second, economists have already begun to develop theories of the interpersonal economy, but these are incomplete and in some ways misleading. Building on the work of Gary Becker (1976, 1991) authors such as Ainslie (1992) and Sugden (2005) have shown how individuals take account of their feelings for others in their decisions, and how they gain satisfactions from sharing in each other's pleasures, or consolations from receiving empathy and understanding.

However, the paradigm for all such analyses by economists is 'exchange' between individuals, rather as in markets for commodities. This is most obvious in the work of Avner Offer (2006) whose attention to 'the economy of regard' is furthest developed.

In his work, individuals' interactions with others in relationships can be understood as a series of reciprocal 'gifts' to each other of love, friendship, support or empathy, which give each in turn a 'warm glow'. This 'trade' consists in taking turns to supply the other with such tokens of their regard, which confirm and communicate these positive feelings, and create a 'self-enforcing bond' between the individuals (Offer, 2006: 77–83).

This is clearly a very limited view of how relationships work, and paints a picture of them which is much too similar to the trade which takes place in markets. Although Offer acknowledges the crucial importance of 'regard' for well-being, his analysis is narrow and mechanistic. Relationships create value, they do not simply trade in it.

The third reason for social work to intervene in this debate is that it can improve this model, and provide a better link between the interpersonal economy of reciprocity between individuals, and the wider issues of justice, equality and inclusion among citizens. Because economists tend to be committed to the principle of 'methodological individualism', they are suspicious of any theory which deals in shared resources, such as meaning, membership and belonging.

When social work writers such as Shulman describe their 'interactional model' as implying that individuals are 'interdependent actors within an organic system' (Shulman, 1999: 35) what they are claiming is that a society consists of ideas, images, practices and institutions which are created by its members' interactions with each other. These relationships are not simply exchanges which produce a 'warm glow'; they are the ways in which members give each others' lives meanings and purposes.

The relational basis for social work which Adams et al. (2005) describe as 'transformational' is the process by which people come together to *create* these ideas, practices and organisations, and to *change* existing ones in this process. In other words, the 'relational goods' which are constructed in the 'interpersonal economy' are the stuff of social work practice with groups and communities, as well as individuals (Jordan, 2006b, Chapters 3 and 4).

So, when people interact they produce 'goods' which are personal and private to their particular exchanges, but also ones which contribute to and transform the wider culture and structure of their society. The first kind of goods can be called 'intimacy' – the close feelings generated by partners, family members and friends. But interactions also produce 'respect' (Sennett, 2003) the culture of civility between citizens, and 'belonging', the sense of loyalty and commitment between members of the same group, community or society.

As soon as we recognise that the interpersonal economy generates such powerful emotions, ideas and social forces, we can see that it is potentially damaging and harmful as well as beneficial. It can produce very large reductions in individuals' well-being, as well as gains. And social work is directly concerned with both these processes – how people's interactions can be enabled to have positive outcomes for well-being, and how harm and damage can be limited. For example, a report by Elinor Stobard for the UK government in June, 2006, detailed 38 cases of serious child abuse connected with witchcraft, mainly by parents of African origin. In these cases, with their echoes of Victoria Climbié, children were beaten, cut, stabbed or otherwise injured because they were believed to be possessed by evil spirits. The report advocated, among other things, that places of worship should have better child protection procedures (BBC Radio 4, 2006b).

This illustrates that faith communities, and the cultures of immigrant groups, which are a source of strength and solidarity to such families, can also promote practices which are severely harmful for vulnerable individuals. Social workers are required to deal in both aspects of the interactions among such members – those which give the sense of belonging, and the resources for survival in an unfamiliar environment, and those which mobilise families and congregations to scapegoat and abuse certain children.

Case Example

Social workers and community workers are constantly required to assess and intervene in complex systems of relationships, which create anxiety and depression as well as joy and self-assurance; which generate stigma and blame as well as respect and dignity; and which mobilise antagonism and exclusion as well as cooperation and belonging. This example is meant to show how the interpersonal economy can work both positively and negatively, contributing to or detracting from the well-being of participants.

Susan and Neil are a couple in their 40s; their daughter, Rachel, is nine years old. They live on a non-descript modern estate, and Rachel attends a very average primary school, yet their lives are beset by several problems.

Neil is well-educated and cultured, but lacks self-confidence. He works hard in a manual job, and worries about the family finances. Susan has long-term health problems which prevent her from gainful employment, though she is active in several associations, and is a strong and forthright character.

Rachel is bright and a high achiever at school, but has been picked on and bullied by some classmates. She has missed schooling through illness, and her mother has raised the question of bullying with the school authorities.

Neil is currently attending a mental health facility for counselling about his fears and anxieties, especially his tendency to overwork, which is affecting his relationship with Susan.

Some of the children who pick on Rachel live in the same cul-de-sac as the family. Susan confronts them when they chase Rachel into the house, and they throw rubbish at her. When Neil goes out to speak to them, he is 'ambushed' by two of the fathers, and assaulted, sustaining injuries which require medical treatment. Rachel witnesses all this, and is very distressed.

This example is chosen, not to illustrate a challenging set of issues for practice, but rather to show how the interpersonal economy affects individual well-being. The family unit is loving and loyal, but neither Neil nor Rachel is particularly confident or assertive. Despite their intelligence and sensitivity, both have suffered at the hands of more dominant and physically aggressive others.

Susan, by contrast, is someone who is resilient and redoubtable, despite her health problems. She does battle on behalf of her daughter and her family, and may unintentionally attract hostility for doing so.

The culture of Rachel's class at school is probably average for current UK children of this age-group, which amounts to saying that it is quite rough and challenging. The immediate neighbourhood too, though by no means materially poor, is one where men are expected to stand up for themselves, and artistic appreciation is not highly valued.

In other words, neither Rachel nor Neil benefits greatly from their membership of the school or immediate neighbourhood. The cultures of both tend to devalue their contribution, even to stigmatise and exclude them. They derive little positive in terms of respect or belonging from their interactions with classmates and neighbours.

This raises many obvious questions for any human service professionals who might try to intervene, to improve their situation. At an individual level, can Rachel and Neil be helped to be more assertive? This may already be one of the goals of the mental health workers consulted by Neil – perhaps individual counselling or a group might be considered? Maybe a school social worker could help Rachel in similar ways?

On the other hand, another approach would be to see whether Susan could become less of a battler on their behalf, and more of an enabler and confidence-booster. Is her strength and assertiveness itself a factor in their timidity, or might she lend some of it to them? A form of family work might look at their interactions, with these questions in mind?

But at another level, there are important questions about the social milieux in which they live their lives. Should the school be more focused on changing the culture of the class group, reducing bullying, and allowing children like Rachel to be more accepted and valued? Might a community worker look at how this local neighbourhood could be more involved in improving their quality of life together? After all, Susan is something of a leader in the civic life of the town, through her memberships of several associations. Could she not be involved in mobilising the locality for some more positive purposes?

The point here is that all these different levels of interventions can be understood as sharing a common perspective – turning the relationships in which these three individuals are involved into ones in which they can contribute more to each other's well-being, and participate more fully in membership of groups and communities that are equitable and inclusive. These are not mutually exclusive goals, but professionals are likely to have to make choices about the best way to improve the well-being of these individuals and this neighbourhood.

Of course there is another whole approach to the situation – for Rachel to change schools, and the family to move to another district. For the current culture of UK and US social relations, this is probably the most likely approach to be adopted. Neil will continue to get some individual counselling about his anxieties, and the family will adopt an 'exit strategy', in relation to education and community.

In the final part of the book, I will consider the relevance of this culture of mobility between options for well-being. At this stage we can simply note that this offers an alternative for those involved in relationships which jeopardise their well-being.

Whatever strategy they adopt – 'exit', by moving, or 'voice' by participating more actively in the school and community (Hirschman, 1970) – they too will 'economise' by directing their time and energy towards the activities and people they see as most potentially rewarding.

Conclusions

The case example just given does not propose any novel or groundbreaking approach to social work or community work practice. It simply restates some very orthodox and agreed alternatives in these professions' analyses in a form which is accessible to economists, and the policy makers who are influenced by economics. The interpersonal economy is the everyday stuff of theory and practice in the human services, and its dynamics do not require distortion to be reframed in these terms. Why then bother to make the effort to express such obvious points in this way?

The reason, I argue in this book, is that this is a necessary step towards asserting the hidden value of social and community work. Since they deal primarily in relationships, and relationships are the main source of the value which contributes well-being, their chief contribution is in improving relationships of all kinds, and in this way transforming cultures, and the situations of disadvantaged and vulnerable people within them.

The main points about the interpersonal economy to be made in this chapter are as follows:

1. People's well-being is more influenced by the quality of their relationships with others than by the quantity of the material things they own or consume.
2. People *create value* in their interactions. Positive interactions, which generate such emotions as closeness, respect and belonging, are the main components in high levels of subjective well-being (SWB).
3. People also *diminish value* in their interactions, by generating negative emotions, through rejection, abuse, disrespect and exclusion. For this reason, interventions in relationships are potentially important contributions to well-being.
4. Close relationships, between partners, family members and friends, are the most significant for well-being, both positively and negatively. This implies that interventions in close relationships require great skill and sensitivity, because they can do much good or much harm to well-being.
5. Relationships with neighbours and other associates, schools and workmates and other fellow citizens are also significant for well-being. Interactions with others are the means by which people gain or lose in terms of the value which makes up well-being. Hence work which influences these relationships is significant for empowerment and inclusion of citizens, and for equality and justice in society.
6. Social work and community work therefore intervene in the interpersonal economy, to enhance well-being. The hidden value of these professions' activities can be made clear, in economic terms, only if the interpersonal economy is recognised as the main source of individual and collective well-being.

All this would have seemed very obvious to the generation of social and community workers, which emerged in the UK in the period after the Second World War (Jordan, 1984, Chapter 6). Indeed, it would have been equally obvious to their counterparts in the USA in the 1940s (Sennett, 2003, Chapters 1–3). But the dominance of economics in public policy, which has led to the 'reform' and 'modernisation' of the public sector, has largely obscured the main contribution of these professionals to well-being in these societies.

It has only been the discovery that levels of SWB have stalled since that period that redirects the attention of economists and policy makers to these aspects of the quality of life. I have argued that this opens up an opportunity for social work, which should not be missed.

In the next chapter, I shall analyse the ways in which the main value of human service work came to be concealed, and their organisation and accountability came to be reframed in narrow economic terms. As we shall see, these reforms were based on many mistakes in economic analysis, and have had negative effects for the evaluation of social work, and for its relationship with community work.

Chapter 2

Service Delivery and the Value of Practice

Introduction

The reform and modernisation of public services in the UK and the other Anglophone countries has been driven by two main principles – value for taxpayers' money and choice for consumers. The first principle requires that professionals in human services such as social work, teaching and medicine are able to demonstrate the outcomes of their work in improved social functioning, behaviour, skills or capacities. The second requires a variety of suppliers (public, voluntary and commercial), and competition between them.

Both these principles derive from the economics of markets. Demand by individuals and firms is related to the price and quality of what is supplied; sales and contracts flow from the value bestowed on purchasers by products. Efficiency among producers is achieved through competition, which ensures that the best use is made of labour power and raw materials, and that the diversity of needs and tastes among consumers is satisfied.

Governments in the Anglophone countries have followed a simple logic in these reforms. The service industry has been the most rapidly-expanding sector of the advanced economies. In 1948, only 39 per cent of the UK workforce was employed in services of whom 10 per cent were in the armed forces, and 16 per cent in government service (Feinstein, 1976, Table 59). By 2001, around 70 per cent of the workforce were employed in services, mostly in commercial banking, finance and insurance, or in miscellaneous services such as retailing, hospitality, leisure or home care. The growth of private services was taken as the model on which the public sector should be modernised.

As I shall show in this chapter, new theory in public finance enabled these shifts, by explaining how services which were shared by members could be more efficiently supplied (Buchanan, 1965; Cornes and Sandler, 1986). I shall argue that many of the principles of this approach have been misapplied in the reform of public services, so the modernisation process has caused distortions, and had unintended consequences.

Finally, the reforms of public services in the Anglophone countries have accelerated a major factor in the expansion of service employment – the increased labour-market participation of women. Some theorists argue that it has been this combination of commercialisation of the service sector and increased female employment that has given the USA and UK the edge over the Continental EU Countries (such as Germany, France and Italy) in economic growth (Esping-Andersen, 1999; Iversen and Wren, 1998).

However, the evidence of stalled well-being in the affluent countries presented in Chapter 1 suggests that these reforms have not contributed to raising average SWB in these societies. Indeed, sociological research suggests that rises in household incomes have been offset by increases in stress and insecurity in the USA (Lane, 2000), Australia (Pusey, 2003) and New Zealand (Kelsey, 1995). Women are more involved in the public sphere, and especially in the economy, but also subject to more pressures and anxieties.

This chapter examines how social work and community work understand the organisation of services as a factor in professional activity, and how this might enter the debate about the value of such activity, and its contribution to well-being. If practitioners see their work primarily in terms of improving the quality of social relationships (as we saw in the last chapter), what does this imply for the way that services are organised and managed?

It is difficult to give a direct answer to this question, because the organisation of social and community work services has varied so much over time, and between countries. In general terms the professions draw their own legitimacy from *ethical* arguments (Koehn, 1994: 59). The practitioner cannot usually contract directly to provide a service to a client (as in the case of a company supplying a holiday or a hairdo), because the transaction is often open-ended, because the client cannot always know exactly what is on offer, and because there is sometimes a third party involved, the legal arm of the state. So the profession's pledge to observe certain ethical standards in its work with those who use its services, under the law, seems the best legitimacy it can offer.

In the past century, the political reality was that this gave governments much scope for deploying social work according to their ideological or political priorities. After the Second World War, liberal democracies incorporated personal social services into welfare states as part of more comprehensive systems to provide for the welfare of citizens. But state social work agencies became the dominant forms of professional organisation only in the Scandinavian countries and Britain; elsewhere, voluntary and charitable agencies were still the main employers of social and community workers, even if they were funded in part by the state. And in the Soviet Bloc, state socialist countries had no social workers, because their governments refused to recognise the need for such services (Jordan, 1997a).

In the UK, the expansion of public sector social work between 1948 and the late 1970s encouraged the profession to allow its identity, its methods and its organisation to be closely aligned with the welfare state, which in turn commanded broad political support. Since then, the break-up of the consensus in favour of state provision has created a far more fragmented situation:

Those people doing social work – even if they are not called social workers, but instead are labelled care managers, youth offending workers, personal advisors – are working in an increasingly diverse range of settings with often complex employment arrangements.

(Horner, 2003: 101)

In one sense, the fact that social workers are now scattered among a wider range of local and national government agencies and partnerships, and 25,000 private and voluntary sector bodies, seems appropriate to the theoretical and ethical basis of social work. It never accepted the 'thin' liberal conception of society and its members' well-being, as made up of free individuals pursuing their own purposes, under an impartial system of law. It has always stood for a more communal conception of the good life, in which people share in common cultures and polities – albeit increasingly plural and varied ones (Clark, 2000: 121–7). Hence it appears to be appropriate for practitioners to be dispersed into many organisations, reflecting this diversity in the ordinary life of our society.

However, fragmentation has also been accompanied by a much stronger emphasis on management and financial accountability, even in the voluntary sector. Along with the emphasis on value-for-money and choice has come a 'new managerialism' (Clarke et al., 1994) in which professionals are required to demonstrate efficiency and effectiveness in service delivery. The new approach:

. . . gives managers the right to manage, ensures the disciplined use of resources, the pursuit of objectives aimed at reducing costs and improvement of organisational performance. It also increases the use of information technology to bring about changes.

(Gibbs, 2000: 229)

Yet these are not the only themes in the reform and modernisation of the public sector, or the development of social work and community work. In the UK, the New Labour government has also recognised the need to balance individual choice and competition with policies for social inclusion and (more recently) 'community cohesion' and 'respect'. Programmes which target deprived communities have used very different methods, and espoused different philosophies, from those in social care and child protection. These have drawn practitioners into projects for community development, youth and outreach work, and various kinds of support groups.

The result has been a kind of 'twin track' approach to the organisation of services, in which the communal aspects of deprived citizens' lives have been addressed through different agencies from the ones focusing on their individual vulnerabilities (Jordan with Jordan, 2000).

Concerns about relations between communities have been heightened, first by the intercommunal violence in northern English cities in the summer of 2001, and more recently by the suicide bombings on the London transport system in July 2005. These events have raised awareness of how social relationships have implications for order and security. The new initiatives on 'community cohesion' (Home Office, 2004a; Blunkett 2003) and 'civil renewal' (Blunkett, 2004) were followed by specific negotiations with leaders of the Muslim community, to promote harmony and positive interactions.

All these issues will be analysed in detail in Part 3 of the book. They have tended further to divide social work from community work as instruments of government policy. The former is seen as a way of delivering specific services to individuals; the latter as concerned with the integration of diverse elements into a viable society.

My focus in this chapter is on how the economic view of service provision has come to dominate social work organisation, and how that view fails to encompass the value of social services for well-being. This leads me to argue for a different approach to the structure and management of these services, which is more in line with social workers' own understanding of well-being.

Service delivery: the packaging of care

At the heart of the reform and modernisation of the public services in the UK is a very specific concept of their value. This is shown in the framework for 'best value' in the commissioning and delivery of social services, adopted by the New Labour government in 2000. It can be traced back to the National Health Service and Community Care Act (1990) which made local authority social services' departments responsible for *purchasing* care for members of their population in need, and introduced such notions as 'packages of care'.

The central idea in this model is that services can be broken down into constituent elements, each of which can be measured, both in terms of its price and its outcomes for service users and carers. This can be applied to such services as foster placements and behaviour modification programmes as well as domiciliary, day and residential care. New Labour's reforms of the Conservative blueprint for community care (such as commissioning and partnership) do not challenge this key feature, but consolidate it more deeply.

So best value is explicitly concerned with economy, efficiency, effectiveness and 'quality'; it involves measurement and comparison, competition and consultation with service users and local residents (Fletcher, 1998; Thompson, 2002: 101). This imposes a particular rationale on all who wish to have their activities and facilities funded. For instance, therapeutic services and therapeutic communities must demonstrate that they are 'delivering' very tangible outcomes for children and adults who use them (Pavilion, 2006).

The New Labour government insists that its reform agenda is concerned with empowerment of the disempowered as well as protection of the vulnerable, but that this can be achieved only by sharpening the quality of services through focusing on measurable outcomes. Its modernisation agenda proclaimed that what mattered was quality of service, not the structure in which it was delivered (DoH, 1998). But in fact, this agenda has driven the fragmentation and diversification of suppliers, and especially the growth of commercial providers in all aspects of personal social services. This is not surprising, given the government's admiration for markets and private sector firms. Addressing the Annual Social Services Conference in 2002, the Secretary of State for Health, Alan Milburn, said:

> *We live in a consumer age. People demand services tailor made to their individual needs . . . People expect choice and demand quality.*

(Milburn, 2002: 2)

The model to which services should aspire is explicitly commercial. Banks and supermarkets set standards of flexibility and efficiency which are benchmarks for the public sector services (DSS, 1998: 26).

Why this insistence on packages and delivery? The answer lies in the economic analysis of how services are used, and how they can be priced. If we start from the notion that services are *consumed* by individuals, in much the same ways as goods are, then it is obviously necessary to identify when a particular unit of service begins and ends, and what costs go into producing, marketing, distributing and delivering it. The paradigm for social care and child protection becomes a particular experience, supplied by a firm such as Disneyworld or expedia.com.

This implies that the well-being of those who need care is best assured by supplying them with access to a series of such experiences, each with a measurable outcome in terms of consumer value. For those who need protection or rehabilitation, the government contracts with experts who can show their effectiveness in producing quantified results. Specific tasks, such as assessment, advocacy, interviewing and reviewing will be commissioned and delivered, in pre-sliced segments of service (a bit like a pizza).

Within this paradigm, the training of social workers focuses on competences which can be listed and tested, and which correspond to these tasks. Tasks are characteristically structured around skills, with checklists and bullet points. The government emphasises practical applications and problem-solving. As the minister put it when introducing the new degree in social work, it is:

> . . . *a very practical job. It is about protecting people and changing their lives, not about being able to give a fluent and theoretical explanation of why they got into difficulties in the first place.*

(Smith, 2002)

The analysis of social work as a series of separate tasks for skilled practitioners, and discrete experiences for service users, also influences the research agenda, and what is counted as 'evidence' for good quality practice. The idea of 'evidence-based social services' is derived from a technocratic model of practice, and drawn from studies of 'what works' within the paradigm of measured specific inputs and outputs (Sheldon, 1998, 2001; Macdonald, 2000). In the evidence-based practitioner framework:

Research use is seen as a rational, linear process in which individual practitioners access, appraise and apply research finding to a practice problem.

(Walter et al., 2004: 39)

In this chapter, I aim to show that the whole model of service delivery promoted by the New Labour government is derived from the economics of commercial services – their production and consumption – and from innovations in the field of public finance. But these analyses are deeply implicated in the failure of economics to explain or address the problem of stalled well-being. Far from providing a reliable basis for the organisation and management of social work, they compromise its future, by linking it to a narrow and mechanistic understanding of the role of services.

The hidden value of social work will not be made manifest until it can show how it helps people make better overall sense of their lives, and their relationships with others. Unlike goods, which are inert until they are activated by human agency, human services are interactional, and work according to the principles of the interpersonal economy, not the material economy. Social work theorists and practitioners understand this better than economists, and should make this clear in the well-being debate.

Services in economics

The distinction between *goods* (material commodities) and *services* is a fundamental one in economics, but there is remarkably little theory and analysis of services in modern economics textbooks. A leading student text starts with the following definitions (and then says little more about services in its next 675 pages):

Goods are physical commodities, such as steel and strawberries. Services are activities such as massages and live theatre performances, consumed or enjoyed only at the instant they are produced.

(Begg et al., 1997: 2)

These examples are revealing. To say that items are 'consumed or enjoyed' only at the instant they are produced conveys nothing about the benefit they confer. Strawberries are of little nutritional value, and are hard to store (they do not freeze palatably). But massages may bring pain relief or relaxation that lasts many hours or days, and a great production of a play may enter the canon of the classics, and become a landmark of a culture.

What the definition really implies is that steel can be kept and sold later, or used as part of an investment (in plant and machinery) – even strawberries can be sold on at a profit (if you hurry) or used as an ingredient of another (value added) consumer good, such as a cake, pudding or ice-cream.

But the examples of services show that such experiences, however valuable, cannot be stored or reused, or deployed to make something else.

This gives us a clue about the distinctiveness of services which is not analysed in modern economics. Because there is some form of interaction in both the examples, they involve a *joint exchange* of emotions. Even in a theatre performance, the audience enters into the occasion, and its response to the opera or play becomes part of the value that is created. This is why recordings of certain live concerts are regarded as more valuable than studio recordings, and indeed why people pay more to attend live concerts (which are one-offs) than buy records or videos of the same performers which can be played many times.

As in the analysis of interactions in the previous chapter, this has positive and negative consequences. An apathetic or restless audience can detract from the performance of the players, taking away some of the value from attentive and appreciative individual members. There are also issues of power and exclusion at stake in a live show. Great performers can move audiences in dangerous as well as inspiring ways; a rabble can ruin a show and disconcert the players; and an elitist milieu can make part of the audience feel small and ignorant.

All this is even more obviously the case in those human services which rely on engaging pupils, patients and service users in a process. Even the most expert teachers and doctors cannot instruct, diagnose and treat without some interaction, in the form of responses, accounts of symptoms and willing participation. Social work and community work are the clearest examples, because they rely on communicating about their lives with people, and on this being translated into actions when the communications are no longer taking place.

What's more, they deal directly in the interpersonal economy – in service users' interactions with each other, and the feelings these generate. They aim to influence these, to give rise to interactions which are more positive, more inclusive, fairer, and hence more conducive to well-being. So it is obvious that social work and community work are more similar to the everyday transactions of the interpersonal economy (producing and distributing the 'goods' of intimacy, respect and belonging) than they are to the material economy, or to the commercial production and consumption of services like banking or retailing (Jordan, 2006b).

After all, these services have not always been provided by professionals, nor are they supplied today by professionals in many developing societies. In the past, poor people in villages got 'health services' from 'wise women', elders or kin; they received instruction from their parents or competent neighbours, and advice from anyone willing to give their time and attention. These aspects of the traditional interpersonal economy (or 'moral economy') have been professionalized, adding the value of scientific expertise and training, ethical commitments and external funding to the informal system. But professional work is not ultimately different in kind from the traditional interactions it replaced.

In other words, expertise and ethics are the *additional* value which is appended to the core of human services, which is interactional in nature. This fits well with the understandings of social work of Shulman (1999) and Adams et al. (2005) which were quoted in the first chapter. Social work is primarily a relationship which is about relationships, in their broadest sense – with fellow citizens as well as partners, families, friends and kin. Its value must be understood in terms of the interpersonal economy (Jordan, 2006 a and b).

This has important implications for the organisation of services, as we shall see. But first it is necessary to consider the other influence from economic theory on the reform and modernisation of public services – public finance.

Choice and collective services

As I mentioned in the opening section of this chapter, social work is not a predominantly public sector occupation in most countries; it is organised by the voluntary sector in most, albeit often with heavy government funding. However, in the UK, as in Scandinavia, it had become concentrated in local authorities by the 1970s, so the fragmentation, privatisation and commercialisation of personal social services has been part of a rationale applied to the whole public sector by Conservative and New Labour governments since the early 1980s.

This rationale was generated by economists who criticised many of the assumptions behind welfare states, and claimed that greater economy, efficiency and quality could be achieved by giving citizens more choice over services like education, health and social care (Buchanan, 1965; Hayek, 1960). These economists became very influential throughout the Anglophone world in this period, and their analyses are still government orthodoxy in the UK, USA, Australia and New Zealand.

First, we must consider the economic reasons why certain services might be regarded as suitable for governments to fund and provide, and on what terms. The standard arguments for state services include:

- A 'good', important for economic and social value, cannot be supplied by firms through markets, because no individual can be excluded from benefiting from its provision. For example, defence, law and order, pollution control and environmental conservation are valuable for all, but any one can gain this value without paying a specific supplier. If some pay, others can be 'free riders'.
- A 'good', important for individual well-being, cannot be accessed by all citizens, because it is too expensive for those who need it to afford to pay for it at the time they need it. Examples are health and social care for old people (who have no earnings), health care for sick people, and education for children. Society as a whole benefits from a healthy, educated and harmonious population.
- The most disadvantaged people are least able to insure themselves against the risks for which they are most vulnerable, e.g. disability, chronic illness and unemployment.
- Insurance companies are least likely to offer viable terms to people with the highest risks of such conditions (adverse selection).
- People are often unable to assess their needs for and possible gains from expert services. They do not know enough about the future, about their own health and well-being, or about the expertise available, to do what is best for themselves.

The first of these arguments concerns 'public goods', which are by nature indivisible into the kinds of portions that can be sold in markets. Defence, law and order and clean air are 'collectively consumed'.

But the other four arguments are about risks and conditions for which some individuals can and do pay and use services individually, even thought they may involve a degree of sharing among users. So, for example, rich people pay to educate their children in private schools, better-off citizens join insurance-based health care plans, and also arrange their own social care from commercial sources.

Because welfare states were concerned with winning the loyalty of all their citizens, with creating common interests between them, and with increasing equality and inclusion, they used the latter arguments to justify universal services such as the NHS, free and compulsory schooling in a predominantly state-run education system, and local authority provision of social care. The shared use of state services was part of the common experience of citizens, and helped to unite them.

So the rationale for the public sector services was primarily political rather than economic, and economists who were market-minded were, from an early stage in the welfare state's development, critical of its efficiency from the standpoint of cost and quality, and quick to point to alternative possibilities. In particular, they emphasised that shared facilities like hospitals, schools and care homes were not *collectively consumed* in the same sense as defence, law and order or clean air.

For example, one way in which individuals would choose which amenities like parks, libraries, streets and sewers they wanted to use was simply by moving to a residential district with the quality they could afford. Each local authority supplied a set of such amenities for its citizens, at a cost charged through local taxes. Individuals sorted themselves into residential districts by selecting in this way – 'voting with their feet' (Tiebout, 1950). Later, companies built gated communities which provided most of these amenities for a service charge paid by residents (Foldvary, 1994).

Another way in which individuals could choose which shared facilities they preferred was through membership clubs. Sports, recreation and cultural facilities can charge members to contribute to their costs, but exclude non-members from access (Buchanan, 1965). In this way, individuals can choose with which others they wish to share, as well as what quality of amenity they are prepared to pay for. A whole branch of 'club theory' in economics explained the patterns which emerged from this process of individuals sorting themselves into collective but exclusive membership groups (Cornes and Sandler, 1986).

In the 1980s, neo-liberal governments, like those of Margaret Thatcher and Ronald Reagan, looked for ways in which these analyses could be put into practice. The privatisation of some aspects of public services, and the encouragement of choice and mobility between options (in terms of geography and membership systems) were features of public policy.

Under New Labour in the UK, the private sector was more involved in financing and managing schools, hospitals and social care systems, as parts of various government initiatives.

So it became an orthodoxy of public finance that individual choice could be reconciled with collective services through enabling citizens to select the facilities which suited them best. This was more efficient, it was argued, because those agencies which supplied education, health and social care would specialise in providing for certain specific needs and tastes, and therefore save on costs of trying to cater for all. Instead of mediocre universal services ('one size fits all') there could be high-quality, tailor-made facilities – specialist academies, faith schools, hip-replacement clinics and beacon social care centres. The economics of 'public choice' enabled this transformation of the public sector in all the Anglophone countries.

Individualised packages and social contexts

UK government policy documents discuss issues of social care in terms of a dichotomy between old-style public provision (standardised and low-quality) and modern, individualised, tailor-made, flexible services (often supplied by firms or voluntary agencies). Because it analyses service 'consumption' as a series of separate experiences, based on choices among options, New Labour thinking pays far less attention to the possible role of services in giving people an overall context for well-being, and a means of making sense of the various relationships with others in their society.

The Green Paper *Independence, Well-being and Choice* (DoH, 2005: 9) describes a 'vision' for social care in which:

> . . . *services help maintain the independence of the individual by giving them greater choice and control over the way in which their needs are met.*

One of the main means by which this is to be achieved is the idea of 'individual budgets' arising from new methods of assessment, and allowing users to take a more active role in planning their own support, and eliminating paternalistic procedures:

> . . . *high levels of bureaucracy, repetitive assessments and piecemeal approaches to meeting individual needs indicate that extending the scope of individual budgets to closely allied services would benefit the individual. People who are currently the passive recipients of services become consumers with the ability to shape and control the services they are willing to buy and shift the culture of care planning.*
>
> (pp. 34–5)

These changes on the demand side should in turn transform the supply of support services. The new system will:

> . . . *stimulate the social care market to provide the services people actually want, and help shift resources away from services which do not meet needs and expectations.*
>
> (p. 35)

The example given of how these arrangements might work is revealing:

> *Taking control of his own support arrangements allowed Mr. Clarke to go on a fishing trip accompanied by his assistant, while his wife took a break from her caring role and went on holiday. Mr Clarke paid £100 for three nights away and 24-hour*

assistance, paying extra from his own pocket to cover the costs. He said this was much more enjoyable, and cheaper, than institutional respite care. 'It's brilliant'.

(p. 33)

This example is designed to give two messages, which are the main thrusts of the proposed reform. The first is that people who need support are willing and able to make their own arrangements. The second is that these are often more efficiently provided by those they pay, either because they are able to select facilities used by others who do not receive social care, or because providers adapt to meet specific needs of certain service users.

However, it should also be noted that the example falls within the economic paradigm of services uncritically adopted by the New Labour government. The support package is a one-off holiday, rather than a long-term set of relationships. It could have been chosen by Begg et al. (1997: 2) as an example of a service which is 'used up in the instant it is produced' – or indeed by Adam Smith (1776: 330) who defined services in the same way.

In fact, of course, what is taken for granted by the example of Mr Clarke's 'independence' and 'choice' is the long-term interdependence between him and his assistant, who is conveniently on hand to accompany him on his holiday, and between him and his wife, who is set to return from her holiday to resume care for him (not much choice there, one suspects).

Individual options such as these are certainly important for well-being, but not the main story. The hidden value of social care is to be found both in the huge volume of support and practical assistance given by partners, offspring, friends and neighbours, and within the relationships between service users and care assistants, social workers and other professionals.

The new model owes much to the campaigning of younger people with disabilities who want better access to the labour market, to civic participation and to independent living arrangements, in which they have more control over their lives, and their support systems. Important elements of these same approaches are common to all people who need social care services.

The consumerist model of care highlights the value of experiences like the fishing trip, which are like commercially-packaged holidays or one-off visits to a theme park. It conceals the value of long-term interactions, including those of memberships and belonging. A better example of the hidden value of the interpersonal economy would have been if a service user spent his individualised budget on a season ticket for a football club he had supported all his life, or for a subscription to a local association which was part of his cultural community.

Example and discussion

Some local authorities which are planning to introduce this system are conducting small-scale research into service users' reactions to these proposals. In one focus group conducted in an older people's day centre, the participants were very critical of the idea of individual budgets and self-directed support, because of the anxiety it would induce, and the time and energy it would consume. They recognised that there had been a time when they wanted to organise their own lives in the ways envisaged by the model, but said they were now too disabled and confused to do so without a lot of help.

When it was suggested that the social services department was now accusing itself of being paternalistic, and not allowing them control and choice, they rejected this, saying they had found care managers helpful and respectful, and had welcomed their interventions.

Eventually one member of the group did acknowledge that he *might* spend part of the budget currently allocated to day care at the centre to buying and feeding a dog, because of the companionship it offered.

Sid: People get good companionship from a dog.
Elsie: He'd probably find himself a St Bernard. We wouldn't see him again.
Mary: Let me shake hands with you before you go.

The members all emphasised that the value of the day centre to them lay mainly in their relationships with each other and the staff, and that this enabled them to integrate other aspects of their social lives, such as membership of the wider community, their past associations and interests. This indicates the other source of hidden value in care facilities – as contexts which supply reality, meaning and the sense of belonging.

In the third part of this book, this aspect of the value of social and community work will be more fully explored. At this stage, it is simply important to note that the consumerist model fails to recognise how systems of relationships within groups and communities supply meaningful contexts.

The interpersonal economy of relationships between individuals produces much more than emotions. It also generates the ideas and images which make up a *culture* (our everyday ways of understanding and doing things, by which we orientate ourselves to others, and coordinate our actions with theirs).

These are the *shared resources* that allow us to distinguish between superficially similar social situations (a strike, a riot, a community play, a festival) and know how to act appropriately (Jordan, 2006b, Chapter 7). They are also the *restraints* that limit our scope for self-indulgent and ultimately self-destructive behaviour, such as eating or drinking too much, or being disloyal to partners and colleagues (Offer, 2006).

The UK government does not discount the interpersonal economy's role in the care of people with disabilities and chronic illnesses. It constantly refers to the essential role of informal carers. But it does convey a very narrow understanding of the value of services for well-being. It fails to take account of the ways in which even the most expert services resemble the informal interpersonal economy in how they generate intimacy, respect and belonging. And it ignores the role of services in creating contexts for meaningful lives, through cultural resources and restraints.

Children's well-being and social contexts

It is a central tenet of social work with children that their development depends on an emotional environment which is loving, stimulating, comforting and challenging. Perhaps relationships of this kind are more recognised as essential for children's well-being than they are for those of adults. Close and reliable bonds with parents and kin are obviously the main factors in nurturing young children.

But education and socialisation rely on children making sense of a variety of settings and social environments, and gaining skills which transfer between them. So these relationships are of great significance for the development of young people who are able to contribute to the work and civic life of society. Here interactions with peers at school and in the neighbourhood are as important as those with teachers, youth leaders and adult members of associations and clubs.

So it matters how these different organisations mesh with families, and how children and parents are supported in connecting with this wider social world. Social and community work are often concerned with these links, as well as with the functioning of the family unit.

Recently, researchers have begun to try to compare children's well-being across countries, just as they have compared adult SWB (see Chapter 1). Using published data from the European Union archive, Jonathan Bradshaw, Petra Hoelscher and Dominic Richardson (2006) have brought together statistics from the 25 member states in a groundbreaking study. They used a multi-dimensional approach to indicators, based on UNICEF's framework of child poverty and well-being analysis.

This resulted in a child well-being index with 613 variables, arriving at maximal comparability and coverage. They put the data on 81 variables with 30 sub-domains and 12 domains into four clusters entitled *children's personal resources* (health from birth and children's subjective well-being, including personal, educational, financial and health self-assessments); *education* (attainment, participation and aspirations); *family and immediate environment* (including family relationships, economic situation, safety and housing) and *children's social resources* (quality of peer relations, civic participation and risk behaviour).

They then scored the 25 countries on each of these clusters, and compiled league tables for each, together with an overall table of child well-being in the EU. Although they insist that this is work-in-progress, their findings are important and interesting.

The UK scored very well for education, especially educational attainment; it was fourth in this, behind Finland, the Netherlands and Belgium (Bradshaw, et al., 2006, Figure 9). Italy, Spain and Greece were among the lowest rated in this cluster of domains, and Poland and the Czech Republic scored well – above Germany, whose performance was surprisingly mediocre (Figures 9–12).

However, the UK scored very poorly for child health (third worst of the 25 countries) and even worse in children's relationships, being lowest of the 21 countries with adequate data for relationships in families (Malta, Greece, Spain, Italy and Slovenia were the top five), and second lowest for relationships with peers. Overall the UK came bottom of the league in relationships (Figures 17–20). In subjective well-being (including risk and experience of violence) the UK was 22nd out of 25, above only Latvia, Estonia and Lithuania, with Spain, Cyprus, Sweden, Malta and the Netherlands the top five (Figure 28).

Finally, the researchers presented an overall table in which these clusters were combined to give a league table, reproduced below with their permission. The median score is represented by 100, with deviations, both positive and negative, shown on a scale. The left hand column represents all 25 countries, the right hand one the 21 for which over 70 per cent of the data were available.

These figures are striking because some poorer countries with few services for children do much better than some richer ones with far more services. It is not

Table 2.1 Index of child well-being

25 EU Member States		21 EU Member States	
1. Cyprus	110	Netherlands	108
2. Netherlands	108	Sweden	107
3. Sweden	107	Denmark	106
4. Denmark	106	Finland	103
5. Finland	103	Spain	103
6. Spain	103	Slovenia	103
7. Slovenia	103	Belgium	102
8. Belgium	102	Germany	102
9. Germany	102	Ireland	101
10. Luxemburg	101	Austria	100
11. Ireland	101	France	100
12. Austria	100	Italy	99
13. France	100	Poland	99
14. Malta	100	Greece	99
15. Italy	99	Portugal	98
16. Greece	99	Hungary	98
17. Poland	99	Czech Republic	98
18. Portugal	98	United Kingdom	96
19. Czech Republic	98	Latvia	94
20. Hungary	98	Estonia	91
21. United Kingdom	96	Lithuania	99
22. Slovak Republic	95		
23. Latvia	93		
24. Estonia	91		
25. Lithuania	89		

Source: Adapted from Bradshaw et al., 2006, Figures 30 and 31.

surprising that the Netherlands, Sweden, Denmark and Finland come at the top of the tables. These are states with extensive public welfare systems; the Scandinavian countries in particular are well known to have among the best pre-school provision in Europe, with high quality facilities that offer loving and play-orientated environments. Sweden and Denmark have 48 and 64 per cent of pre-school children (3–5 years) in day care kindergartens (OECD, 2001). They are also high in the league tables for educational attainment.

But the Mediterranean states (Spain, Italy, Slovenia, Greece, Cyprus and Malta) have very few such facilities. For example, Denmark's proportion of pre-school day care is ten times that of Italy, Spain and Greece (OECD, 2001). So these countries are in the top half of the league table of children's well-being in spite of an absence of state provision, and in spite of the mediocre or bad performance of their educational systems.

The reason for their position is that they score very well for children's personal resources, children's subjective assessments of their health and happiness, and their relationships with parents and peers. And this in turn seems to reflect societies in which the different spheres in which children and families live their daily lives are *consistent and coherent* – they support and reinforce each other, rather than pulling children and parents in different directions.

Just as Scandinavian kindergartens support the high proportion of mothers in employment in these societies, and schools and families seem also to be mutually supportive, so in the Mediterranean countries kinship networks, local communities and churches appear to provide good contexts for childhood and family life. They do not present parents and children with incompatible or stressful demands, and they sustain good relationships for development.

By contrast, the post-communist countries of central Europe, despite their good educational systems, do badly in the overall league tables. They are still poor, they have undergone a huge process of change after the collapse of the Soviet Bloc version of state socialism, and their social infrastructures in particular have been destroyed in the transitions. The nurseries and youth groups which were part of the socialist system have been disbanded, and parents are having to accept far more responsibility for their own lives than under the previous regimes. This implies that the various spheres for social activity are not (yet) congruent or coherent, and that families and children face conflicting pressures.

Among the large, rich countries of the EU (Germany, France, Austria and the UK) performance on child well-being is disappointing. But the UK does especially badly, mainly because of its dismal figures for children's personal resources, subjective well-being and relationships. Here again it seems likely that the lack of congruence and coherence between the social spheres is a large part of the problem. Parents are heavily committed to earning a living, work longer hours than in the other large rich states, have far less support from state services than in the Scandinavian countries, and live in a highly competitive and individualistic public culture.

It is easy to see how the ideology and policies of the UK government reinforce all these aspects of social life. New Labour's notion of services as experiences which are 'consumed' in the instant they are 'produced' leads it to see education and child care as a series of specific inputs. It distracts attention from the context for relationships, and from the overall coherence of the systems in which children grow up (Jordan, 2006b and c). Children grow up in the same culture of individualism, materialism and competition, which is reinforced by the emphasis on achievement in schools. This culture is now coming under criticism from educationalists and child care experts (*Daily Telegraph*, 2006). It has led to the setting up of an Inquiry into the Nature of a Good Childhood by the Childrens' Society (in September, 2006).

The policy document *Every Child Matters* (DfES, 2004) makes proposals for integrating children's services with education, in a more coherent system for realising children's potentials. The notion of 'well-being' has been introduced into the discourse of education, and especially early years education. Important steps have been taken away from a narrow emphasis on acquiring skills, and towards recognising the importance of communication, play, enjoyment and creativity. These developments are discussed in the last section of this book (pp. 140–9).

The value of services can only be fully realised if they pay attention to wider contexts, which enable good relationships, and to the overall coherence of their lives in families and communities.

Conclusions

In this chapter, I have argued that the lack of a convincing analysis of the economics of services has led the UK and other Anglophone countries to policies which are ill-conceived. The notion of services as goods which are 'instantly consumed' by individuals leads New Labour to overlook much of their potential value for well-being.

Individual autonomy and mobility are important aspects of well-being. This is why health is so significant as a factor affecting SWB; people with chronic illnesses and disabilities lose control of their lives, and access to many dimensions of membership. So they lose some of the respect and belonging which are central to exchanges in the interpersonal economy of citizenship.

But autonomy and mobility are means to the ends of membership, not 'goods' in themselves. They enable people to interact with others, and form relationships of equality and sharing. Personal freedom gives people the chance to seek happiness, but it does not give happiness in itself.

The UK government's model for human services puts a high priority on individual choice and the chance to switch between options. Services are packaged and delivered so as to enable this. It also emphasises efficiency and effectiveness, breaking down therapeutic services, family interventions, child protection and youth training into specific pieces, so that these can be priced and evaluated. These are then commissioned under contract in ways which allow precise costs to be accounted, and outcomes recorded.

This model loses a very substantial part of the value of services, because it fails to recognise:

- That human services involve interactions between professionals and service users, in which emotions such as empathy, closeness, respect and belonging are at stake. Services use the mechanisms of the interpersonal economy to produce much of their value.
- That social services deal in long-term interdependencies, not one-off experiences. Social care is not about 'independence' but about the quality of relationships in systems of relationships where people give and receive support over many years.
- That social services create cultures and contexts in which both professionals and service users make sense of the world, interpret and experience it. This is why anti-discriminatory and anti-oppressive approaches to practice are so important; the cultures and contexts created by social services should be sensitive to gender and ethnic differences, and create a diversity of understandings, in which groups can engage in dialogue about society and social interactions.
- That social services are also crucial for the congruence and coherence of people's experiences in various parts of their lives. They can promote this coherence in how they engage with service users and with colleagues in other organisations. This is not so much 'joined-up thinking' (which focuses on partnerships to achieve specific outcomes), as an approach which tries to mitigate the tensions and contradictions between the demands on people from different aspects of their social participation.

Of course this does not mean that New Labour's policies have completely undermined the interpersonal and contextual elements in services. For example, the service users who are interviewed in qualitative research on social care (such as those in the examples given in this chapter) constantly emphasise relationships with each other and with staff as the most positive features in provision. They do not subscribe to the view of services as segmented packages, each with a price tag, delivered in sequence, but with no overall continuity of relationships or meanings.

In the case of children, too, the new structures for services do potentially provide ways in which schools and child care facilities can be meaningfully linked, turning the context of children's experiences into a more coherent whole. The language of well-being permeates these reforms, even if the concept is not clearly defined, nor the economic model adequately modified. Although this approach is potentially undermined by government agendas on anti-social behaviour and security, it is developing in a bottom-up way, from the level of practice (see pp. 147–9).

The research and evaluation agenda also throws up findings which rebut the narrow version of service delivery. The preliminary study of the effectiveness of Sure Start found that local programmes made significant improvements in relationships between parents and children, but failed to do so in the much more specific learning and behavioural outcomes which were central to the initiative (NESS, 2004). In other words, the multidisciplinary staffs of local programmes were able to support the development of bonds between children and parents in deprived districts, even when they could not demonstrate the achievement of skills and capabilities. This implies that they were – in spite of the requirements of the policy and guidance – working within very supportive relationships, and through relationships.

Similarly, the headteacher of the primary school which came top of the national league table in SATS tests (at Witney in Oxfordshire), when asked about how she achieved such excellence, replied that she took no notice of test results. She focused on employing teachers who loved children, and creating an atmosphere of positive commitment among pupils (BBC Radio 4, 2006c).

In later chapters I shall argue for specific changes in the organisation of services which are indicated by the alternative analysis of the role of services for well-being outlined in this chapter. The main point here is to note that packaging and delivery of services is appropriate for a model in which consumer choice on the one hand, and contracts for effectiveness and cost-efficiency on the other, are central principles. Once we recognise that these do not give rise to optimal levels of well-being, the case for this model is greatly weakened.

The other side of the model, individuals who are 'independent' and move between options, is also a questionable basis for the social relations of well-being. High rates of geographical mobility, and switches which lead to concentrations of individuals of similar incomes and tastes (and of poverty, disability and exclusion) are not conducive to trust, cohesion and community participation (Jordan, 2006 a and b). Social services which aim to provide a context for equal citizenship and social justice should be accessible for all, and should promote interactions between different groups and communities. This is often incompatible with the economics of self-selecting residential districts and collective facilities.

Chapter 3

Relationships: The History of an Idea in Social Work

Introduction

So far in this book I have analysed the doubts emerging in affluent societies, about the material basis for individual well-being, and drawn attention to an alternative account of well-being in the literature of social work practice. I have presented a critique of the economic principles which inform the organisation of personal social services provision, and shown how they ignore the contribution of interpersonal value to people's SWB, and of cultures and context, to well-being in societies.

In this chapter, I shall show that augmenting the hidden value of relationships of all kinds through relationships with service users and communities has been the dominant rationale of social and community work since their emergence. Historians who have charted the birth, growth and transformation of the professions have emphasised the differences between the various stages of their development, and the schools of thought which sustained these distinctions. I shall consider the common features of professional thinking and activity throughout this period, and their roots in a kind of resistance to the consequences of commercial and capitalist social relations.

In Chapter 2, I argued that personal social services and community work are largely substitutes for (or complements to) the interpersonal economy of mutual support among families, kin and neighbours. This traditional system of relationships was disrupted by the advent of commercial economic systems and the growth of industrial and urban social organisations. In the face of ideas and lifestyles which gave priority to work, earning and consumptions and which disrupted all forms of social unit through a process of 'creative destruction' (Polanyi, 1944; Schumpeter, 1934), social and community work focused on the bonds between people as more reliable sources of well-being.

An accelerated version of the same pattern has been evident in Central Europe since the collapse of state socialism in 1989. There the institutions being destroyed by commerce and capitalism were the ones which sustained Marxism-Leninism – state enterprises and unions, cultural and sports centres, youth groups and kindergartens. With their collapse, and the shift towards a new culture of self-responsibility and accumulation, social work rapidly re-emerged, to deal with the casualties of this process (Jordan, 1997a, 2004).

My purpose is to trace the common themes in 150 years of writing about social work, and show how these reflect a response to the commercialisation and industrialisation of social relations. In social work education, it is far easier to teach about the differences between, say, the Charity Organisation Society in the late nineteenth century and the services which emerged as part of the welfare state in the UK after the Second World War. But the common themes indicate how social work is embedded in the interpersonal economy, and the value which it creates and distributes.

What has changed over time was the cultural and political context in which relationships were understood. In the late nineteenth century, leading figures in the charitable societies which sponsored social and community work saw relationships as part of a 'moral economy' (Scott, 1976). They had a Christian conception of the value of people to each other, and of the kind of society practitioners should promote. This involved the traditional virtues of individual and family life, but also new forms of 'friendship' between members of different classes (Jordan, 1984).

In the first half of the twentieth century, awareness of the impact of collective factors such as class and power, and of the collective impact of economic forces on income and employment, added new dimensions to the moral analysis of relationships. This paved the way for the post-war emergence of public services, in which democratic membership and social justice supplied a more politicised context for practice (Cole, 1945).

This in turn was further nuanced and refined by the acknowledgement of identity and diversity, as factors in the experience of social problems, leading to practice which reflected a fuller awareness of gender, sexual orientation and ethnic group membership as dimensions of the cultural context (Dominelli and McLeod, 1989; Dominelli, 1988). Yet the fundamental model of well-being in society promoted by social work has remained similar throughout. Adams et al.'s definition (2005: 2) – helping them 'in such a way that enhances their social relationships and well-being' – has held throughout this history.

I shall analyse how social work theory tries to combine practices which stem from the liberal values of individual moral responsibility and freedom with the values that arise from critical perspectives on power and exclusion – anti-oppressive, anti-discriminatory and emancipatory principles. My argument will be that a focus on the interpersonal production and distribution of value, in the form of emotions and cultural resources, dissolves many of the apparent contradictions between care and control, individual and collective methods, and the various schools of thought that have vied for influence on practice.

In my account of the history of a central idea in social work, I shall emphasise the continuities in this development. Practitioners have always tried to balance individual freedom with bonds of love, duty, mutual responsibility and equal membership. Differences between 'schools' of thought have been ones of emphasis rather than fundamental principle. This means that social work can contribute to the debate about well-being in a coherent way, which emphasises the value of relationships for SWB.

Origins and Foundational Ideas

In the standard texts about the origins and basic principles of social and community work, the nineteenth century founding organisers of practice, the Charity Organisation Society (COS), are usually portrayed as being concerned primarily with the morals of the poor. In this version, the individual should be self-responsible, and make provision for 'the ordinary contingencies of life' (Loch, 1895: 698–9). The family should be the basic support unit for the health and welfare needs of all its members (Loch, 1884: 8–9). Hence the Society saw all social problems and needs as requiring 'self-dependence'.

> *The possibility that the fault could lie, wholly or in part, in the economic set-up of society did not enter the collective mind of the COS. To them, character, not circumstance, was the explanation of failure.*
>
> (Woodroofe, 1962: 34)

In similar vein, Younghusband (1981: 12) wrote that 'Both the religious urge and the prevailing individualist philosophy led the pioneers to concentrate on the individual, on what they called "character", to be supported if it was there or deplored if it was not'.

However, new scholarship shows that this was only part of the story. The founding organisers and practitioners drew their inspiration from moral philosophers whose vision of society was not individualistic, and who opposed the materialistic basis of capitalist social relations. In particular the British Idealists – T.H. Green, Bernard Bosanquet, Henry Jones, Sidney Ball and Charles Gore – were personally known to them; Bosanquet's wife, Helen, was a leading member of the COS. Although the Idealists – now claimed to be the progenitors of 'Ethical Socialism' (Carter, 2003) – did indeed emphasise individual character and family self-dependence, they did so in a particular context of social relationships:

> *. . . Bosanquet argued that a moral socialism, which is founded on a notion of the common good and an organic society, 'is the only thing for which any healthy human being, at the bottom of his heart, cares a single straw'. It was the emphasis on social interdependence and citizenship in many socialist doctrines that Jones also found most appealing: 'It is Socialism in some form or other alone that evinces any consciousness of the deepened solidarity of modern citizenship'.*
>
> (Carter, 2003: 147–8)

So it was the 'moral economy' of social relationships rather than the material economy of capitalist, industrialised urban development that the Idealists saw as providing the basis for a socialism of the common good. Compare the following two statements:

> *. . . man is, in his essence, united into society with his fellows, and that his inner self can only realise itself through a social Polity, which is himself, though it be more than himself.*
>
> (Holland, 1900: 31)

> *[Interactional social work assumes] a relationship between the individual and his nurturing group which we would describe as 'symbiotic' – each needing the other for its own life and growth, and each reaching out to the other with all the strength it can command at a given moment.*
>
> (Schwartz, 1961: 146–7)

The latter sentence is taken as the main source of inspiration for Shulman's model of practice (1999: 10) in his guide to practice. The former is by a leading British Idealist; the words omitted at the start of the sentence are 'Socialism teaches that . . .'

So the Christian ethic which inspired the COS pioneers was far from being individualist; its morality was deeply social, and specifically claimed to be socialist. Its approach to relationships was very similar to the one claimed 100 years later by a basic social work text, and it claimed that the true value of a society lay in the bonds between individual members, which should reflect the pre-eminence of the social over the individual, and a community working together for the common good (Gore, c 1900: 11).

This gave rise to practice which promoted close personal attention to the lives of poor people, based on empathy and respect. The earliest of the educated, middle-class women who adopted these methods was Elizabeth Fry, who visited women in Newgate prison from 1813, and organised sewing classes for them; she also persuaded the Home Secretary of a thoroughly oppressive Tory government to modify the disciplinary system in favour of a regime for reformation and moral improvement. Later, Josephine Butler ran homes for prostitutes and women with illegitimate children which adopted similar principles.

These ideas were formalised by the COS, which started to train its visitors in the final quarter of the century. One of its leaders, Octavia Hill, expressed the values behind the new professional approach very clearly. The best practice was supposed to bridge the gap between the social classes with an offer of 'friendship', which avoided the patronising and arrogant style of earlier good works. Her own projects for social housing were practical contributions to material as well as moral regeneration for the inhabitants of city slums. Above all, they were based on generous supplies of personal attention, given in a spirit of humility and common humanity. Octavia Hill argued that what the poor needed was 'not alms but a friend':

> *By friendship she meant giving all her resources to the common pool of daily life in which she shared as an equal.*
>
> (Cormack, 1945: 97)

She brought to all these relationships an attitude of 'respectfulness' which gave full recognition to her tenants' dignity, and to the moral significance of all the interactions between them. She encouraged them to meet in a communal room, for a social centre and a crèche, she provided a playground for children, and involved the tenants in all stages of the organisation of her scheme. But her ideal of the relationships of friendships and equality did not stop her pursuing and challenging fraud and false pretences by applicants for charitable aid.

Octavia Hill, like the COS's secretary, Charles Loch, thought of charity as a 'social regenerator' (Woodroofe, 1962: 50). She wanted to improve the social relations of poor districts by these methods:

Only when face meets face, and heart meets heart; only in the settled link with those who are old friends . . . is [there] more opportunity . . . to grow and shine.

(Hill, 1891: 169)

While all these pioneers (including Canon Barnett, who founded the Settlement Movement, and is regarded as the originator of community work) were connected with the British Idealist philosophers, and influenced by the principles of ethical socialism, they were also bearers of an older cultural tradition. Just as T.H. Green, Bernard Bosanquet and the other Idealists looked to Hegel and the German School for their inspiration, social work practitioners must have been conscious of a literary sensibility from the English novelists of the earlier part of their century.

After all, Charles Dickens had conveyed a vivid and detailed account of interactions between middle-class women philanthropists and the denizens of London's under-world. Especially in *Bleak House* (1852) (recently adapted in a brilliant TV series by the BBC) where Dickens presented both the self-deluding Mrs Jellyby and the patronising Mrs Pardiggle as grotesques, and their impoverished clients as grimly realistic survivors. By contrast, the heroine Esther Summerson is represented very much in the terms of Octavia Hill's social worker; she is respectful, modest and self-effacing. Similarly, the novels of George Eliot portray a rich tapestry of social relations, in which certain women characters (such as Dinah Morris in *Adam Bede*) play a key role in enabling the moral improvement of flawed characters.

In this section I have drawn attention to the similarities between the principles of the nineteenth-century pioneers in the UK, and the interactionist model adopted in current social work theory. While individual moral autonomy is important in both models, this is located in a context of interdependence and the common good. The main difference is the overt Christian content of the founders' ideas, in the UK and USA.

Summarising the contribution of the Idealists to these principles, and to ethical socialism, Carter writes:

Green and his colleagues presented a philosophy that rejected the atomistic individualism and empirical assumptions which were believed to have underpinned Classical Liberalism. Instead their idealism emphasised a unity in the thought and understanding of the world, which in social terms . . . was reflected in the coming together of individuals in an organic society . . . [His followers] repeated his new philosophical settlement in a host of different domains, from the top table at the Charity Organisation Society to the pulpit of St Paul's.

(Carter, 2003: 188)

If the main source of value in an ethical society was relationships of friendliness, equality and common interest, this involved the rejection of materialistic and mechanistic versions of socialism and the role of the state. This set the scene for a confrontation in the next century.

Social work, socialism and the state

In the orthodox narrative of the development of social work in the UK, the Royal Commission on the Poor Laws (1905–9) is represented as a watershed. The Majority Report, whose protagonists included C. S. Loch, Helen Bosanquet and Octavia Hill, represented the view of the COS, and prescribed a limited role for the state in the provision of social protection and social services. The Minority Report, chiefly written by Beatrice Webb, had behind it the sponsorship of the leaders of the Fabian Society – her husband, Sidney Webb, Bernard Shaw, H.G. Wells and the rest. In the orthodox narrative, this was a confrontation which postponed the reform of the Poor Laws, and delayed the implementation of the welfare state.

This view is now disputed. The disagreement between the COS and the Fabian Society was not liberal individualism *versus* socialism, but a battle between two alternative versions of socialism. The Idealists objected to Marxist theory, on the grounds that it reduced people to the pawns of economic forces, much as capitalism did:

> *Human affairs are not governed by mechanical laws and do not move towards necessarily determined conclusions . . . [I]f there is no change in the spirit among men, the class war might proceed to revolution and to the victory of the proletariat, but it would not really ameliorate the lot of men or give them liberty, it would only substitute a bureaucratic tyranny for a plutocratic.*
>
> (Gore, 1922: 10)

The COS members of the Royal Commission were indeed concerned that large-scale state systems for relieving poverty were too mechanistic and impersonal, and could undermine self-reliance, community organisation and self-help associations, as well as the traditional virtues of prudence and thrift.

The Fabians wanted state schemes for pensions, health, education and employment, and in this sense did anticipate the development of services which came into full function only after 1945. It is a fascinating 'what if?' question of history to speculate which of the Fabian recommendations would have been adopted by the Liberal government before the First World War, if they had been able to persuade the majority of the Commission. As it was, of course, Lloyd George as Chancellor of the Exchequer did introduce state pensions, unemployment and industrial injury insurance, against strong opposition from the House of Lords, but the Poor Law itself was reformed rather than abolished.

In defending a system which stigmatised and punished destitute citizens through the workhouse system (however modified) the COS representatives on the Commission did associate the charitable tradition of social work with an anti-state political stance, and this was to haunt the voluntary sector for the next 80 years.

Because Charles Loch, Helen Bosanquet and Octavia Hill were so determined to uphold an ethical version of the role of services, they were implacably opposed to the *style* of argument for state systems adopted by the Fabians. But they did concede much to the critics of the Poor Law. For example, they allowed terms such as 'systems of help' and 'public assistance' to be substituted for the old, harsh vocabulary of 'pauperism' and 'outdoor relief', and advocated more regulation of employment, more technical education, labour exchanges and public works.

The standard view of the Commission recognises that 'the majority showed a greater understanding of human need' (Younghusband, 1981: 18). As Horner points out, the Fabians paid little attention to *personal* social services, and the few they would have created in the public sector would have been punitive in their nature, because they thought the mainstream welfare services would meet most needs:

> *Their concession to a residual social work function would be – and here is the irony – that of a social control nature, as they saw the need for enforcement, recommending detention colonies for a residual group of the 'work-shy and lazy'.*
>
> (Horner, 2003: 24)

After the First World War, as issues of poverty, unemployment and class conflict sharpened, the divide between the advocates of state-led socialism and those in the ethical tradition of Green, Bosanquet and the Idealists became institutionalised. But several intellectuals of the left bridged this divide, and continued to link the latter principles (and voluntary sector social work) with the Labour Party and the Fabian Society. One of these was R.H. Tawney, generally regarded as the leading British socialist thinker of the twentieth century.

Tawney was an undergraduate at Oxford during the dominance of the Idealists, in the early 1890s, and absorbed the spirit of their philosophy. He worked closely with Edward Caird, one of that school, and – along with his future brother-in-law, William Beveridge – visited Toynbee Hall, the first University settlement in East London. He was also associated with Scott Holland and Charles Gore (the Bishop of Oxford), followers of Green, and with R.B. Haldane, a politician raised in that tradition.

The most obvious sign of their influence in his writing was his insistence on the value of the *spiritual* over the mechanical or scientific in human life. He argued that economic power and economic efficiency supplied an inadequate version of the good life, and that belief in God was a necessary condition for equality:

> *The Social problem is a problem not of quantities, but of proportions, not of the amount of wealth but of the moral justice of your social system.*
>
> (Tawney, 1922: 18)

Tawney specifically attacked the theory of value of the Fabians and Marxists, because of their mechanistic approach, which equated what workers deserved with their productivity, rather than their social function:

> *Ideally conceived, society is an organism of different grades, and human activities form a hierarchy of functions, which differ in kind and in significance, but each of*

which is of value on its own plane, provided that it is governed, however remotely, by the end which is common to all.

(Tawney, 1926: 34)

As parts of such an organic society, individuals' relationships with each other contributed to this common good (Carter, 2003: 174–5). Capitalism undermined the functional order, and concealed the value of relationships. The shared values and culture of a society should enable individuals to have equal access to social opportunities, despite economic inequalities. Equality demanded:

. . . not necessarily . . . an identical level of pecuniary incomes, but of equality of environment, of access to education and the means of civilisation, of security and independence and of the social consideration which equality in these matter usually comes with.

(Tawney, 1926: 17)

Another leading figure in socialist thinking between the wars, G.D.H. Cole, was also instrumental in trying to bridge the factions of the movements. Although he was closer to the Fabians on the question of state leadership and economic power, his version of Guild Socialism (in the tradition of Ruskin and William Morris) argued for decentralisation and workers' control. This was to be implemented through collectives of workers and co-operatives of consumers and providers of public services. He deplored the 'capitalistic character' of health and education professionals, and thought that public servants should avoid 'the spirit of greed, grab and acquisitive struggle' (Cole, 1920: 96–7).

This was a period in which the modern orthodoxy in economic analysis was taking shape, through the writings of Lionel Robbins (1931) and A.C. Pigou (1920). But there were also many who challenged the idea that all value was to be measured purely in terms of abstract 'utility' reflected in the price that consumers were willing to pay for goods and services. Writers such as Bertrand and Dora Russell (Russell, 1918) C.H. Douglas (1920a and b) and A.R.Orage (1935) proposed reforms in banking and credit which would allow entirely different forms of economic measurement of value to be deployed.

In professional social work, these political debates were reflected in continuing disagreements about the role of the state. But while these focused on economic power and class among the socialist societies, within the profession it was the nature of relationships themselves, which was the main topic of dispute and innovations. As much as unemployment and poverty, Marxism and fascism, practitioners had to come to terms with the writings of Freud and his followers during this period.

From the second decade of the century, social work educators and practitioners turned towards psychology and psychiatry as the basis for their expertise, at the expense of a *moral* analysis of relationships between members and citizens. The inner worlds of individuals, as much as the bonds between them, became a new focus of interest. In the 1930s, and especially in the USA, Freudian psychodynamic theory became the standard ideology, as well as analytic framework, in some social work schools. Describing what she called the 'Psychiatric Deluge' in that country, Woodroofe wrote:

> *By 1940, according to one American writer, any deviation from Freudian psychology in the theory of social work 'was looked upon by some with the same horror as a true Stalinist appraising a Trotskyite' [Miles, 1954: 9]. The reasons were the same in both cases: both had become a religion with a theology, an organisation and an inquisition to discover and punish heresy.*
>
> (Woodroofe, 1962: 130)

This was undoubtedly an exaggeration. There were, at the same time, many developments within local and national government in the USA which incorporated social work into the New Deal, as part of policies to address poverty and unemployment. Indeed, after describing the 'Psychiatric Deluge', Woodroofe's next chapter was entitled 'The State as Social Worker' (Woodroofe, 1962, Chapter 7).

Practitioners in these new public agencies adopted a new approach, which was less intrusive, and less concerned with morality and character:

> . . . *the social worker, who sat at an application desk in an unemployment relief office, realised as never before that the casework relationships was a reciprocal one in which she had to 'accept' herself and her client equally. Too many of the applicants were people like herself with much the same or sometimes better cultural background, education and previous earning capacity. She knew that, but for the grace of a relief programme, which put a premium on her work, she would be on the applicant's side of the desk.*
>
> (Woodroofe, 1962: 167)

In the UK, these processes of change in both directions was slower. Only in the early child guidance clinics did social workers truly embrace psychodynamic approaches; only in public hospital almoning were they closely involved in state agencies. As Younghusband (1981: 19) put it, 'initiative and fresh discovery died down in social work itself for almost the first 40 years of the twentieth century'. But the Second World War ushered in a new political climate, in which the profession became part of the welfare state.

Collective services and the welfare state

The New Deal in the USA required social workers there to embrace 'a new democratic approach to the people who sought the caseworker's aid' (Woodroofe, 1962: 167). By the end of the Second World War, the same kind of relationship was recognised as being needed for the services which would be constructed by the Labour Government. Writing in a volume about *Voluntary Social Services: Their Place in the Modern State*, the socialist author G.D.H. Cole (1945: 29) both evoked the ethical theory of the British Idealists, and looked forward to the new political settlement that was taking shape, under the guidance of the Beveridge Report (1942). Social work:

> *... transforms itself ... into communal service, designed to widen and deepen the expression of the spirit of democratic cooperation. As long as there are rich and poor, this will tend in some degree to reflect inequalities in class and income. But under modern conditions there can and does enter into them much of a different and more egalitarian spirit. This democratic element is fostered by the growth of the salaried professions upon whose members an increasing amount of the actual work devolves.*

Cole and his contemporaries were arguing for public services which modelled new forms of social citizenship, in which relationships among fellow members of society were expressed in the way that these professionals related to service users. Elizabeth Macadam, who had pleaded for a broader outlook before the War, considered that all the new public services of the welfare state should share this ethic and political philosophy:

> *Social services have now no hard and fast boundaries. They cover all efforts preventive and curative which are concerned with the attack on the giant evils of the Beveridge Report ... Our former limited ideas as to the scope of social work must be cast aside ... It extends to the community as a whole and is concerned with all the efforts to generate throughout the world equal opportunities – physical, economic, intellectual and spiritual for all.*

(Macadam, 1945: 126, 134–5)

So this was as much a political as a professional project. Welfare states were designed to win the loyalty of citizens, after a devastating conflict, in which fascism had been defeated, but state socialism in its Soviet form now ruled over a substantial part of Europe, and threatened to spread throughout the globe. The founding figures of the welfare state, taking their lead from Beveridge (a Liberal) were keen to emphasise that the new politics preserved individual liberty and party contest, while including working class organisations and interests.

The aim was to create a more regulated, planned and collectivised economic and social environment, but one in which private property and enterprise still supplied the main structure and dynamic. Services balanced and compensated for the harsher features of urban and industrial life: social housing schemes, for example, attempted to create more convivial context for interactions among the families of workers.

It was as if the Fabians had won the battle over the Labour government's economic programme – the nationalisation of key industries, the planning of investment and production, and the redistribution of income – while the ethical socialists had had some influence on the programme for public services (the NHS and education system, as well as the local authority personal social services).

But the weakness in this model was that there was no integration between the economic analysis on which the two programmes were based. Planning, industrial policy and redistribution reflected the ideas of J.M. Keynes (another Liberal), who argued that the aggregate demand for goods could be managed by government action, keeping incomes up and unemployment down. But there was no counterpart in an economic account of the role of public services because, as we saw in Chapter 2, there was very little in the way of an economics of services.

Indeed, the most influential figure in the *Economics of Welfare*, A.C. Pigou, had nothing to say about health, education or personal social services in his 1920 account of the subject. In the long run, as we have seen, this reliance on political arguments for public services made them vulnerable to market-minded and individualistic critics, who could present arguments from efficiency and choice for their fragmentation.

In the field of social work, the most forceful case for the reform of the remnants of the Poor Laws came from the inquiries into the human consequences of their operation, especially for children. The first, on the death of Dennis O'Neill, a child in the care of Newport (Monmouthshire) Education Department, found that lax supervision, poor coordination and tardy action all contributed to his fate at the hands of a brutal foster father. Sir Walter Monckton's committee reported that the overriding failure of the local authority officials was lack of awareness of the human needs of children, especially for warm and caring relationships:

> The 'fit person', local authority or individual, must care for the child as his own; the relation is a personal one . . . [There was not] sufficient realisation of the direct and personal nature of the relationship between a supervisory authority and a boarded-out child . . . the administrative machinery should be improved and informed by a more anxious and responsible spirit.

(Monckton, 1945: 15, 17, 18)

The second inquiry, by a Committee chaired by Dame Myra Curtis, was on the care of children deprived of normal family life, and recommended the establishment of a single local authority department with this responsibility. Although the term 'social worker' was not used, the Committee was 'increasingly impressed by the need for the personal element in the care of children, which Sir Walter Monckton emphasised in his report on the O'Neill case' (Curtis, 1946: 146). The department should be headed (ideally) by a social science graduate with experience of children and good administrative activities:

> Her essential qualifications, however, would be on the personal side. She should be genial and friendly in manner and able to set both children and adults at their ease.

(Curtis, 1946: 149)

So the new culture in the Children's Departments (and the local authority welfare services for older and disabled people with social care needs) attempted to combine sensitivity to emotional and family factors with a wider commitment to equality, democracy and community. This was reflected in the numerous university and college training courses for social workers which sprang up at the time, as these agencies recruited the bright young graduates from working class families who were the first generation to get secondary and tertiary education as part of the social citizenship of the welfare state.

The high water mark of public sector social work came in the late 1960s and early 1970s, when the local authority Children's and Welfare Departments were merged, following the Seebohm Report. This created large, generic agencies, intended to be a Fifth Social Service, almost on a par with health, education, social security and housing. But the reforms of that period mainly addressed issues of coordination and management, against a background of growing political radicalism in the public services:

> *The vision behind this re-organisation was ambitious – a comprehensive and universal social work service, which embraced community alternatives to hospitals and other institutions for adults and children, and used group and community work approaches to a range of social issues.*
>
> (Horner, 2003: 87)

The authors of the Seebohm Report, which drew up the blueprint for the new agency, were optimistic that it would enjoy wide public support, and provide leadership and direction for a changing society. They defined its tasks broadly, as to:

> *. . . enable the greatest possible number of individuals to act reciprocally, giving and receiving service for the well-being of the whole community.*
>
> (Seebohm Report, 1968, Paragraph 2)

It was not only in social work that this period can be seen as the high point of collectivism, led by an organising state, in the UK. It was also the era of massive urban rebuilding, the construction of outer-city, council estates, and the rapid expansion of comprehensive education. It might be perceived as Britain's attempt to emulate Sweden, by developing a public infrastructure which shaped the context of citizens' lives, and their interactions with each other from cradle to grave.

But this attempt carried the seeds of its own destruction, which were clearly visible at the time. Industry was in decline, unable to compete with the USA and Germany or the newly industrialising South East Asian states in world markets. Collective action was directed as much against the state as towards new solutions to the challenges faced by the country. The long traditions of possessive individualism and class struggle did not recognise the new collective institutions as reliable ones in which to settle conflicts of interests.

In social work, the symptoms of the malaise of this period included:

- A new trade union consciousness amongst the staff of social services departments, which mobilised on the side of forces resistant to many of the government's strategies and policies.
- A new radical, critical perspective on practice (Bailey and Brake, 1976; Statham, 1978) which highlighted issues of power and injustice, implicating social work and other public services in the structural disadvantages of citizens in need.

- More negative public images of social work, reflecting the resistance of the popular press and sections of public opinion to what was seen as an over-mighty alliance between government and the public service professions. This deployed evidence of the child protection scandals, such as the death of Maria Colwell (Parton, 1985) against social workers, portraying them as over-politicised and incompetent.

All these factors contributed to the public services' (and the collectivist model's) vulnerability to a neo-liberal backlash. Margaret Thatcher drew on the ideas of elderly economists like F.A. Hayek (1960, 1978) and Ludwig Von Mises (1966) to attack the economics of Keynesianism and the socialism of Tawney and Cole. Her revolution was to insist that individuals in markets supply the basic units of society, and that social services should be a last resort. The consequences of this revolution are still being felt by practitioners today.

Individualism and social work practice

I have argued throughout this chapter that the theory on which social work practice is based has had relationships (both close and civic) at its heart. But the 1970s and the 1980s saw a sudden shift between a somewhat state-led, collectivist approach to the organisation of social work, to a radical individualism which used social services as a safety net for those unable to keep pace with change, competition and the struggle for survival. During this period, it was harder for the profession to hold its bearings, because the political culture in which it was embedded was so volatile.

After 1979, one manifestation of this instability was the sheer volume of need – unemployment, destitution, homelessness and personal disintegration – which followed from the new government's reforms. A large section of society found itself without the structural supports (from workmates and neighbours as well as services) which had sustained it for the previous three decades. The social services departments had to try to deal with the consequences of this deterioration within a hostile financial and political climate.

In this context, it was not surprising that analysts focused on power and oppression, and developed ideas about how to counter them. Anti-oppressive principles, which promoted equality and justice, became prominent in its literature (Jordan, 1990; Thompson, 1993).

On the other hand, the new culture of individualism emphasised self-reliance, self-development and self-improvement (Rose, 1996). The expectation by the government (and gradually people's own expectations of themselves) was of being 'independent' – autonomous-mobile, shifting and switching between options. Margaret Thatcher's property-owning democracy was made up of citizens with mortgages, who looked to the bank rather than the state for support, and who regarded the market as the source for identity and self-expression through consumption (Jordan, 2004).

Just as a politics of identity and diversity emerged within this society, so the literature of social work reflected issues of ethnicity (Dominelli, 1988) and gender

(Dominelli and McLeod, 1989). Practitioners themselves were encouraged to be aware of power dimensions in their own lives, and develop themselves as well as enabling service users to be self-realising (Lishman, 1998).

But (as we saw in Chapter 2) the background to these theoretical innovations was the relentless fragmentation of social work organisations, and the emphasis on efficiency, effectiveness and managerial control. Practitioners faced an uphill struggle to make space for reflection, and for work which allowed them to interact with service users in a way which did full justice to their thoughts and feelings about their overall situation.

As a consequence of all this, practice has become a hectic round of assessment, risk-management and review. It has become rather formalised, arm's length and office-based, involving check-lists and standardised procedures. Child protection work has become more accountable to courts, guidelines and timetables. The scope for interpersonal negotiations has narrowed (Jordan with Jordan, 2000). In voluntary agencies these pressures are less intense, but still of the same nature.

Under New Labour, there have been many new initiatives around social inclusion, focused on deprived groups and communities, where social problems became concentrated in the Thatcher era. But these have drawn community work away from its connections with social work, and deployed a range of new support, outreach and specialist workers, with new titles and tasks. As Mark Drakeford puts it:

> . . . when the government acted in generous mode – in the Sure Start Scheme for disadvantaged children to take just one example – the term 'social work' almost never appeared in official discourse, even when the tasks undertaken – advice, guidance, practical help and so on – appeared very close indeed to social work itself. Only when the government turned to authoritarian mode – in its treatment of 'anti-social' children, the regulation of the family, or the compulsory treatment of the mentally ill – did the place of social work seem secure.
>
> (Drakeford, 2002: 35)

This brings us up to the present, and to the new debate about well-being, prompted by psychological research and the breast-beating of economists. As we saw at the start of Chapter 1, social work principles and the teaching of practice have not deviated from an interactionist perspective, which sees the interpersonal economy of intimacy, respect and belonging as its domain, and relationships as its means. But government policy and the requirements of audit and quality control use a very different yardstick to evaluate its work.

In some ways this is surprising. I have traced the origins of these ideas to the writings of the British Idealists, whose ethical socialism was a response to the cruelty and squalor of nineteenth-century capitalism. Their view of an organic community, in which the quality of relationships and contribution to the common good was more valuable than the production and consumption of material goods, had a profound and enduring influence on social and community work.

Paradoxically, this tradition is more obviously alive and well in the UK now than at any time since the Second World War. New Labour, in rejecting the Fabian view of a collectivist welfare state, and the leading role of the public sector in social life, has returned to the ideas of the ethical socialists. Its rhetoric is very similar to that of T.H. Green, Bernard Bosanquet and Charles Gore. As Matt Carter, until recently the General Secretary of the Labour Party, puts it:

> ... Tony Blair provides the best example of a generation of Labour leaders who have recorded a link with these traditions. Blair is significant because he has also been influenced by the work of Green and the Idealists, primarily through the work of the philosopher John Macmurray. Blair's own definition of ethical socialism also strongly reflected the ideological settlement established by the idealists with notions such as common good, rights and responsibilities, and an organic society, in which individuals can flourish only by working together, placed central in his thinking.

(Carter, 2003: 189–90)

But this is perhaps the central paradox of the story told in this chapter. Just as the COS was unable to detach its ethical version of the good society as a community of harmonious relationships from its commitment to the freedom of individuals, property and enterprise, so too New Labour locates its version of socialism in an individualistic culture and a free market. It is ironic that social work, which was incorporated into the fabric of the welfare state during the intervening period, should be one of the main victims of this unresolved tension between individual moral autonomy and communal mutuality.

This is why the debate about well-being provides a new opportunity, and a challenge for social work. The critique of economists like Layard and Offer of their own discipline, and of Tories like David Cameron of the Thatcherite legacy, allows the question of how well-being relates to value, and how value is analysed, to be re-opened, with capitalism on the back foot.

Conclusions

I have argued that relationships have always been central to the idea of practice, and that social work has always encompassed a view of society in which value is created by relationships of empathy, equality and justice. Social workers use their relationships with service users to add to this value. They *produce* value through these interpersonal transactions, and *enhance* the value that their clients create in their relationships, by improving them (if possible).

This emphasis has sometimes been misunderstood, both by those outside the profession and by some inside it. The 'use of self' which was emphasised by theorists from the earliest beginnings to the present is not something precious and pretentious, but a realistic description of what social workers do. To describe practice in terms of 'personalised help' is simply to distinguish it from the impersonal provision of money or goods, just as the ethical socialists distinguished their view of the moral economy from the Fabians' model of a mechanistic economy, driven by impersonal forces, to maximise material production.

In his book, *Social Exclusion and Social Work: The Idea of Practice*, Michael Sheppard (2006: 122) is critical of my work, along with that of Keith-Lucas (1972), Ragg (1977) and England (1986) for giving too much importance to the personal elements in practice, and to the empathy involved in transactions. He describes this as an individualised approach, evoking the criticisms made of the COS in the early twentieth century. But this is to misunderstand the significance of relationship-based social work (it deals in the value created in the interpersonal economy) and its scope (it applies to wider social relations, as well as close ties among family and friends).

Sheppard's own preference is for social work which focuses on rational autonomy and rational action, and which concentrates on improving and widening service users' capacities in these respects. He sees the transactions between workers and clients as 'rational conversations', involving negotiation and persuasion. He also locates the justification for practice in a consensus around the nature of social problems, and the legal power to intervene to ameliorate them, meet need, or control behaviour.

The difficulty with this approach is its stance on issues of structural inequality and injustice. In a society based on private property and capitalist enterprise, issues of value are determined by a logic of consumer choice and ownership of resources. Sheppard is critical of Marxist and other structural critiques of society, because they cannot be derived from the consensus or the law.

But, as we have seen in this chapter, social work's origins lay in just such a critique of capitalism and its consequences. From the start, social workers, like the ethical scientists, insisted that:

- The value created by a society consists more in the quality of feelings and interpersonal bonds generated by its relationships than in the quantity of material goods it produces.
- Social work practice aims to improve the quality of relationships, and cooperation for the common good.
- This includes all relationships by members of society with each other, and hence has a collective dimension, which can be enhanced by the policies and organisations of the state.

This stance sets social workers in a half-oppositional stance to the mainstream of society, under a system of private property, markets and capitalism, because it refuses to recognise that economic criteria are paramount in issues of value. This stance cannot be adequately captured by Sheppard's 'objective', 'rational' and 'realistic' version of the profession, which places it too firmly within the mainstream.

The debate about well-being allows social work to emerge from a position of covert resistance to the logic of markets, choice and independence, and engage actively in issues about well-being. These will be more fully explored in Part Two of this book.

Chapter 4

Constructive Social Work in Public Services

Introduction

If the hidden value of social work lies in its ability to improve relationships in society, and hence well-being, how is this consistent with its statutory role? Practitioners are required to intervene in child abuse, truancy, drug and alcohol misuse and delinquency, as well as serious mental illness, often against the wishes of the clients. Surely these duties imply a controlling function, which addresses anti-social behaviour and corrects deranged or irresponsible individuals, rather than seeking to produce value by positive interactions?

This point has been made in two different ways in the literature of social work. On the one hand, it has been asserted by those who emphasise that practice is concerned with the social functioning of individuals (with adjustment to social norms and legal standards), and with the efficient working of the economy and social system. On the other, it has been used by critical theorists (Marxists and others) to castigate their opponents (including the functionalists) for aligning practice with the power of property, the state and the law.

Between these two poles have been many intelligent and fair-minded commentators who have simply drawn attention to the political and legal basis for social work under democratic regimes, and concluded that practice is inescapably conducted under rules which connect practitioners with the mainstream institutions and ideas of a society. For instance, Michael Sheppard (2006: 100–10) argues that social workers' powers under child protection and mental health legislation, connect practice with the need which some clients have to overcome 'internal constraints' on their capacity to act rationally. This is an 'objective need' – for instance, the fact that some parents are factually unable to control their tempers, and hence put their children at risk:

> Just as there is an explicit connection, in British legislation, between need, harm and adequate child care, so there is also a direct connection with the notion of rationality. Indeed, there is a direct connection between all three, and social work intervention. The standards of behaviour which social workers are expected to maintain and support, in the legislation, are those of the 'reasonable parent' – reasonable being derivative from rational. This is apparent from the Children Act,

Section 13, under which a care, or supervision, order may be granted, if the child is suffering, or is likely to suffer, significant harm, and the care provided by the parent is 'not what it would be reasonable to expect a parent to give him'.

(Sheppard, 2006: 103)

The implication of this is that statutory social work consists in helping clients to develop an improved ability to put rational decisions into action, by overcoming their 'internal constraints' (uncontrollable tempers, addictive desires or psychotic delusions). If practitioners' interventions fail to achieve these goals, this warrants such actions as care orders or compulsory hospitalisation. The focus for practice is therefore a skilled input of behaviour- or thought-changing work, which modifies actions, leading them to legal and social acceptability.

On this account, social workers act on behalf of the rational authority of the state to bring about change in the behaviour of those who deviate from the standards required of self-responsible citizens. This is certainly a different model of practice from the one presented in the first part of this book, because it implicitly accepts:

- That there are, in any society, rules deriving from current distributions of property and power, in current social roles, and with current freedoms to challenge these distributions, which in themselves warrant compulsory interventions.
- That the goal of practice is to restore states of self-control and adjustment to these rules which allow clients to behave in ways that do not violate them; or to substitute arrangements or treatments that overrule their choices.
- That the skill of practice, and the method of practitioners, lies in the ability to carry out rational persuasion, negotiation and counselling which brings about these outcomes, either voluntarily or compulsorily, so as to protect the clients and others from avoidable serious harms which might otherwise ensue.

This version is a logical deduction from a view of society which derives current distributions of resources and power, and current roles and freedoms, from the rational exercise of authority by a democratic government. But the view of society and social work taken in the first part of this book (and implicitly or explicitly by mainstream social workers from Octavia Hill to Adams et al.) is considerably more nuanced than this.

If the value which makes up well-being in any society is comprised of the products of the interpersonal economy, as much as or more than the formal material economy, this challenges the hegemony of the economic and institutional regime of that society. For example, if the value of the care given to children, disabled people and frail elderly people by their female relatives is greater than the value given for money by firms and voluntary agencies, but this value goes unrecognised, then this challenges the rules under which distributions of resources and power are made by officials and politicians. And if the respect and sense of belonging available to members of ethnic minorities, or refugees and asylum seekers, comes mainly from informal sources in their own communities, this challenges policies under which various state benefits are rationed or withheld, or sanctions (such as detention) are applied to immigrant and asylum-seeking members of those communities.

In other words, people whose 'rationality' is questioned by practitioners, intervening under the democratic authority of the law, may have 'objective' reasons (derived from the interpersonal economy) to dispute the interpretations put on their actions, or on the consequences of their actions, by the legal authorities. Social work is as much concerned with mediating between the informal and interpersonal worlds of the client's interactions, and the institutional world of the government, law and agency management, as it is with imposing standards of rational and responsible behaviour.

This is because, as the founding figures of social work recognised, there is often a conflict of interests and values between what is being produced and distributed in the interpersonal economy, and the systems of power and production in the formal economy. Just as T.H. Green and the ethical socialists sought to include the value of relationships and associations in the resources and roles to be fairly allocated for the common good, so too today social workers must try to deal in the relational goods of families and communities, as well as in formal systems. Because property and power are intertwined in the institutions which generate law and bureaucracy, practitioners cannot simply assume that poor people, minorities and disadvantaged communities are being 'irrational' in resisting the imposition of their standards.

However, this does not imply that statutory social work can escape the responsibility to protect children, to challenge offending and anti-social behaviour, or to restrain mentally ill people who may harm themselves or others. It means they must do so in ways which respect and take full account of their interpersonal relations, and the cultures generated by them, and try to turn those resources to good account, building bridges between the official, material and interpersonal worlds.

To confine practice to a role of advocacy over rights to material goods, money and resistance to official authority is too limiting, because it fails to make possible connections between oppressed groups and the mainstream. But to side uncritically with the official line is potentially oppressive, if it misses opportunities to build on the strengths in services users' networks and associations.

In this chapter, I shall analyse the ways in which statutory social work can claim to use the same values, methods and principles as work which is consensually undertaken. I shall argue that it is justified, and seeks to achieve outcomes, primarily in terms of improvements in the relationship-based well-being of the most vulnerable individuals in situations, and that it mobilises the interpersonal economy for these purposes.

Maintenance, control and empowerment

One of the main claims of this book is that many of the most fundamental and divisive disagreements in the theory of social work stem from a muddle over its contribution to value. The debate over well-being allows this muddle to be clarified, and in the process these divisions and disagreements are dissolved.

Once we recognise the two streams of value, material and interpersonal, and the different ways they are produced, a clear analysis of practice can emerge, especially in relation to the interpersonal sources of well-being.

Case Example

A neighbour in the block of flats complains to the child protection team about Belinda C's care of her daughter Jasmine, aged three. She alleges that Belinda is living with a known drug abuser and petty hoodlum, Paul B, who is violent to her, and possibly to Jasmine also. Loud music, shouting and banging are coming from the flat at night, and Belinda has been seen with bruises to her face.

The social worker carries out an investigation of alleged child abuse. She sees Belinda and Jasmine, who is a lively, healthy and well-developed child. At first, Belinda is defensive and angry about the neighbours' report, but after a while she becomes tearful. She says that Paul B is not living with her, but does spend some nights there. He has been violent to her, and she is wanting to end the relationship. She feels isolated and miserable, and that the neighbours are all talking about her, but none are friendly.

With the social worker's support, Belinda does tell Paul she no longer wants to see him. She also arranges for Jasmine to attend a nursery, with some help from local authority funding. She is introduced to a group of mothers in a nearby block of flats, and is now thinking of retraining for future employment.

Discussion

This case example could be selected by any of the various schools of social work to illustrate their analyses of practice. Each would put a different spin on what happens.

According to writers such as Davies (1994) the social worker has helped Belinda to *cope*. This could be seen as an example of social work as a *maintenance* activity. On behalf of the social consensus on deprivation, the practitioners have conducted an authoritative assessment of an allegation, have found no evidence of abuse, and ensured that Jasmine is protected. Belinda's own strengths have been enlisted to overcome the problems with Paul, and she has been re-connected with a social group.

This fits in well with the perception of social work as a specific activity connected with improving the functioning of individuals and of society. It is consistent with current government thinking, in that the intervention is brief, time-limited and purposeful (Reid and Epstein, 1977) and produces measurable changes in the situation. It is also a response to 'objective need' which engages Belinda's rational agency, so that she makes better choices for Jasmine's well-being (Sheppard, 2006).

However, much the same aspects of the intervention might fall short of satisfying the Marxist and critical analysis of practice. The social worker has perhaps not helped Belinda to make the connections between her isolation and depression, and the structural features of her situation. As a lone parent on benefits, and a tenant of a poor-quality council flat, she has reason to feel that she has been marginalised within the economy and mainstream society. Her lack of savings, property and work skills have condemned her to a life of long-term disadvantage and exclusion.

According to Corrigan and Leonard (1978) and their school of thought, Belinda and Jasmine would be better served in the long run if she was encouraged to join a social movement which addressed these structural issues (such as a claimant's union or a tenants' group), rather than simply seeking the company of neighbours, or a low-paid, part-time job. Membership of an oppositional movement would heighten her consciousness, and might lead her to take more effective *collective* action, with wider political goals. Without this element, the social worker may have colluded with a process of social control.

Finally, the social worker's intervention could be seen as anti-oppressive, and as *empowering* (Adams, 2003) Belinda, by those who emphasise the differentials in power experienced by women and minority ethnic citizens. In her relationship with Paul, Belinda has experienced oppressive use of male violence, and the workers' support in resisting this has enabled her to develop her capacity to challenge this abuse. Belinda is black, so her exclusion among the group of residents has a racist dimension; here again the intervention empowers Belinda by connecting her with a group of other (mainly black) mothers, who have experienced similar discrimination and exclusion (Dominelli, 1998).

My argument is that these perspectives are not mutually exclusive, once we adopt an analysis of well-being in terms of the workings of the interpersonal economy:

- Belinda's relationship with Paul is producing more negative emotions – hurt, insecurity, shame, fear and depression – than positive. She is hanging on to it because she feels lonely and excluded. With the support of new friends, and of the social worker, she can feel better about herself, and also interact more positively with Jasmine.

- Jasmine will soon experience anxiety and confusion over Paul's behaviour if she is not doing so already. She loves her mother, but needs more outlets for energy, more company, and more opportunity to explore the world. The nursery will help her in all these ways.

- Belinda is being made a scapegoat and excluded by her neighbours, who show her no respect, do not allow her to feel she belongs, and instead confer stigma on her. Through improving her self-confidence, and her support network of friends, Belinda may in time be able to become a full member of the community in her block of flats. In the meantime, she can at least hold her head up – the first step towards receiving respect form her neighbours. In this sense she is already empowered.

- Belinda and Jasmine are indeed suffering structural disadvantage and oppression, like all their neighbours and like many other members of her ethnic group. There is a whole dimension to her oppression and exclusion which has not been addressed by the particular intervention of this social worker. However, in the longer term, if the child protection team is well connected with community workers and community groups in the district, it may be possible to link Belinda with an action group or social movement, and so allow collective action. Others like herself have become activists in a local voluntary agency's community centre, and have gone on from this to become community workers.

By analysing Belinda's situation, and the social worker's intervention, in terms of the emotional, civic and associational value produced by their interactions, we can reach a more reliable understanding of how the intervention has affected her well-being. The relationship with Paul was producing negative value, as was that with the neighbours. By ending her abusive connection, by having more value-enhancing friendships, and by challenging the stigma of her neighbourly interactions with her new demeanour, Belinda has increased her own well-being. Jasmine's has been enhanced by participation in the nursery, and by removal of the threat from Paul's presence. But their well-being could be further improved in future, by membership of wider community organisations and social movements.

In other words, neither 'maintenance', nor 'control' nor 'empowerment' adequately clarifies what has happened, because they do not specify the respects in which interactions create value, both positive and negative. The different schools of thought argue about what is 'really' at stake for Belinda and the social worker, but dispute the meanings of their encounter in ways which cannot be settled within their own terms.

The 'interpersonal economy' analysis allows us to show:

- That Jasmine's well-being has been improved by the intervention in the ways shown.
- That Belinda's well-being has increased, because she is relating better to friends and neighbours, and has ceased to experience negative feelings, from her relationships with Paul and those who stigmatised her.
- That the social worker has contributed to their well-being, by showing empathy for Jasmine and Belinda, by supporting Belinda in her stand against Paul's violence and the neighbours' disrespect, and hence creating positive emotions of self-confidence and self-respect.

So it is not simply the changes in *behaviour*, and hence in Jasmine's *physical safety*, which stem from this intervention. It is the improvement in their well-being, which can be accurately demonstrated – measured, if necessary – by asking them to assess their overall happiness with their lives, and their feelings about various dimensions of it.

Once we recognise that these subjective factors contribute directly to well-being, which is the main aim of social work interventions, then this provides a much clearer *economic* justification for statutory social work. Instead of trying to do a cost-benefit analysis simply on the basis of risk assessments, which measure only potential *harms*, we can look at practice in terms of the concrete gains in well-being from these interpersonal transactions.

Economics should not be about nothing but money. As Layard (2005) and the well-being theorists recognise, it should be about how we use our personal resources, including our capacities to relate to others, to create value, and to receive value, through our interactions. Social work will only be properly valued by society when this form of analysis is applied to all its activities.

Social work with families and children is taking steps in these directions. The closer links between education and child care provision are leading to a new focus on children's well-being. These developments are discussed in Part 3 of the book (pp. 99–149).

Subjective well-being and social construction

One of the reasons why social work academics and practitioners have been hitherto reluctant to assert the importance of relationships and feelings in professional activity is that the public sector has become a hard-nosed economic environment. The insistence of government guidance and funding on targets, outcomes, quality control and best value as the basis for evaluation and finance makes these factors seem 'soft' and vague. Yet the well-being debate opens up the opportunity to get them back into the equation, and to improve theory and practice in that process.

Another theoretical dispute in social work in recent years has concerned the validity of subjective ideas and emotions in the analysis of practice. If the justification for funding professional activity is to be purely in the public provision of services to meet objectively-measured needs, and to change objectively-measured risky or harmful behaviours, then the scope for introducing these elements into the evaluation of practice seems limited. As Sheppard argues, to claim that the ideas and feelings of abusive parents, drug-crazed addicts and psychotic patients are as valid as those of a professional assessment of need, risk or harm undermines the objective, legal and realistic basis for social work intervention (Sheppard, 2006: 124–33).

But this argument distorts the nature of how both social workers and service users think, communicate and negotiate decisions. We are only able to reflect on our situations, deliberate about them with others, and choose how to act, by using ideas and images from the cultural resources at our disposal. The words we use, and the way we combine them in concepts and meanings, are all derived from our education, socialisation, and everyday interactions; they are created in the social environments in which we live. Social workers bring their ideas and images from their personal lives, their professional training, and the wider culture of politics, the media and civil society. Service users are likely to be more influenced by their immediate social environments, and the cultures of the locality, community and informal groups.

The concept of Subjective Well-being (SWB) recognises that we draw on this stock of experiences and cultural resources to construct our identities, our ways of relating to others, and our understanding of the social world; we also assess our happiness with our lives by relating our projects and commitments to standards and norms which we derive from that cultural stock. SWB is a self-evaluation, according to the person's own assessment, using personally and culturally-derived criteria. By demonstrating that SWB is a robust basis for comparisons over time, between individuals, and between societies, Kahneman et al. (1999) have validated these subjective and culturally specific standards, and economists like Layard (2005), Sugden (2005), Offer (2006), Frey and Stutzer (2002) have shown that these findings undermine much of their discipline's analytic framework.

However social work can play an active role in reconstructing that framework, to take account of subjective, emotional and relational factors (Jordan, 2006b). It can show in detail, if necessary through research, how relationships with service users do create value, in the ways I have outlined above. In this process, it can contribute to the reformulation of the economics of well-being, as well as modifying its own accountability to government and taxpayers.

Meanwhile, this process can also clarify a dispute within the theory of practice. The position I have just outlined on the nature of thinking, communication and choice in social interactions is close to that of 'social constructionism'. This insists that the individual is not a 'black box', simply making decisions on the basis of preference for the 'utility' of a specific bundle of goods, or pursuing a rational strategy of self-interest. He or she is a *self*, using language and other cultural resources to form an identity and make sense of the world (Howe, 1993; Seligman, 1995). This identity then enters into conversations with professionals, and is the way in which service users attempt to preserve themselves, and have control over their experiences, as they receive professional interventions (Howe, 1993: 195).

The situations assessed by social workers (such as the allegation of child abuse in the example given) are complex and ambiguous. The term 'constructionism' (or 'constructivism'), comes from sociology (Spector and Kitsuse, 1987) and seeks to capture the process by which professionals interpret such situations, and define them by the use of categories. In social work, concepts like 'child abuse' have been broadened and refined over time, and distinguished into 'physical', 'emotional' and 'sexual'; all this has developed since the 1970s when the terms were introduced from the USA (Parton, 1985).

From a social constructionist perspective, a statutory intervention (such as an investigation of child protection issues, an assessment for a court report, a review of a child in care, or a mental health tribunal) is a process through which professionals and clients seek to interpret and define situations, conditions (such as abuse, addiction or mental illness) and people.

Although there is more legal terminology and rhetoric in a court hearing or a tribunal than in an informal interview, both use resources from the official world of law and regulation, as well as the interpersonal world of family, kinship and neighbourhood relationships, to reach a kind of negotiated version. Even when the parent, offender or patient rejects the conclusions reached by the professionals or the court, their identity and interpretations of that situation enter the discussion as elements to be taken into account.

This approach sounds entirely different from the one taken by economists. In modern micro-economic analysis, individuals communicate through their behaviour, and especially through how they allocate resources – energy and time, as well as money. I know whether someone likes me by seeing how often they ring, visit or write, not by the rhetorical flourishes of their calls or letters.

Marks and Spencer knows what customers think of their food and clothes by how many enter their shops, and how much they spend. However, even Marks and Spencer are curious to find out what lies behind such decisions. Do customers see their shops as dowdy or trendy? Do they regard the clothes as suitable for a young image, a successful entrepreneur or an active lifestyle? How does the customer's self-identity interact with the popular perception of M&S, to influence sales? Only by engaging with the public, through market research, and by projecting messages by advertising, can the company ensure that it is successful in competition with Tesco and Sainsbury's.

In other words, social life and the choices which make up individual lifestyles are constructed out of intersubjective ideas and meanings, as well as prices, costs and profits. The cultural resources that enter into these intersubjective transactions are created, as much in the interpersonal as the material economy. In the same way, the interpretations of professionals, courts and tribunals are constructed from concepts and images which mix official and everyday street language.

The economists who are now studying well-being are coming to recognise that their model of choice and action is too narrow and limited. But their scope for adapting it is constrained by their commitment to *methodological individualism*. This means that any social phenomenon must be explained according to the individual decisions which form components in its makeup. So, for instance, a group, club, trade union or collective action movement must be formed from the decisions of individual members that this is in their interests, and then held together by a continuing perception of this collective interest, or a balance between the individual advantage of remaining a member, and the sanctions against defection or exit (Olson, 1965, 1983).

The only exceptions to this rule are systems and social habits which come about because people get benefit from them, and participate, without conscious cooperation (Elster, 1985; Douglas, 1987). For instance, Adam Smith (1776) showed that people created markets for personal gain, but benefited from their optimal distributions for *overall* efficiency without being aware of it; and John Locke (1690) argued that people chose to use money as a kind of experiment, for its convenience, making property, trade and markets (with all Smith's claimed advantages) possible (Jordan, 2004).

These exceptions imply that methodological individualism *can* explain some collective phenomena in the social world. But this seems a rather small concession, given the importance of language, culture and the interpersonal economy, all of which involve a huge proportion of *shared* resources. Any adequate account of social life – and especially of social work – needs to analyse how these are created and used in a great variety of circumstances. This is what social constructionism tries to do.

Economists are inching towards some such analysis. For instance, Offer seeks to argue that commercialised consumerist affluence is undermining well-being in advanced economies, because instant gratification (consumer goods, access to sex, drugs, drink, fast cars and fast food) leads them to reject the habits of restraint, prudence, fidelity, abstinence, and so on, which their parents practised:

> *Choice is fallible. The main difficulty is in reconciling immediate desires with the commitment required to achieve more remote objectives. Since individual calculation is not reliable, people fall back on social conventions, norms and institutions. These 'commitment devices' form the fabric of civilisation. To achieve a set of desires encompassing the present and the future, it is necessary to ensure the enduring commitment of other people, and also of one's own self ... It also requires a capacity for social interaction ... People vary in their capacity for commitment ... in their access to the tools of commitment: the heritage and conventions of the social and national cultures, of institutions, law, governance and commerce.*

(Offer, 2006: 358)

This is radical for an economist. But Offer does not explain the relation between (socially constructed) 'commitment devices' (arising from social interaction) and *politically* constructed formal systems, such as law and governance. Nor does he explain how the former may interpret, modify and transform the latter in practice. As a methodological individualist, Offer does not easily see how 'commitment devices' in the form of norms (informal) and legal systems (formal, institutional) can act both as *restraints* on immediate gratification, and *resources*, for the construction of narratives of resistance, survival and change.

This is because cultural resources are not like individually-owned private goods. Ideas, images and norms are constructed in interactions, and shared among those who use them: they belong to all, and can be modified for use by a group or association. Offer's 'conventions', such as prudence, chastity, respect and abstinence, are not simply eroded or weakened, they are transformed for current conditions as much by young people in internet chatrooms as by older people who meet and gossip in the village green (Jordan, 2006b, Chapters 9 and 12).

The construction and transformation of cultural resources is an important aspect of community work, and is relevant for all social work practice. The idea of norms which restrain individual selfishness, yet enable trust, cooperation and reciprocity, is attracting the interest of economists (North, 1990) sociologists and political scientists (Coleman, 1990; Putnam, 2000) who use terms like 'social capital' to analyse these phenomena (Home Office, 2005b).

All this implies that practitioners do not meet the public or service users in a vacuum; they encounter each other and interact within a web of language, images and expectations, and a legal and political system. Statutory practice is part of a continuum of such encounters, in all of which services users will be aware of the social workers' power and authority, and often wary of it. This power must always be acknowledged and negotiated, interpreted and explained. It can never be imposed.

Constructive practice

Social constructionism's emphasis on language, images and culture leads to the idea of 'constructive practice'. This is *more*, not less, important where the social workers' power is being involved, i.e. in statutory practice.

The danger is that, in situations such as the investigation of alleged child abuse, or the writing of a court report, the official framework and legal language will come to define the interaction and the outcome. Terms like 'neglect', 'harm' or 'addiction' come to be accorded an 'objective' status by the practitioner and the client, who may internalise them. This, of course, is in the nature of the legal and medical models: situations are defined and classified according to categories which justify decisions. But the role of the social worker is always to keep open other possibilities, which engage the client's own 'narratives of resistance' to these labels, and to the patterns of behaviour they imply (Parton and O'Byrne, 2000, chapter 5).

Constructive social work tries to use interactions to open up conversations about individual action, relationships and the social world, so as to allow new possibilities for change. Seeing relationships as the basis for thought, speech, meaning and identity, practitioners use an encounter (or a longer-term contact) to generate new meanings (Gergen, 1999: 49) and hence new patterns of social life (Gorman *et al.*, 2006: 24). Constructice practice looks for 'narrative solutions to problems' – ideas and images which give clients more control over their lives, and forge new identities, which are positive and resistant to old patterns (de Shazer, 1991, 1994; White and Epston, 1990; O'Hanlon, 1993).

This approach looks for stories of survival, resistance and overcoming problems – ways in which people who are perceived, and perceive themselves, as irresponsible parents, anti-social residents or isolated depressives, can recognise new possibilities for change. It seeks exceptions to apparently negative sequences of experiences, and sets goals for taking charge of events. This is partly about coping (as in Davies, 1994) but also about transformation (Parton and O'Byrne, 2000, Chapter 6).

The case examples given by Parton and O'Byrne in their book (Chapter 7) are from the field of statutory social work, concerning adopted children who are 'out of control' and a child in care who has been sexually abused. They involve dialogues which redefine experiences and identities in ways that enable the services users to regain control over their lives, and move forward. Examples from child protection (Berg, 1994: Turnell and Edwards, 1999), crime and offending (Gorman et al., 2006), mental illness (de Shazer, 1994; Bertolino and O'Hanlon, 1999), residential work with young people (Durrant, 1993) and substance abuse (Berg and Miller, 1992, 1995), all elaborate methods appropriate to these issues. In the case example given at the start of this chapter, Belinda might have tried to cover up her distress, used Jasmine's good health and demeanour to rebut the allegations, and continued to associate with Paul. The social worker might, through pressures of other work, reluctantly have accepted that there was nothing more she could do at the time, despite some doubts about the situation.

In that case, the family could have been re-referred several months later, in a far more serious situation. Jasmine's health and development could have been clearly jeopardised by Paul's violence; Belinda could have become addicted to drugs, and committed offences. A set of child protection measures could have been set in train, affecting them all for a number of years.

But at every stage in that process there would be possibilities to engage with Belinda, Jasmine and Paul, on the lines suggested by constructive social work principles. If they are not amenable to these approaches at the first intervention, and if court orders are eventually required, there will be many later opportunities to open up discussions of new possibilities for development and change.

For example, in their book on *Constructive Work with Offenders*, the contributors to Gorman et. al.'s (2006) analysis give instances of these methods in work with those in court, on probation, in prison and in groups:

> *When the negative effects of crime on their lives and their relationships are talked about, the majority of those who have a close relationship with crime can engage with conversations about these effects and begin to be alienated from offending so that they start to stand up to the invitations, supported by the worker. . . . It is recognised that an offender's 'local' knowledge is as, or more, important than knowledge which has been derived from 'scientific' research and which has been disseminated, and embedded in a variety of new systems and service packages.*
>
> (Gorman et al., 2006: 27)

This last comment indicates that practice is always located in a wider culture of policy and guidance, with its own terminologies and constructions of social problems. In the UK, this context is the New Labour government's 'tough love' climate (Jordan with Jordan, 2000) with its emphasis on choice, enterprise, property and social cohesion. In order to gain support from working class voters and property owners, it has denounced 'benefit cheats' and 'bogus asylum seekers', adopting punitive postures on issues of crime and disorder, and a technocratic approach to interventions with 'deviant' groups. Playing on fears and insecurities, the tough elements have been more evident then the loving ones.

But some aspects of the prevailing public culture do favour constructive work. The idea of citizenship as self-responsibility and self-improvement (managing one's own developmental trajectory through a 'project of self') includes the elaboration of a narrative of identity, survival and the overcoming of problems. This is in line with the principles of self-development and change in constructive approaches (Jordan, 2004, 2006c). But clients must first overcome negative stereotypes of residents of poor districts, and of minority ethnic citizens, in order to develop self-esteem and problem-solving skills.

The high value put on enterprise in Third Way ideology can also be deployed to advantage. Service users are likely to be living in districts where the economy has been impoverished, through the withdrawal of commercial firms as well as government agencies. Much of the income-generating activity in such neighbourhoods is 'informal' – hustling, drug dealing, petty crime, prostitution and begging (Jordan and Travers, 1998). Practitioners who try to help service users adopt more positive identities can encourage ideas of independence and self-responsibility which are part of the political culture. More ambitiously, they may be able to help them set up in small, legitimate businesses (Capisarow and Barbour, 2005).

Finally, constructive practice can deploy New Labour rhetoric on activism, participation and social cohesion to foster group and community identities which are more positive, and which encourage bonds of mutual support (Worley, 2005). Many statutory clients are not isolated, but well-embedded in local networks; constructive practice can engage with these, to seek to strengthen them, and connect them with mainstream activities and proposals.

Conclusions

In this chapter, I have responded to the challenge that statutory social work cannot primarily address Subjective Well-being (SWB). I have given examples of how services which address official definitions of need, risk and harm can and do respond by engaging with service users' own understandings of their identities, and the quality of their lives.

Indeed, I have chosen an example from child protection work to illustrate exactly how a social work intervention could be justified, as a contribution to well-being. This involved showing that:

- It reduced harmful emotions and actions, and enhanced positive ones.
- It contributed to the mother's and child's prospects for developing better self-esteem, and control over their lives.
- It enabled better relations with friends and neighbours, improving membership and participation, and hence respect and belonging.
- It could, if extended, lead to activism in a social movement, and hence to engagement in collective action to improve social justice and inclusion, and confound racism and oppression.

In other words, I have shown that the approach to practice which analyses problems and interventions in terms of an 'interpersonal economy' can encompass statutory work because:

- It can demonstrate the value of interventions, in creating positive emotions and bonds, and in improving problem-solving capacities.
- It can address 'objective' issues and legal requirements within a framework that includes subjective interpretations and local perceptions of social issues.
- It dissolves many issues about 'coping', 'control' or 'challenging oppression' by showing that the same intervention creates value and improves well-being in all these dimensions.

The perspective in social work literature which is useful for illustrating this approach to practice stems from social constructionism. It is directly in line with the central thesis of this book, that relationships are the most important source of well-being (Parton and O'Byrne, 2000, Chapter 1). It also deals in people's subjective meanings and interpretations: 'It invites people to reflect, ponder, re-examine, try out, dream and construct differently' (Parton and O'Byrne, 2000: 48).

This is very different from the understanding of social work in terms of 'service delivery' – the specific provision, for service users' consumption, of an experience which is 'used up in the instant it is produced' (see pp. 18–21). Instead of trying to assimilate services to goods, as in the orthodox micro-economic model, it recognises that they involve joint construction of meanings, negotiated between practitioners and clients, even where they stem from statutory interventions.

The constructive practice movement stems in part from a critique of the technocratic approach to service delivery that was derived from the neo-liberal and Third Way economic analysis of the public sector. Writers like Nigel Parton saw this style as potentially oppressive, and social constructionism as a way of understanding practice that was truer to its philosophical and ethical roots:

> . . . practice is better characterised as a practical-moral activity rather than a rational-technical one, and . . . attempts to increase realism and objectivism are likely to be misguided. However, we do not fall into an ethical abyss or sink into moral nihilism but rather make even more explicit the moral choices and responsibilities that are central to social work practice.
>
> (Parton and O'Byrne, 2000: 3)

This explicit reference back to the foundations of social work in ethical socialism re-inforces the arguments in this book for a relationship-based approach to practice, for the sake of improved well-being.

But this is not inconsistent with the insights gained by the more rigorous application of research methods to practice (Walter et al., 2004) and of evidence-based approaches to practice. Like the law and guidance, such evidence and research can be used to advantage in practice, so long as it is imaginatively introduced into an approach which recognises the validity of service users' own interpretations of their social worlds.

The schools of thought which promote objectivity, hard science and cost-effectiveness often write as if the past was a dark age, when professionals practised in self-interested or self-indulgent ways, under a cloak of personalised and ethical integrity. However it is difficult to find an area of statutory practice in which the new approaches to service delivery have improved outcomes in a convincing way. Numbers of psycho-social disorders among children and adolescents (Rutter and Smith, 1995; *The Guardian*, 2006c) are higher than ever; prisons are fuller, with over 80,000 in custody at any time.

This reflects a decline in the relative situation of poor, ill and disadvantaged people in UK society. Greater material inequality has been accompanied by increases in types of behaviour which signals despair (such as self-harm) as well as rebellion and resistance (such as anti-social and disorderly conduct). The public services can increase well-being through their interventions, and in this way reduce social problems.

To try to find technical fixes, or to clamp down by tough measures, has not proved successful. Above all, I have argued that the perception of services as serial one-off experiences, to be delivered in occasional packages, is counterproductive. Nowhere is this clearer than in substitute care for children. In the 1960s, frequent moves of placement was recognised as a problem for long-term adjustment and educational attainment (Parker, 1966). But almost 40 years on, these issues are as prominent as ever.

A Barnardos report (2001) has highlighted the failure of children in public care to achieve GCSE passes. Whereas around 50 per cent of mainstream children achieve five such passes, only 6 per cent of children in care do so. They are 37 times less likely to get to university (BBC Radio 4, 2006c). A child who left school with no qualifications, despite obvious brightness, attributed this to frequent moves, and the lack of parental guidance; no-one had ever attended parents' evenings for her at her many schools. Around half of all children in care end up in prison, homeless or as prostitutes.

Care, like education, is not a series of separate experiences. It involves the creation of value, by positive and consistent exchanges between adults and children. Public services, above all others, should see the creation of such value, through coherent contexts and consistent practices, as a statutory responsibility.

Chapter 5

Independence and Well-being in Social Care

Introduction

The idea of 'social care services for adults' has entered the vocabulary of social policy as a portmanteau term. Like 'utility' in economics, it stands for anything and everything that someone who is not fully able-bodied, or who suffers from a chronic physical or mental illness, might require to help them lead their version of a full life. It comprises a range of services from 24-hour assistance with feeding, toileting, dressing and moving around a building, to a season ticket for a football club or theatre.

While this is a revolutionary and welcome change from the days (most of the nineteenth and twentieth centuries) when most such people spent their lives in institutions, outside mainstream society, it also begs many questions. What should be the social roles of frail elderly, physically disabled and mentally ill people, and those with learning disabilities, in a high-tech, commercialised and consumerist society? Is their citizenship the same as those who are in full-time jobs and education, or different? What should society expect of them, and how can they best contribute and belong to it?

The great change of the past 25 years in countries like the UK and USA has been that social care services have become orientated towards enabling all these groups of people to live as 'normal' (i.e. non-institutional, non-segregated and non-stigmatised) a life as possible, and as involved in the mainstream as they are capable of being.

But this goal is deceptively complex. It has been perceived primarily in terms of the transfer to 'the community' of the hundreds of thousands of citizens who inhabited mental illness and 'mental subnormality' hospitals (as they were called) and similar institutions for people with physical disabilities or the mental frailties of old age. Even if they lived in smaller 'homes', with full-time carers, this was seen as bringing them closer to mainstream society (albeit often as occasional spectators, being taken out for a walk, rather than as active participants).

At the same time, new cohorts of working-age adults were being squeezed out of the labour force, and consigned to a life on various kinds of incapacity benefits, on the margins of the economy. There are currently about 2.8 million claimants of these benefits (and their various supplements) in the UK, far more than those claiming unemployment-related job seekers' allowance, or lone parent benefits. Most of these are people with mental health problems sufficiently serious to affect their capacity to work and earn, but not to warrant treatment in a hospital or day clinic.

In other words, as our society has been shifting towards trying to include more of its traditionally exiled and institutionalised members, it has also been pushing an even larger number of its previously active participants into passive and impoverished roles. This applies particularly to men in manual occupations living in depressed regions, where rates of this kind of employment have slumped (McVicar, 2006). Whereas women who were previously home-based have joined the workforce, men in these regions have become less economically active. Government policy now seeks to re-activate them, and many other claimants of incapacity benefits, but in exactly which economic roles?

To develop the kinds of social care services which will promote well-being, we need to have a clear analysis of these issues. We have seen that levels of SWB are strongly related to health, relationships and work-role satisfaction. Although the health status of these groups is probably almost as varied as that of the general population, all face some constraints on their levels of activity. These in turn do limit their work roles – for some, the type of work they can do, for others the duration and stress levels of what is required of a particular employment. Relationships are the least likely to be limited by these conditions, but other people may be required to give practical or emotional help of various kinds, so interdependence must be a realistic expectation of any long-term set of relationships.

The physical and mental constraints on people with these conditions can be put on a continuum, with young people with purely physical disabilities at one end, and very old people with both physical and mental frailties at the other. The former have successfully and justifiably campaigned for society and the government to recognise that they can, with sufficient supportive help from paid and unpaid carers and from technology, live a life in which they are full members of the workforce and of civil associations (Oliver, 1990, 1992; Oliver and Sapey, 2006). As we saw in Chapter 2, innovations like direct payments have allowed people of working age with disabilities to purchase their own services for assessed needs, and the National Service Framework enables people with long-term physical conditions to receive lifelong support (DoH, 2005). Research such as that done by the Joseph Rowntree Foundation (1999) has fuelled campaigns for independence and control over 'care packages', and criticisms of professional criteria and judgements. The focus for change for this group of service users is therefore on enabling full participation, in work and civil society.

But older people are equally clearly entitled to 'time out' from active work (by virtue of their earlier contributions to the material economy), and may have a limited desire to be involved in the life of culture, recreation, sport and politics. They may, at a certain point, prefer to withdraw somewhat, and be among those who have done so also.

Between these two poles lie many possible combinations of ability, aspiration and need for involvement and contribution. The UK government now seeks to cut through the professional, bureaucratic and political processes of assessing people's capacities, of classifying their needs, and assigning them services. Instead it plans, where possible, to allocate them money, so they can be 'independent', make choices, and control their lives.

As Tony Blair wrote in the preface to the Green Paper on social care:

> . . . *we have already seen in social care how the use of direct payments, for example, has helped improve services and transform lives. Our task now is to continue this transformation right across the field of social care for adults so people are given more choice, higher quality support and greater control over their lives. We need to ensure the services we deliver are flexible and responsive enough to meet the differing needs of individuals.*

(Blair, 2005: i)

However this is not the whole story. At the same time, the UK government is introducing new procedures, criteria and initiatives into the system of incapacity benefits, to channel claimants of these payments into employment, and away from long-term reliance on state support (Fothergill, 2006). And the majority of those who remain outside the workforce by virtue of physical or mental disabilities or illnesses do not qualify for social care support because they do not meet the local authority eligibility criteria, either because of their income and savings, or because their needs for support are not sufficiently severe.

So the state will continue to be involved in processes of defining and shaping the roles and contributions of citizens in these groups. On the one hand, there are new 'personal advisors', like the ones who have steered claimants of jobseekers' allowances into education, training and employment over the years since 1997. These personal advisors are doing tasks which in many ways are social work ones (Jordan with Jordan, 2000) but in the Department of Work and Pensions, and under its training and supervision systems. On the other, social workers will continue to carry out assessments of people in all the other groups, most of whom will be outside the workforce, to see whether they are eligible for support payments, to help them manage their 'individual budgets', and to ensure that they are informed about the range of services from which they can choose. The role of local authorities in regulating service providers, and promoting a range of 'appropriate' support services, will continue; at local and national levels, government will still shape the 'market' in social care, according to its vision of the social roles of people with disabilities, illnesses and frailties.

In this chapter, my starting point in the analysis of issues of well-being for people who need social care services is the idea of their *human rights*. As Dean (2004) points out, the whole discourse of human rights, pursued by the United Nations since the Second World War, but gaining momentum since the end of the Cold War in 1989, implies that each person has an entitlement to the full development of their capacities (Sen, 1985). This vision has been taken up by the European Union in its Charter of

Fundamental Social Rights of 1989, further extended by the Maastricht (1993) and Amsterdam (1997) treaties, and claiming that the EU is funded on 'indivisible', universal values of human dignity, freedom, equality and solidarity' (CEU, 2000: 11). Finally, the United Nations has adopted a new Convention on the Human Rights of People with Disabilities, on 26 August, 2006 (BBC World Service, 2006a) which will extend these to previously unacknowledged citizens of developing countries.

The UK government frequently uses the rhetoric of human rights in its pronouncements and policy statements. For example, speaking to the Global Ethics Foundation in 2000, Tony Blair said:

> ... the belief in the equal worth of all [is] the central belief that drives my politics ... Note: it is equal worth, not equality of income or outcome; or simply, equality of opportunity.

(Blair, 2000: 4)

The uses of the word 'value' in the EU document, and 'worth' in Blair's speech, imply something about the economics of human life and citizenship. In analysing the social roles of those who need care, and how these are best supported, we should start with more clarity about this 'value' and 'worth'.

The value of human beings

In New Labour's version of citizenship, the worth of each person is contingent on their willingness to contribute to the material economy. Tony Blair made this clear in the speech quoted above that benefits of all kinds are payable only to those incapable of work, or of earning enough for subsistence (i.e. needing tax credits to top up wages). This was part of his (and New Labour's) commitment to the credo of 'no rights without responsibilities'. If 'equal worth' implies a human right which is conditional in this way, then human rights demand work effort from all who cannot prove they are incapable, once the government creates an economy with employment opportunities:

> Opportunity to all; responsibility from all. ... I don't think you can make the case for Government, for spending tax payers' money or public services or social exclusion ... without this covenant of opportunities and responsibilities.

(Blair, 2000: 4)

This 'covenant' was the New Social Contract for Welfare, laid out during the years after New Labour took office (DSS, 1998: 80) in which the duties of the state are 'making work pay', 'making financial products safe' and meeting the needs of those incapable of work, while the citizen must earn, save, take responsibility for family members and avoid being a burden to taxpayers if possible.

But, by tying the value (or worth) of able-bodied, working age citizens to a contribution to the material economy, and to saving for property ownership and financial independence, this ideology leaves it unclear how the value or worth of the rest of the population is manifested. Is it that they make some other kind of contribution, and if so what is it? Is it that they have made a genuine effort to contribute, but are prevented from doing so by forces beyond their control? Or is their value or worth of an entirely different kind, by virtue of some other qualities?

These questions arise only because of the insistence that rights are linked to responsibilities, and specifically *economic* responsibilities, by New Labour. In the Catholic constitutions of many European countries, a person's worth is established simply by being a *soul* (perhaps specifically a *Christian* soul) – it consists of something like *spiritual* value or worth, which is independent of any sort of performance of an economic or social role. The New Labour version might be regarded as a Protestant notion of equal human rights, in which individuals justify themselves by their works, rather than by faith alone (Tawney, 1923).

In order to try to relate the questions to ones of well-being, and to the social care services which sustain adults outside the material economy, we need to return to the concept of the value produced in relationships. Both the notion of citizenship and the idea of well-being imply the existence of a society in which the members' flourishing depends on their relationships with each other. We saw in Chapter 3 that this concept of well-being was central to the views argued by social work theorists, both ethical socialists and modern interactionists, throughout its history. Whether we regard society as an 'organic whole' or a fairly contingent system of membership under a political authority, the interdependence of citizens is taken as a basic assumption.

This interdependence means that all are included (for the better or worse) in each other's fates, because we are inescapably linked by bonds of membership – as voters for a shared government, as contributors to and beneficiaries from collective taxes and services, as producers and consumers in the material economy, and as fellow citizens and participants in a community. My well-being is affected by all others and theirs by me. We cannot dissociate ourselves from this interdependence and interconnectedness, except by permanent emigration. The 'common good' is not simply an ideal; it is a fact, because we share a culture, institutions and traditions.

If the basic value or worth of all members stems from this interdependence, then this applies to children, people with serious disabilities and frail elderly people, as well as the economically active and those with property holdings. Their ideas and actions can influence the culture and institutions of our society; their feelings and behaviour can have a direct effect on our well-being. They are inescapably part of us, as a society. For example, people with learning difficulties are now seen as an important group for inclusion in citizenship through a modernised and reformed set of public services. The new rhetoric of rights and participation insists that they should have a voice in decisions, and the chance to be full members of society (National Disability Authority, 2003). The ideas of independence, choice, control and inclusion in mainstream activity are as strongly applied to them as to people with physical disabilities (DoH, 2000). Citizenship is seen as requiring advocacy (Goodley et al, 2003) for the full exercise of rights (Reinders, 2000).

But people with learning difficulties are not held responsible for economic independence, self-development and material contribution in the same way as mainstream citizens, or even as people with mental illnesses (who are perceived as requiring treatment, rehabilitation, and a gradual, phased return to a full economic role). Their 'full participation' in society is not primarily as consumers, producers or any other performative competence. How then can their value or worth to society be defined?

One suggestion, advanced by Steve Smith (2001), is that they are allowed to be 'affective' or 'communicative' citizens – members whose contribution lies in the responses they give to others, and that others give to them. The stereotypes of a learning disabled person is of someone who is simple, loving and kind, who gives affection and trust unconditionally, and in return 'brings the best out of' informal carers and professionals.

On this account, it is therefore through their relationships with others that people with learning disabilities contribute to value, and have personal worth. If this is in any sense so, then it has implications for all other groups who require social care. Once it is recognised that any citizen can have value because of the emotional and relational responses they make to others, and evoke from others, why should this not apply to other groups also? Children need and give such responses, as do many older people, and people of all ages with physical disabilities do so also, where they receive positive, enabling care. In a good society, such relationships of interdependence should be the norm.

Being able to choose with whom to form close relationships, and on whom to rely for help, are clearly important aspects of well-being, for people with disabilities as well as able-bodied citizens (Vernon and Qureshi, 2000: 256). But unstigmatised need for care is a feature of a society in which interdependence is recognised as a matter of fact, and people with disabilities are not seen as 'burdens' to others. An 'ethic of care' (Tronto, 1994; Sevenhuijsen, 2000; Meagher and Parton, 2004) will enable this recognition, and allow people with disabilities to be seen as having worth, despite relying on others for their daily needs.

Social care policy and practice should constantly be trying to balance two factors – the rights of individuals and minority groups to choose distinctive ways of living their lives, according to their own priorities and projects; and the interdependence of people with disabilities or long-term health conditions and other members of their social units.

Rights protect freedoms, including the freedom to choose; interdependence sustains well-being (quality of life) through an ethic of care and mutual support. In social care policy and practice, service users should be free to select with whom to engage in long-term relationships, and from whom to get short-term assistance or entertainment. Rights and interdependence can be balanced, but only if this is a conscious aim of policy and practice in social care.

Why then does the government emphasise independence and choice as central to the well-being of these groups, when it is obvious that *inter*dependence is the reality for them, even more than for the rest of us? One part of this seems to be that, in a

Example: The In Control Scheme

Ahead of the government's policies for switching from care management to 'individual budgets' for social care, several local authorities in England have pioneered a scheme for learning disabled adults which adopts many of the same principles.

With help from their family or paid carers, these service users are having their needs assessed, and individual payments made to their bank accounts, according to resource allocation principles which allow for informal as well as formal support. Brokers can also be used to negotiate and purchase services if appropriate. The aim is to agree a support plan, which will then be managed by the service user, broker or family carer.

It is difficult to fault the support plan format which has been developed in the pilot authorities. The one I have seen, *In the Driving Seat: A Booklet to Help Me Plan My Support*, is in straightforward language and falls into two parts, 'Deciding Where to Go – How I Want My Life to Be' and 'Getting There: Getting Support to Make it Happen'. Part I has 12 questions, with sub-sections:

1. *What money do I have for my support?* – The amount of money specified by the local authority on the basis of the assessment and resource allocation schedule.
2. *Who can help me make important decisions?* – Including a list of these decisions, and how the service user can participate, who else will help, and who has the final choice.
3. *Who do I want to help me put the plan together?* – What help do I want, from whom, in planning my support? The service user is invited to think about the people who are most important to them, how much time they spend together, and what they might do.
4. *What's working in my life now? What's not working?* – What makes me happy and unhappy? What do I want to change?
5. *Who am I?* – The good things, what I do well in.
6. *What would be a great day for me?* – Who would I be with, what would happen?
7. *What would be an awful day?* - Who would be there, what would happen, where could I be?
8. *What would be the best ever future for me?* – If I had a magic wand, what would my life look like?
9. *What is most important to me?* – In order of precedence.
10. *How can people support me well?* – Who can help make sure the plan really happens?
11. *How can we communicate?* – Who will I communicate with and by what means?
12. *How do I keep healthy and safe?* – If I take some risks, who can look out for me, and how?

highly individualistic culture of self-responsibility and self-development, it is only someone who can be represented as exercising choice who can be accorded respect and value. In a symbolic way, learning disabled people must be seen to be acting in ways that are exercising the power of choice, and participating in decisions, even if this requires the frequent intervention of carers, advocates and spokespersons (Redley and Weinburg, 2006).

The potential advantages and disadvantages of this approach to the provision of social care can be assessed from the following example:

Discussion

This list of questions presents an excellent balance in the promotion of the well-being of individual service users. It emphasises that they can choose how to spend their time and money, but allows them to prioritise relationships and contexts as well as activities. It does not imply, in the ways the questions are asked, that a series of one-off experiences is what is at stake; instead, it allows them to identify sources of well-being – for example, to substitute time spent with friends for time spent in a care centre, or to seek a living situation away from the family home.

It is encouraging to see a planning instrument which gets this balance right. Choice and individual control are fine, as long as what is being chosen are defined in a way consistent with a balanced understanding of the sources of well-being.

In some ways this is easier with learning disabled people, both because it is obvious (from their own patterns of behaviour, and from the reactions of others) that relationships are the most important component of their well-being, and because many are not burdened with the requirement to work, earn, save, accumulate property, etc. So the important questions are always about which bonds and contacts will create the most positive emotions and good experiences, and which contexts create the best cultures for positive engagement, participation and creativity. These should be the relevant questions for all service users' support plans, but there is a risk that other priorities may intervene, for ideological reasons.

Unfortunately, however, there may be a gap between the assessment and planning processes and the implementation of In Control plans. The scheme has not yet been evaluated (a national process of research is under way), but some small scale investigation of the lead-up to its introduction in one local authority points to some possible weaknesses. For example, traditional day services for adults with learning disabilities were withdrawn or changed, as part of a Day Service Modernisation programme. A qualitative study of 20 parents and paid support workers was conducted, to get their views on this programme's outcomes for them, choosing those whose day service had been changed, and who were expected to have positive or negative responses. Generally there was agreement in the assessments made by family carers and paid carers of the consequences for individual service users of the changes.

These interviews showed that 12 of the family carers and six of the service users were unhappy or very unhappy about the changes, and only four carers and three service users were happy or very happy. The main reason for those who welcomed the programme was that they were more active in mainstream activities and associations, including education, and had virtually left the learning disability services, a major improvement. But those who were highly critical, especially the parents, felt that the service users had lost access to activity and participation, and especially to contact with their friends in traditional day care.

The working group summarised the findings as showing that:

. . . there is a clear perception of winners and losers from Day Service Modernisation so far. The loss of fellowship and friendship, the range of activities and amenities and the group encouragement to participate plus the comfort and security of routine are all keenly felt.

(NDPG, 2006: 35)

Issues in self-directed support

The pitfalls identified in this research report are present on an enormous scale in the strategy for social care proposed by the UK government. In other countries which have introduced schemes with some similar principles and possibilities, such as Germany and the Netherlands, the sums available are paid as entitlements (after medical assessments) on the basis of social insurance contributions. This means that all citizens have rights to social care payments, without assessment of their incomes and savings, purely on their needs for care.

In England and Wales, each service user is first assessed on their means, and then on their match with the eligibility criteria for the care budget. These are set very high; applicants have to need a substantial amount of support to qualify. This is a major difficulty for those who (unlike those with learning disabilities) require care to enable a good quality of life, rather than just to dress, eat and move about. Even if the principles behind the (self-) assessment and care planning processes are excellent, if the eligibility criteria are too stringent, then the very group who might most benefit from this approach will be the ones who do not have access to budgets.

In the research interviews referred to in Chapter 2 in which a local authority was testing service users' reactions to its plans for self-directed support, both frail elderly and younger disabled people identified this potential weakness. While they approved of the principle of being able to buy support from mainstream commercial suppliers of transport, leisure facilities or holiday companies, to build on or sustain their lives as members of communities; they thought that this was most appropriate for a stage before they would qualify for payments. Some younger disabled people said that they had been deemed ineligible when they sought such support under the existing system.

The older people attending a day centre defined a moment in their lives when they had welcomed the intervention of a social services care manager, to help them plan and organise their week, as well as pay for support. They saw this as a kind of crisis, or watershed, before which they had valued independence and choice, but after which they had needed guidance and care in the overall running of daily life, over and above practical help with mobility and access to mainstream facilities.

In this view, care management and services were not paternalistic or usurping their autonomy, as the statutory authorities were now alleging against themselves, but enabling. As Reg said:

. . . we can't, the brain doesn't, I know mine doesn't [work], I couldn't do it without the help of staff here doing it, I couldn't get her to organise a bus to get here, and pay for it, the brain is going . . . It comes to a point, you'd opt out, rather than worrying with it . . . you wouldn't do it, you'd be tied to your home every day of the week.

It is difficult to disentangle the elements in these service users' views, forcefully expressed by those who took part in focus groups. Partly they stemmed from loyalty to the day centre and group in which they participated as members, were valued and supported by each other, and in turn gave the sense of belonging. They asserted the importance of each other's support and friendship, and that of the staff, against the individualistic assumptions they saw as lying behind the proposed reforms, and in favour of the collective ethics of their group. They felt that self-directed support somewhat subverted their membership, in favour of a suspect notion of 'independence' which was unrealistic for their situation.

The idea of some kind of 'watershed' in the need for care, which signalled an end to the aspiration for independence and choice, in favour of a more protective type of care, was common to all groups, and to the perceptions of those who saw themselves as having reached that stage, and those who did not. However, the advocates of self-directed support can argue that this is a self-imposed limitation, which is reinforced by the care management approach. If people were to encounter the support system for the first time as one which helped them plan on the lines of In Control, they might be able to sustain independence and participation in mainstream activities for longer.

Another theme of the focus groups was the lack of information about what was available for service users to purchase from their individual budgets. They found it hard to visualise a planning process in which they would really have the knowledge to make informed choices; some said that they might not have tried out what subsequently turned out to be valued facilities. They were surprisingly uncritical of the care management system, valuing the way in which they had been steered towards support services, in ways that took account of their preferences and commitments.

After all, the justification for a public system of social care does not lie simply in the difficulty of citizens in saving enough for their needs of disability and old age. It also lies in the difficulty for people, often in distress over a crisis or emergency, to make decisions on imperfect information. Advocates of self-directed support are confident that advice and brokerage roles in the new system will deal with these difficulties; service users were more sceptical, feeling that it could be stressful to have to go through the complex processes.

This was linked to another point arising from the focus groups – the demands in terms of accounting, employing, contracting, invoicing etc. – of buying one's own care. Here again the older service users were fearful that more would be lost than gained, and that some more confused or nervous people might do much less than under the present system, because of the complexity of managing their budgets. It might also cost more, if they had to pay to have all this administration done for them.

In a more general way, there is an issue about the cost of individualising care budgets. In the past, when local authorities were the main providers as well as funders of social care, large-scale facilities like training centres and day care, as well as residential care, were relatively inexpensive to run, because of their collective method of cost-sharing.

Individualisation is expensive, if no costs are shared with others, for instance in the arrangements which give people company, occupation and support during the day. The response from advocates of self-directed support – that service users could spend more time at libraries, community centres or garden centres – was treated with scepticism by members of focus groups.

Finally, there are issues about the range of suppliers of support and care that would be evolved by the self-directed system. The model postulates that these could respond in market-like ways to the needs of service users. In the idealised scenario of some advocates of the new approach, budget-holders could do the rounds of providers, making their requirements clear, and negotiating about prices and detailed quality standards. For most service users in the focus groups, especially the older ones, this was unrealistic.

The fear was that public, commercial and voluntary sector providers would have no easy way to know about the needs of budget holders. If imaginative, creative and innovative new schemes of care and support are to be developed, a large element of risk would be involved. Without the possibility of negotiating block contracts with the local authority, investment in buildings and staff would have to be made in advance of a clear indication of demand. The danger would be that some bad or mediocre providers would survive, while the more innovative ones could go to the wall, or some good-quality existing facilities decline, because budget-holders did not know enough about what they could supply.

After all, it is not that the existing situation, especially in residential care, is all rosy. There has been a succession of scandals about neglect and cruelty to residents, especially in the commercial sector. For example, an investigation by *Face the Facts* (BBC Radio 4, 2006d) found that there had been 269 complaints, 80 per cent of which had been upheld, against Four Seasons Health Care, between April, 2002 and May 2006, concerning their 50 homes in Scotland. Four Seasons is one of the largest providers of residential care in the UK, with 20,000 staff and 17,000 residents in the 350 homes. In one case, involving the death of a resident, it was found to have allowed him to develop multiple bedsores, and to become emaciated and dehydrated. Other investigations have found malnutrition to be commonplace in the care sector generally.

Self-directed support and individual budgets will not, on their own, address these problems in the supply of poor-quality care. Local authorities will still have to act as information exchanges between service users and providers, stimulators and regulators of facilities, as well as assessors, monitors and accountants.

It is important that they do not become intoxicated by the rhetoric of independence and choice, or the economics of individualisation in packages of care. The In Control scheme gives some indication that a balance may be struck, so long as the needs of those with long-term dependency are not relegated below those capable of using mainstream facilities.

Interdependence and the ethic of care

I have argued that the 'equal value' or 'equal worth' of citizens with disabilities can be understood in terms of the interdependence of members of a society. Our well-being consists mainly in the benefits of our relationships with each other.

But there are also costs that arise from interdependence. The need for care creates duties and tasks, which are not evenly distributed among the population, but fall disproportionately on certain individuals and groups.

Part of this is just luck, or fate. To have a child with a disability, or a spouse with a mental illness, or a parent who becomes very frail, is something which can happen to anyone. But the other part is socially produced, because women are expected to take on the main responsibilities of the role of carers, unless they are in a position to buy substitutes (usually other women) or there are other family members (sisters or daughters) close at hand to take on the tasks.

If the value of people who need care is their contribution to the interpersonal economy, and if interdependence is the stuff of that economy, then it is paradoxical that caring should be burdensome. Why should women feel that it is unjust that they do more of it than men, and have fewer other options, or valid excuses?

The answer is that all relationships impose constraints, and all family relationships (which come with birth, and are not chosen) contain an element of enforced obligation. The ideal of equal, democratic, negotiated intimacy between individuals, each of whom brings a reflexive, open and empathetic self into the relationship – 'pure' relationships (Giddens, 1991) – is for unattached adults in the prime of life. Partnership, parenthood and kinship are all more complex mixtures of positive and negative elements, with opportunities to receive support and obligations to give support. So the interpersonal economy creates and distributes work roles as well as value.

Caring, whether it is done informally among kin or as a paid job, can be immensely rewarding. The closeness that comes with caring for a loved relative or admirable service user is a very important source of positive emotions. But it is more likely to involve both gains and losses in well-being. After all, even mainstream mothers of able-bodied offspring see childcare as one of the less rewarding aspects of their everyday lives (Layard, 2005: 95).

Issues about women's role as carers have been much debated within feminism, and in the theory of women's citizenship. Now that women have better access to the labour market and public life – though still far from equal with men's (Lister, 1997;

Voet, 1998) – the focus has shifted to whether they wish to be treated the same as men, or differently. While some see the appeal to traditional female values as potentially oppressive (Young, 1990), others argue that a citizenship that emphasises interdependence and the common good is impossible without a leading contribution by women (Elshtain, 1981, 1998). Both these schools of thought argue for greater recognition for women's roles as carers, and for the work-life balance as a major issue for social policy.

It can be argued that women are now expected to be *both* significant contributors to family incomes from earnings *and* the main providers of care for children and relatives with needs for support (Williams, 2005). They are caught between the Third Way requirement to be active, autonomous and self-responsible self-improvers in the labour market and the civil sphere, but also nurturing of family members and pillars of the community (Jordan, 2006a: 157–61). These tensions have been revealed by research on women's well-being in countries with Third Way political cultures and social policies (Ellis, 2004; Pusey, 2003: 99–105).

This is not helped by the fact that economic policy prioritises activity in the material economy, and offers inducements and puts pressures on women to take employment, while giving very inadequate financial support to carers. The tax credit system in the USA (Newman, 2002) and the UK is designed to 'make work pay' for part-time low-paid jobs, and the New Deal and subsequent reforms of benefits offer counselling and training to lone parent mothers, to encourage them back into employment. All this reinforces those factors in an individualistic culture which put a high value on independence and material consumption, and see caring work mainly in terms of the constraints it places on these.

For these reasons, some authors have argued that the value of care and interdependence, as essential conditions for well-being in families, kinship systems and communities, should be recognised and promoted (Williams, 2001, 2005; Sevenhuij-sen, 2002; Meagher and Parton, 2004). This is in line with the analysis presented in this book. Only when the value created by relationships of caring is acknowledged, and taken into account by public policy, will a set of institutions for enhancing the well-being of citizens be established.

This is recognised by researchers who have investigated new systems for supporting and enabling younger disabled people in the community. They have found that service users put a high value on their relationships with social workers, enablers and carers – 'more than a job' (Marquis and Jackson, 2000). They look for qualities which promote friendliness, sharing, trust and personal closeness (Nicholson, 2006).

The main problem for policy-makers is that the systems of taxation, benefits and services in this field interact in complex ways. We have already noted that the economics of industrial production has created very large groups of people (mostly men in certain regions) who can no longer find satisfying, decently-paid employment, and have found their way onto incapacity benefit rolls. For this reason, the government wants to restrict access to these benefits, and get claimants back to work, even if this involves extra incentives, in addition to tax credits. Much the same applies to claimants of lone parent benefits.

So the government is actively trying to narrow the scope for roles outside the labour market, and its finance for citizens who are not seeking paid employment. This leads it to define disability and its support as restrictively as possible, to target benefits and new services on promoting the labour market participation of disabled people, and to limit payments to carers.

A citizenship of interdependence would reconsider these priorities. It would recognise the value of many activities in the family and the community, which are at present seen almost as 'opting out' of the real business of society. And it would value caring roles much more highly, recognising the special contribution of women (Jordan, 2006a, Chapters 9–11 and 14).

This approach would see the role of government as to promote *full engagement* between citizens, rather than 'full employment'. Being active in the community's cultural, sporting and political life would be as valuable as stacking shelves in a supermarket, or more so (Jordan, 2006b, chapters 7–12). The production of positive feelings of closeness, support, respect and belonging between members of a community would be as much a contribution to well-being as doing a paid job.

This could be enabled by giving financial support to all those who are active in roles, not just as carers, but as volunteers and community activists. But to test whether they were doing this work would require a great deal of bureaucratic checking. A 'Participation Income' (Atkinson, 1995) would be expensive to administer, even if it created measurable improvements in SWB for participants and the general population.

The radical alternative would be a 'Citizen's Income' or 'Basic Income' which would be *unconditional* and paid to all as a regular allowance, instead of benefits, tax credits or tax exemptions. This would trust them to be active in some combination of paid and unpaid roles, finding their own balance, both of work-life activities, and of contributors within families and communities (Jordan, 2006a, chapter 14, 2006b, chapter 11). The implications of this will be discussed in more detail in Part Three.

Conclusions

The issues discussed in this chapter show that the concept 'social care' conceals much complexity. The UK government presents it as being simply about the support services chosen by those who are outside the labour market by virtue of disabilities and illnesses. But the roles of service users and carers are constructed by policies on employment, taxation, benefits and public finance, as well as the type of support available from a range of suppliers.

Consider the example of a couple, David and Sheila, who have just retired when David is diagnosed as having one of the several forms of 'dementia' – a condition which causes loss of short-term memory, confusion, disorientation and occasionally personality change and inability to sustain any kind of social functioning. Suddenly the couple are both deprived of the period of their lives they have worked and saved for, and looked forward to. Instead of having an active life of adventurous holidays, involvement in voluntary associations and clubs, and engagement with their grandchildren, they can expect a gradual shrinking of their social contacts, and a restricted lifestyle.

First, apart from medication from his GP, David can expect no active medical intervention in his progressive condition. What's more, because of their savings, the couple will not qualify for public-funded services until they run down their bank balance, as they live in England. Third, they will receive nothing more by way of income than their state and occupational pension until they can prove David's need for extensive practical help with everyday tasks. The fact that Sheila has to take full responsibility for organising the family finances, paying bills, thinking ahead about all contingencies, and planning from day to day, qualifies them for nothing; nor does the time she needs to spend with David, making sure that he is safe from possible hazards and harms.

Sheila's task is to make sure that David's life is a balance between stimulation and novelty he can handle, and continuity which is familiar and reassuring. She must aim to keep him active in things he can still do, and not make it obvious that she is taking responsibility for most of the essentials. She must not expect him to coordinate his actions with hers, because he cannot take in what she is doing; but she must spend time working or recreating in parallel with him.

She can achieve much of this by a round of contacts with friends and family, which she plans and choreographs. Sheila has mixed feelings about her new role. She has got over the panic and self-pity that set in for the months after the diagnosis, just as David has got over his initial shock and depression. She still loves him, and it is rewarding to see him happy, and hear the sincere compliments he gets from friends and family, who love him too. It is not the life that either of them anticipated, but it is far better than the one they feared when his condition was diagnosed.

When they do eventually need support services it will be important that these fit into the joint strategies they have adopted to preserve the valuable elements in their relationships, in their social life, and in their self-respect as individuals. Sheila is looking for tactful ways to involve younger people as company for David. He loves gardening, and it may be possible to pay a young man who is at college nearby to help, on the pretext of learning more about plants and horticulture. This is not so much to allow her to escape into a life of her own (which she no longer craves) but more to provide the sort of companionship which is difficult for her, or his friends of his own age, to give.

In the longer term, Sheila thinks it may be necessary to spend their savings on an extension to the house, to have live-in help. This will fairly soon run down their remaining balance, to the point that they will qualify for social services help. She will want continuity in his care if possible, and will use day and residential care only as a very last resort.

This example illustrates some of the central points of this chapter:

- The social roles of people who need care are not fixed and given. They evolve from their lives and circumstances, and are very varied.
- The role of retired couples with an occupational pension is a relatively privileged and statusful one. The early onset of dementia is a major loss of status, and also of well-being, because it jeopardises a whole set of relationships with others, such as friends living at a distance, who are important sources of rewarding contacts and good experiences. It also reduces opportunities for active engagement in the community.
- The roles of carer and cared for in partnerships modify the ways in which couples relate to each other. They change patterns of interaction, making equality and mutuality more difficult to sustain, in all aspects of the relationships, and not always in predictable ways.
- Well-being can be maintained if carer and cared for can reach a new equilibrium in every aspect of their lives, from their sexual relations to everyday practicalities and social contacts. This can be helped by discussions with friends and professionals, who can bear to share the pain of loss and fear, guilt and resentment.
- Care services cannot be prescribed in standard ways, but need to reinforce the couple's own strategies, to create the most effective contributions to well-being. They should focus on rewarding relationships, and enabling the maintenance of satisfying roles and contacts, not simply on dealing with practicalities.

[Note: this may be read as a slightly idealised version of caring, especially by feminists. Some would argue that the expectation of care by spouses of people with dementia is oppressive. In fact, almost as many men as women care for partners with dementia. Those, like Williams (2001, 2005) and Ellis (2004) who advocate an ethic of interdependence and care as the basis of citizenships and social relations would subscribe to something like the version given here, I think.]

My contention is that, despite the individualistic, market-orientated model for social care developed by the UK government, and the lack of an adequate economic theory of services noted in Chapter 2, there is much positive potential in the proposals now under consultation. But this potential will not be realised unless entitlement criteria are generous, the local authorities take responsibility to coordinate a full range of support services, and – in the longer term – the national tax-benefit system sustains a more open-ended scheme for supporting the roles of cared-for and carer.

This is turn raises more issues about the kinds of community and engagement which are condusive to well-being and conviviality, and social work's role in promoting it. That will be the topic introduced in the next chapter, and developed in Part Three.

Chapter 6

Community, Cohesion, Diversity and Deprivation

Introduction

It can be argued that the focus of social work has always been social deprivation and exclusion (Sheppard, 2006). As we saw in Chapter 3, it emerged as a profession in the context of urban poverty in the UK and USA, as a means of sustaining the links between the social classes (by casework and community work), as well as a way to improve the morals and characters of the poor. Statutory social work in the UK still takes as its context government policies, whose stated aims are to promote social inclusion, cohesion and community, in a society which is ethnically and culturally diverse.

In this chapter, I shall examine the well-being perspective on the bonds which connect members of districts, communities and societies together, and give them the sense of mutual respect and belonging. We have already seen in Chapter 1 that these are significant for individuals' SWB. To live in a society where trust is low in neighbours, fellow-citizens and political institutions is to experience lower levels of SWB than those who are citizens of more cohesive and inclusive societies. Relative to their national incomes per head, the Anglophone countries do not enjoy very high levels of average well-being, compared with the Scandinavian countries and Switzerland on the one hand, and certain poor African and South American countries on the other.

It is not immediately obvious what governments can do about this through public policy. The New Labour administration inherited an economy with high inequalities of income by the standards of European countries, in which unemployment and benefits dependence were concentrated in around one fifth of households, and in certain districts and regions (DSS, 1998, Chapter 1). Its first priority was to promote social inclusion through policies for increased labour market participation, through the New Deals.

These policies used education, re-training and personal advice to encourage target groups – of young people, lone parents, people with disabilities and residents in high-unemployment districts – into work. The introduction of tax credits to supplement low wages and 'make work pay' were an important incentive, since much of the new employment was in part-time or short-term service jobs.

At the same time, New Labour launched a series of initiatives, through Sure Start, the Social Exclusion Unit, the New Deal for Communities, and the urban regeneration programme, which aimed to promote social inclusion in other ways (Jordan with Jordan, 2000, chapters 2 and 7). These used methods derived from community development as well as social work, to engage with groups of residents of districts with problems like homelessness, drug abuse, truancy and delinquency, to form partnerships with local authorities and firms, and to try to improve the physical and economic infrastructures of communities.

Since then, this strand of social policy has taken a number of twists and turns, in order to address the changing manifestations of deprivation, disorder, conflict and protest which have continued to provide ammunition for the government's critics. Through a series of further initiatives and working partners, it has shifted in turn to cohesion and civil renewal (Blunkett, 2003, 2004), and then to respect, and finally 'multiculturalism' (*The Guardian*, 2006d). All of these aim to improve social relations among citizens considered marginal, disaffected or dangerous to order, and to integrate them better into the mainstream.

Such initiatives might have been expected to counter the fragmentation of the social and community work professions which was noted in Chapter 2. After all, they were intended to improve the 'glue' of society, by promoting civil relationships, and enabling dialogue between diverse groups. But they did not, for two reasons:

1. New Labour made a rigid distinction, both in organisational and professional terms, between the policies and professional tasks of child protection, social care and mental health work on the one hand, and these new initiatives for communities on the other.
2. It kept each new agency and programme separate from each other, seeing the training for and support of the task, undertaken as specific to that organisation, and shielding them from local authority control (Jordan with Jordan, 2000, chapters 7–9).

I shall argue in this chapter that both social work and community work are primarily concerned with improving well-being amongst members of a society, and that their ideas and methods form a continuum with considerable overlaps. They also come from the same ethical and political traditions. They can draw on the same analyses of the interpersonal economy to argue for the value they create, and the way they achieve this. For these reasons, it is in both their interests to emphasise their common ground, rather than their differences.

However, the recently-emerging theory of well-being in psychology and economics does not help social and community workers achieve this merging of their theories for practice. There are two rather different strands to the practice recommendations of well-being research and analysis, which roughly correspond to social work and community work, and well-being theorists tend to emphasise their divergences rather than convergence.

On the one hand, the psychological research which has launched the well-being movement starts from a neurobiological perspective on individual functioning (Davidson, 2005; Layard, 2005, chapter 1). It addresses happiness and its absence through the experience of pain and pleasure, and regards their social context in the light of a stream of specific, one-off moments, which can be measured, and patterns plotted (Kahneman, 1999). From this perspective, it goes on to consider how individuals can increase the number and intensity of the happy experiences, both by what they do, and by how they interpret what they do.

On the other hand, acknowledging the central role of relationships with others for well-being, the researchers and theorists who compare its levels between social groups and societies focus on social bonds. For example, Helliwell and Putnam (2005: 438) state that there are:

> . . . *robust correlations in various countries between vibrant social networks and important social outcomes, such as lower crime rates, improved child welfare, better public health, more effective government administration, reduced political corruption and tax evasion, and improved market performance, educational performance, etc.*

This large claim focuses on the quality of social relationships in *communities* ('social capital') rather than individuals' experiences, and on policies and practices which address groups, networks and organisations, and how their members relate to each other. This implies a very different set of priorities and targets.

Where there is potential consensus between these views is in their critique of individualism, and the simplistic assumptions of 'rational egoism' in micro-economic analysis. As Kahneman et al. state in the introduction to their seminal text:

> . . . *the economic approach is limited in several ways. First, it focuses on these aspects of life that can be traded in the marketplace. Thus desirable goods such as love, mental challenge, and stress are given little consideration. Second, the economic view presupposes that individuals will choose the greatest amount of utility for themselves; yet a great deal of evidence now contradicts this proposition. Third, economics assesses variables that are only indirect indications of something else – subjective fulfilment.*

> (Kahneman et al., 1999 : xii)

As an economist, Layard is equally critical. He points out that inequality, the effects of others' actions, changing norms and values, fear of loss and inconsistency of behaviour are all inescapable parts of the real world, but economists rule them out by assumption in most of their analyses:

> . . . *economists have no interest in how happy people are and focus instead on their combined purchasing power, assuming that preferences are constant over time. Instead, we need an economics that collaborates with the new psychology.*

> (Layard, 2005: 135)

Layard's policy proposals are broad, and encompass work and income redistribution, work-life balance, restraints on rivalry and competition, and the promotion of community life (ibid. 232–4). Unfortunately, only two of his recommendations have been taken up by the New Labour government – more resources for mental health services, and especially for individual Cognitive-Behavioural Therapy (CBT), and more attention to 'personal education' in secondary schools. Indeed, some newspapers describe Layard as the government's 'Happiness Czar' because he has been so influential on these two initiatives (*The Observer*, 2006).

This signals that New Labour has decided that well-being belongs in the 'children's services and social care' box in its public policy thinking; it is part of the education-childcare nexus on the one hand, and the mental health for adults-independence-and-choice agenda on the other. This separates it from the other fields to which Layard's recommendations apply (tax and benefit reform, work regulation, pay and competition, and the role of the public services more generally). It also separates it from community work and the promotion of active citizenship.

In this chapter, I aim to make links between the issues which have been allocated to the Office of the Deputy Prime Minister, and now to the Department of Community Affairs, presided over by Ruth Kelly, who rapidly succeeded David Milliband, for community cohesion, respect and now multicultural issues – the role of community and social capital in well-being and in social life.

But we must also bear in mind issues of order and security, still the province of the Home Office in the UK. After the London Transport suicide bombings of 7 July 2005, ideas about community cohesion shifted. Until then, policies within the broad range of local authority services, as well as new government initiatives, perceived community cohesion in the light of the intercommunal violence in Bradford, Oldham and Burnley in the summer of 2001 (Worley, 2005). This framework addressed the 'parallel lives' led by concentrations of minority ethnic and deprived white communities in such towns (Home Office, 2001a).

But the bombers, although they too came from the north of England, were by no means deprived or excluded. They were well educated, and had good jobs or job prospects; their leader was in special education services. They were active members of sports clubs, a marker for mainstream membership in social capital theory (Putnam, 2000). One was not even an Asian, but a mixed-race African Caribbean who had converted to Islam.

All this has precipitated a re-examination of multiculturalism as the basis for the social order, and a politics of the common good. I shall therefore start with the social worker's stance on the value of anti-discriminatory and anti-oppressive practice, and its contribution to the 'good society'.

Anti-oppressive practice and social inclusion

Social work was one of the first professions to embrace the idea that power in society, exercised to the disadvantage of certain groups of citizens, should be challenged by practitioners. As early as 1989, the Central Council for Education and Training in Social Work stated that social work should uphold anti-discriminatory practice. This initial commitment has been refined and embodied into the BASW's statement of professional values:

> . . . *Social workers have a duty to . . . ensure that they do not act out of prejudice against any person or group on any grounds, including origin, ethnicity, class, status, sex, sexual orientation, age, disability, beliefs or contribution to society . . . challenge the abuse of power for suppression and for excluding people from decisions that affect them . . . support anti-oppressive and empowering policies and practices . . . recognise and respect ethnic and cultural diversity . . .*
>
> (BASW, 2003: 4)

The kind of society promoted by this statement of values was one which was open to change and development in the direction of equality, with barriers in terms of traditional power and wealth being challenged. It encouraged social workers to be reflective about their own power, and about power in relationships within their organisations. But its context was the identity politics of the late 1980s and the 1990s, rather than the class politics of the 1960s. It promoted 'difference' and cultural 'sensitivity' as much as it criticised the distribution of material resources (Dominelli, 1998).

Under the neo-liberal regimes of Margaret Thatcher and John Major in the UK, the radical return to an economy largely unprotected from global economic forces, and the deliberate weakening of organisations like trade unions and local authorities which upheld working class interests, was partially balanced by the growth of lobbies and movements for justice and equality in 'race relations', and for women in the workplace and civil society. It was also more open to participation by service users and carers, albeit against a background of the new managerialism and economic accountability, as we saw in Chapter 2 (Clarke, et al., 1994).

So the UK became at once a more individualistic society, in which citizens were required to take responsibility for their own financial security, and for equipping themselves for a 'knowledge-based' labour market, yet also one in which an individuals' skin colour, gender, sexual orientation and physical capabilities demanded respect, as aspects of their identities. This new culture influenced every part of public policy, including immigration (where good 'race relations' became an explicit factor in limiting access), employment (where new legislation improved the rights of women as mothers) and education (where the expansion of university places allowed previously excluded minorities to participate more fully). This was the context for anti-oppressive practice.

New Labour's initiatives for social inclusion have been taken within this framework of social relations. The flagship programmes, the New Deals and Sure Start, have assumed that people suffering exclusion through unemployment or underachievement at school, could best be helped by improving their capacities for work and parenting and learning, not by increasing demands for workers, or salaries. They have also involved firms, voluntary organisations and community groups in 'partnerships' to regenerate neighbourhoods, and tackle drugs, homelessness, crime and truancy (Jordan with Jordan, 2000, chapters 5–7).

These initiatives were ambiguous in terms of the social theory which underpins anti-oppressive practice, and the notions of social value which it implied. When groups of local women, black residents or disabled people were invited to join partnerships for regeneration, or to address homelessness and crime, were they having their views and identities respected, and engaging in real deliberation and negotiation on these issues, in ways which redistributed power in the neighbourhood? Or were they being co-opted as participants in top-down processes or re-ordering and controlling such communities, according to government blueprints, and in the interests of company profits?

These questions raise the problems posed by analysis in the traditions of Jurgen Habermas's (1989a and b) account of the 'public sphere' of modern society. In his view, social relations should be understood in terms of a dichotomy between 'system' (the formal economy and government agencies' activities) and 'lifeworld' (the interpersonal economy, including associations and civil society groupings). As a legacy of the Enlightenment's creation of an educated bourgeoisie, with its discursive culture and network of voluntary organisations, this lifeworld involved an independent public sphere, in which critical reflection on the economy and politics was developed by members, through discussion.

the bourgeois public sphere may be conceived above all as the sphere of private people coming together as a public; they soon claimed the public sphere regulated from above against the public authorities themselves.

(Habermas, 1989b: 27)

Habermas saw the period after the Second World War as one in which the state, through new institutions, 'recolonised' this public sphere, through imposing a rational-bureaucratic version of social and economic relations on the lifeworld, taking over more and more aspects of its associational practices. Instead of a plural and independent civil society, it imposed a technocratic order, a single uniform public sphere, shaped by the organisations of capitalism and the state. On this account, New Labour has reclaimed control over the marginal, disaffected districts created by Thatcherism, in the name of an instrumental rationality – the logic of markets and individual responsibility.

This implies that voluntary agencies and community groups which participate in the initiatives for inclusion are being incorporated into this order. Instead of operating in their own 'claimed spaces' (self-defined, self-created fields for participation, collective action and contestation), they are taking part in 'invited spaces' where the government and firms have allowed them a voice, but one which can exercise little influence, because of differences in power (Gaventa, 2004: 34–5; Forde, 2006).

This distinction draws on a field of analysis and debate in social and political theory which is fiercely disputed. In the 1990s, representative democracy was criticised by theorists who followed Habermas, and tried to make his very abstract ideas about 'communicative action' – the creative activity which individuals pursue together – concrete, and ultimately perhaps central to political decision-making (Cohen and Arato, 1992). They, like Habermas, pinned their faith on 'new social movements' such as feminism, anti-racism, the gay and lesbian movement, environmentalism and peace activism to achieve this (Castells, 1997).

One strand of thinking in this school advocates 'deliberative democracy' (Dryzek, 1990: 49) arguing that new social movements 'can contribute to the establishment or revival of free discourse in a public space'. More recently, these authors have emphasised that, with globalisation the public sphere is no longer national and state-constructed, but transnational and more fragmented (Dryzek, 2000; Schwartz-mantel, 1998).

Another strand is less concerned with achieving consensus through deliberation, and more with allowing competing groups and public spheres to participate and co-exist (Fraser, 1992, 1997). This can allow the subtler processes of power and control, including incorporation disguised as inclusion, to be challenged. Deliberative processes can then lead to involvement in formal, representative bodies, through the 'strong publics' that can challenge power and influence decisions (Fraser, 1992: 134–5).

All these theorists, and many others, recognised the value of a vibrant, active and engaged lifeworld, consisting of families and friendship groups as well as associations and informal groups, which encouraged critical reflection, and was willing and able to challenge dominant versions of the public sphere, whether emanating from commercial interests or from the state. This is in line with the writings of social work theorists such as Dominelli (1988, 1998) and Thompson (1993, 2002), who emphasise the role of power in constructing the social order, and the need to sustain a diversity of identities and movements to provide alternative relationships.

Yet this ideal can be recognised as especially difficult to achieve in statutory social work. The welfare state itself was ambiguous on this account, in that it did indeed involve an intrusion of instrumental rationality, and the logic of the government's economic model, into the lifeworld, albeit in the name of countering unrestrained capitalism. It meant that public sector social work practice was always simultaneously acting on behalf of this colonisation process, and trying to uphold a vigorous, critical and often dissident lifeworld, interpreting this back to the system in a reflective dialogue.

The important point, as we saw in Chapters 3 and 4, was that social work's own values were derived from the lifeworld rather than the system, and especially that it always took a stand against the purely materialistic interpretation of equality, justice and well-being. The interpersonal economy, which embraces the whole lifeworld, and many of the practices of the statutory services, is therefore the source of value for society which social work must prize most highly, must uphold and sustain.

So it is a very important challenge to understand New Labour's initiatives on social inclusion, community cohesion, civil renewal and respect. These are all attempts to influence the culture and interactive processes of the lifeworld, through top-down interventions, but ones that involve participation and partnership with lifeworld organisations. In what sense are they giving rise to enhanced value, and hence well-being, in the interpersonal economy? Does the controlling impulse behind the Third Way model detract from their potential for improving well-being?

Community, cohesion and respect

From its election to office in May 1997, New Labour addressed the problems of concentrated deprivation bequeathed it by the Thatcher and Major administrations but did so in terms of their problems and deviance and disaffection. The watchwords 'Tough Love' were invented by the media, but willingly adopted by the government (Jordan with Jordan, 2000: 25–6, Box 3). The goal was to include members of these communities by making them more responsible, more able to contribute to the economy and less criminally opportunistic.

This version of 'communitarianism' (which was fashionable in political philosophy during that decade) was conservative, conformist, conditional, moral and prescriptive, and dealt in the duties of individuals towards others and the state (Driver and Martell, 1997). It looked back towards an age of self-help and mutuality, as well as supportive family relationships.

Drawing analogies from small-scale interactions to the obligation of citizenship, Tony Blair said that, 'For every right we enjoy we owe responsibilities. That is the most basic family value of all' (Blair, 1996: 2).

In all this, New Labour drew on the work of the American theorist, Amitai Etzioni (1993, 1998):

> *First, people have a moral responsibility to take care of themselves . . . the second line of responsibility lies with those closest to the person, including kin, friends, neighbours and other community members. . . . As a rule any community ought to be expected to do the best it can to take care of its own.*
>
> (Etzioni, 1993: 145–6)

So New Labour's version of community complemented its notion of active, autonomous, mobile citizens in a market economy, and its initiatives for social inclusion reflect this view. But the government suffered a series of setbacks in 2001, which caused it to re-assess its model for the social order. First, the riots and intercommunal violence in Bradford, Oldham and Burnley during the summer, then the media outcry about asylum seeking via Sangatte and the Channel Tunnel in early September, and finally the destruction of the World Trade Centre on 11 September, all cast doubt on the nature of minority ethnic communities, and especially the Muslim community, and their relations with deprived white residents and the state.

By the end of the year, the government had rushed out a report by an Independent Committee, chaired by Ted Cantle, on the situation in the northern towns (Home

Office, 2001). It noted that different ethnic groups were living 'parallel lives' in adjacent districts:

> *Whilst the physical segmentation of housing estates and inner city areas came as no surprise, the team was particularly struck by the depth of polarisation of our towns and cities. The extent to which these physical divisions were compounded by so many other aspects of our daily lives, was very evident. Separate educational arrangements, community and voluntary bodies, employment, places of worship, language, social and cultural networks, means that many communities operate on the basis of a series of parallel lives. These lives often do not seem to touch at any point, let alone overlap and promote any meaningful interchanges.*

(Home Office, 2001: 9)

The recommendations from this report gave rise to a whole new thrust to New Labour policy – towards community cohesion:

> *In order to combat the fear and ignorance of different communities which stems from the lack of contact with each other we propose that each area should prepare a local community cohesion plan, as a significant component of its Community Strategy. This should include the promotion of cross-cultural contact between different communities at all levels, foster understanding and respect, and break down barriers. The opportunity should be taken to develop a programme of 'myth busting'. We therefore believe that a new Community Cohesion Task Force should be established to oversee the development of local community cohesion strategies and the implementation of the proposals set out in this report.*

(Home Office, 2001: 11)

This represented a change of direction as well as emphasis in government policy, and it was the responsibility of all local authority agencies to implement it. The Home Office produced a guide for local authorities and their partners, *Building a Picture of Community Cohesion* (Home Office, 2003) which gave as a key headline indicator of cohesion 'the proportion of people who feel that their local area is a place where people from different backgrounds can get on well together' (p. 6).

As Worley (2005) points out, the notion of community cohesion was quickly used synonymously with 'social cohesion' (Home Office, 2005a) and then with '*national cohesion*':

> *Fundamentally, national cohesion rests on an inclusive sense of Britishness which couples the offer of fair play, mutual support – from security to health and education – with the expectation that people will play their part in society and will respect others.*

(Home Office, 2005b: 42)

This quotation brings together several of the new themes which came to be linked with the community cohesion agenda – Britishness, security and respect. It illustrates a growing concern that Muslims in particular did not identify with the common values of British society, which should be more clearly articulated. Tighter controls on immigration through the new legislation in 2002, and the changes which introduced citizenship lessons in school, and citizenship classes and tests for those applying to naturalise, were all aspects of this new agenda.

However, it is not difficult to see that these directions in government policy and local authority practice sit uncomfortably with the main overall thrust of public service reform and modernisation. As we saw in Chapter 2, the key driver of this is the idea of choice – that citizens, as an aspect of individual self-responsibility and self-improvement, should be given opportunities to switch and shift between suppliers of education, health and social care, just as they do between commercial firms supplying services. This includes the chance to move to other districts, if this allows them access to better schools or health facilities.

The consequence of this, it has now been well recognised, is that the population has, at an accelerating rate since 1979, been sorting itself into various kinds of 'enclaves' on the basis of income, age, taste and preference, as well as ethnicity and faith (Jordan, 2006b, Chapter 9; Dorling and Thomas, 2003). This echoes similar findings in the USA (Putnam, 2000: 134–5, 140). Increasingly, individual and households group themselves together with others like themselves, in terms of their stage in the life cycle, their cultural proclivities and social aspirations.

This leaves poor people (and especially those with disabilities and chronic health problems) not only most reliant on family, kin and neighbours for informal support, but also least able to afford to move. So deprived districts become 'communities of fate' rather than the 'communities of choice' occupied by the mainstream population.

So, the sorting of those with fewest resources into rival neighbourhoods in the northern towns, and in some parts of the Midlands and South-East England, is a specific instance of the consequence of policies which encourage choice, mobility and the exercise of 'exit options' rather than 'voice' (participation) or 'loyalty' (solidarity) (Hirschman, 1970). The belated attempt to foster contacts and links between communities is up against the whole dynamic of a society organised around these principles, and New Labour's own main reform agenda. The biggest barrier to cohesion is in fact the cultural mindset that seeks affirmation through the perception that others who use shared facilities are the same, or 'better' than oneself.

As we saw in Chapter 2, this type of thinking is promoted by an economics of 'public choice' for the services provided by the state. Since efficiency and cost-effectiveness are supposed to be promoted by allowing citizens to select their own facilities, and the power of politicians and professionals controlled by these processes (Davies, 1992), the anti-collectivist drive of this branch of economics takes no account of the consequences of exit-orientated service use on the political culture. The government was provoked into action as much by the success of the BNP in local elections in Burnley and other local authorities as by the riots and disorder; it sought to counteract what were essentially direct outcomes of its own economic logic.

But these anxieties were raised to the level of alarm by the suicide bombings on the London transport system of 7 July, 2005. These have triggered a more panicky re-assessment of multiculturalism, and the very values which inform the anti-oppressive agenda in social work. Since that time, there has been a simultaneous stream of media articles and programmes questioning the multi-cultural model, and attempts to construct a version of 'Britishness' (or even 'Englishness') which can command common respect, and mobilise the sense of belonging to a cohesive and coherent social unit. This culminated with the appointment of a Commission on Integration and Cohesion, announced by the Secretary of State for Communities, Ruth Kelly, with a promise to subject multiculturalism to critical scrutiny.

A frequent argument in this debate concerns the failure of British society to 'integrate' Muslim youth. This has suggested that the alienation reflected in suicide bombings and bomb plots reflects the fact that young people in these communities are easily drawn into religious extremism, both because their elders have allowed firebrand preachers to take over their mosques, and because they suffer disproportionate unemployment and lack of educational attainment. Disaffection, it is argued, stems from the sense of not belonging to the host society, because economic inclusion, and education for citizenship has not reached the Muslim minority.

Yet this is not reflected in the backgrounds of the 7 July bombers, or of those arrested for the alleged plot to blow up aircraft bound for the USA. These were not young men with no education, jobs and prospects, like the ones who set the French cities ablaze in October and November, 2005. They were, in the main, well-educated, high achievers, with excellent futures ahead of them. Far from reflecting a failure to integrate, they were economically successful and members of sports clubs, for example, interacting frequently with fellow citizens in the white communities.

It seems plausible to argue that these young men reflect a *success* in UK policies for inclusion and integration. Furthermore, they were not protesting about the situation of British Muslims in their communities, but about the government's foreign policies, and specifically the wars in Afghanistan, Iraq and the Lebanon. If they bear comparison with earlier dissidents, it is more with the privileged members of the Bader-Meinhof gang in Germany in the 1970s, or the Red Brigades in Italy, both involving educated, middle class memberships in violent action against capitalist leaders and the state.

Social capital and well-being

All these developments in public policy on community and citizenship raise basic questions about the nature of professional practice in statutory social work, as well as youth and community work. How exactly can we understand those ways of working with groups and communities which address issues of *respect* and *belonging* – the civility of relationships between neighbours, and fellow-citizens, and the sense of membership of a community and a society?

These questions have always been recognised as central for practice, by the nineteenth-century pioneers, as well as present-day authors. For the Ethical Socialists, how poor people treated each other, and how they related to the bourgeoisie was as important for practitioners as their individual characters. As the leading US analyst of professional skills puts it in his comprehensive review of methods:

> *The mission of those early community-orientated agencies included attempting to help immigrant and other poor families to more effectively integrate into our society.*

(Shulman, 1999: 17)

This is still as important today. 'Macro practice can include direct working with groups . . . and applied to work with community groups' (ibid. 802).

Such methods address individual well-being through the quality of interactions with others outside the immediate circle of the family and close friends (those relationships which confer feelings of emotional closeness, warmth and intimacy). They deal in an interpersonal economy of recognition through politeness, consideration and (where necessary) concern, rather than empathy; and in the sense of identity that comes from sharing beliefs, commitments and common practices with a group or community. The former is what is meant by respect, the latter by belonging.

Richard Sennett (2003) has written subtly and imaginatively about the role of welfare state organisations, such as social housing, in the type of respect shown by citizens to each other, and by officials to citizens, in the post-war era. This was eroded by the economic decay of inner-city districts in the 1970s and 1980s, in both the USA and UK. The fragmentation of working class communities, and the concentration of poverty and unemployment in certain districts, undermined the civility and 'bureaucratic respect' of that era.

In the more diverse and dynamic social relations of the present, respect has to be negotiated, and requires a creative imagination, which can enter the worlds of others whose experiences, and interpretations of them, are quite different from our own. Such respect is not intrusive, but recognises authentic identities and ideas, and the practices these generate. It takes an effort to communicate respect to those who do not belong to the same social worlds as ourselves, and thus gives rise to value in civil society – the value of living together in a day-to-day culture of mutual recognition (Harris, 2006: Jordan, 2006b, Chapters 4 and 9).

The value created by groups and communities for their members' identities is a more combustible one. The sense of belonging is both a source of security and a fuel for action. It can mobilise individuals to activities based on bigotry, scapegoating, hatred and revenge, as much as inspire them to acts of bravery for the sake of loyalty, and solidarity. So, belonging divides people into membership groups as much as it unites them. The interpersonal economy of tribalism, xenophobia, racism and violence is testimony to the down side of the ideas, images and emotions generated by these interactions. Belonging in communities of blood, soil and faith is based on a 'blood and guts code' of loyalty which can be oppressive and violent (Jordan with Jordan, 2000: 54–7 and Chapter 8).

But it can also move them to strong collective action for mutual support to defend their interests against oppression, and to day-to-day activities which create positive value, in the shape of informal services. These ambiguities in membership systems, and the kinds of belonging they generate, will be discussed in Chapters 7 and 8 of this book.

Well-being theory has attempted to link with other recent theory to analyse these aspects of a good quality of life. Theorists have tried to explain the fact that activists of all kinds (in civil associations, political and cultural groups and faiths) report higher levels of SWB than those who experience life as passive consumers, and watch a good deal of TV. This has obvious resonance with the idea of 'social capital' – the bonds among family, friends, neighbours and fellow citizens which are generated through formal and informal interactions, and which have been claimed to contribute positively to the effective functioning of democratic political systems and capitalist economies (Putnam, 1993, 2000).

Helliwell and Putnam (2005) make large claims about the contribution of social capital to well-being. They argue that there is research evidence of a 'close connection between well-being and social capital' (p. 435) and that 'social networks have value' (p. 438). They claim that, where there are high levels of trust in dense networks, 'reciprocity and trustworthiness are nearly universally concomitant' (p. 438). 'People who have close friends and confidants, friendly neighbours and supportive co-workers are less likely to experience sadness, loneliness, low self-esteem and problems with eating and sleeping' (p. 439).

This account of the value of social capital does attempt to give something like an economic analysis of its contribution to well-being. However, it conflates respect and belonging as the main elements in the creation of value through social bonds and networks. It is important to distinguish between respect, a 'cool' good, created by politeness, consideration and kindness, with belonging, a 'hot' good, which can generate destructive divisions and conflicts between members of rival groups.

Furthermore, because bonds and networks do produce exclusivity, prejudice, hatred and stigma for outsiders of membership systems, some of Helliwell and Putnam's claims are dubious. For example, they insist that networks contribute to low levels of crime, child neglect, illness, corruption and tax evasion, and to good market and educational performance. In support of this they note various studies such as Sampson et al. (1997) and Knack and Keefer (1997).

But this evidence is incomplete without a parallel investigation of the contribution of networks to intercommunal strife, violence, terrorism and disaffection. Where groups feel excluded from the mainstream by virtue of ethnicity, faith or income, or districts are deserted by markets and the state as 'communities of fate', bonds can help define identities which reject other groups or the whole culture. This form of social capital creates costs for society, and for some members of the group. This will be discussed more fully in Chapters 7 and 8 (see also Jordan, 2006a, chapter 13).

It is exactly these issues (of loyalty to deviant community values and criminal or disaffected mobilisations) that the New Labour initiatives attempted to address. Public sector social workers are now being asked to practice in such a way as to build the strength of communities, and make bridges between those leading 'parallel lives'. As Worley (2005, 2006) has showed from her research, workers find it very difficult to describe or demonstrate how their practice addresses these issues.

This is because the notions of cohesion, respect and participation cut across the dominant cultural themes of the Anglophone countries (individual self-realisation, autonomy and property accumulation), and of New Labour's own agenda for reform and modernisation of the public sector (choice, independence, mobility between options). The attempt to counteract individualism and exclusiveness in groups by some form of participatory engagement remains a vague aspiration, rather than a goal pursued through clear policy priorities by well-defined practices.

This is why the suicide bombings and plots by Islamic activists provoked such a panic about multiculturalism and the common culture of Britishness. If the dominant political ideology promotes the freedom of individuals to pursue their projects of self-realisation through choice in markets and a market-like public sector, loyalty and collective action for the common good will always be the loser. In a sense, there is nothing in British mainstream culture to be loyal to, except the culture of the individual consumer, in search of more and more material satisfactions. Any such ideology is deeply vulnerable to a faith-based code of commitment to a common cause – one legitimated by the crudeness of George Bush's and Tony Blair's adventures in the Muslim world.

Well-being does indeed involve interpersonal interactions which promote respect and the sense of belonging. But this in turn requires us to challenge the culture of materialistic individualism, and the individual bias of the type of social work which is prescribed in today's public sector. It requires connections between social work and community work to be remade. This will be fully analysed in the final part of this book.

Conclusions

Social work's anti-oppressive values are derived from the period when feminism and anti-racism were part of a radical challenge to barriers to equality in the US and the UK societies. These principles were not directly antagonistic to the emphasis on individual liberty which characterised the neo-liberal Thatcher-Reagan era, in that they enhanced a culture of equal opportunity in workplaces and politics. They promoted identity, recognition and difference as values, as well as justice for previously invisible and excluded groups. But they also allowed self-realisation within an overall climate of mutual respect.

At the present time, there is something of a moral panic in the UK about the security implications of the multiculturalism in which these values were located. Leading commentators have questioned whether a multicultural society can create sufficient cohesion and integration of marginal and disaffected groups (Phillips, 2005; Goodhart, 2005). Muslim youth is seen as a special challenge to this agenda, because of the suicide bombings and plots against British and US targets; a vicious circle of fear and resentment threatens to develop between the authorities and this group (Ramadan, 2005; Kureishi, 2005; Gilroy and Ouseley, 2005).

Because the attempt to achieve cohesion goes so strongly against the government-led culture of autonomy, choice and material consumption, and because of the authoritarian streak in New Labour ideology, this panic has quickly translated itself into measures to control immigration and to clamp down on extremist groups. At the press conference launching the commission for Integration and Cohesion, Ruth Kelly is reported to have said that it 'had to engage with the argument made by Trevor Phillips, the chairman of the Commission for Racial Equality, that support for multiculturalism, should be abandoned in favour of efforts to create a more homogeneous society' (*The Guardian*, 2006d: 7). She added:

> There are white Britons who do not feel comfortable with change . . . they see their neighbourhoods becoming more diverse. Detached from the benefits of those changes, they begin to believe the stories about ethnic minorities getting special treatments, and to develop a resentment, a sense of grievance. We have moved from a period of uniform consensus on the value of multiculturalism to one where we can encourage that debate by questioning whether it is encouraging separateness.
>
> (ibid)

Yet none of this was really new. Home Office documents for several years had been emphasising the effort to 'integrate' new immigrants in particular. For example, the White Paper *Strength in Diversity: Towards a Community Cohesion and Race Equality Strategy* (2004) stated:

> Integration in Britain is not about assimilation into a simple homogeneous culture. It is a two way process, with responsibilities on both new arrivals and established communities. Integration is also about more than how we respond to new arrivals. It means ensuring that ethnic, religious or cultural differences do not define people's life chances and that people with different backgrounds work together to build a shared future.
>
> (Home Office, 2004a)

The later paper, *Improving Opportunity, Strengthening Society*, added:

> We will improve opportunities for young people from all backgrounds to learn and socialise together and to develop an inclusive sense of British identity alongside their other cultural identities. . . . This does not mean that people need to choose between Britishness and other cultural identities, nor should they sacrifice their particular lifestyles, customs and beliefs. They should be proud of them.
>
> (Home Office, 2005a, Paragraphs 11 and 14)

For practitioners in the public sector, this effort to create an 'inclusive British identity', in any deeper sense than a material stake in an individualistic, mobile society of atomistic citizens shifting between options, is highly problematic. Furthermore, public policy is ambivalent about processes of integration, both for those who have arrived as workers (such as the 600,000 from the new EU accession countries, mainly Poland, who came between May, 2004, and the summer of 2006) and for asylum seekers awaiting determination of their claims.

For the latter, it has created an agency, the National Asylum Support Service, which gives 'support' to those dispersed to accommodation all over the country, while at the same time they are deliberately discouraged from integrating with the economy and their own communities of fellow-immigrants by this process of dispersal. These support workers, many of them with a social work background, are employed by the Home Office to sustain this situation of 'limbo' for new arrivals (Brown, 2005).

In this chapter, I have argued that it is possible to understand practice which builds respect and belonging between groups and within communities in terms of the interpersonal economy. This approach to the improvement of well-being is different from the one taken by the UK government, because it recognises the value of relationships between people in a very concrete and specific way, rather than as a vague aspiration. Such practice creates value by:

1. Promoting the experience of respect and the sense of belonging between citizens and in communities.
2. Recognising that these are different forms of value, and must be fostered in different ways.
3. Creating respect by learning politeness, consideration and concern as everyday practices in the public culture, and challenging racism, sexism, and all other forms of disrespectful, stigmatising behaviour.
4. Promoting the sense of belonging by practice which engages with group identity and membership, and building relations of mutuality and mutual identification through shared debates and activities, addressing common issues and problems.
5. Challenging bigotry, stereotyping and exclusion, both within such membership groups, and by mainstream organisations against their members.

Clearly this involves addressing change in a way which goes beyond individual casework. It requires intervention in the interpersonal economy in ways that alter the collective ideas, images, norms and cultures of members, and the way they interact on key issues. All this is implied by many of the well-being theorists, such as Layard (2005) Helliwell and Putnam (2005) and so it is disappointing that the media response to the well-being turn in the social sciences has been almost exclusively in terms of individual factors, such as mental health and work-life balance. This was evident in such programmes as *Making Slough Happy* (BBC2, TV, 2005), in which 'hedonic therapists' prescribed activities for the stressed-out residents of that benighted town, or castigated children for their commitment to educational options which would maximise their future earnings.

But this in turn merely reflects the priorities of the leading economist to influence the government's thinking on well-being, Richard Layard. He was described in the press as the new 'Happiness Czar' when it was announced that he would be presiding over a multi-million pound programme for 'personal education' in secondary schools. He had already been strongly associated with the higher priority given to mental health, and especially Cognitive Behavioural Therapy, in the government's health spending plans (Brindle, 2005). This does little justice to the anti-individualist tone of much of his book (2005) and the breadth of his recommendations on redistribution, social relations and the cultural resources of society.

The potential implications of the new evidence on well-being are more radical than this. In the final chapter I shall review the tensions between new approaches to children's quality of life and social development, and the emphasis on security and control.

In the final part of this book I shall turn to the agenda on multiculturalism and cohesion, and the part that social and community work might play in it.

Chapter 7

Accountability and Community Participation

Introduction

In the final chapter in Part Two, I argued that the interpersonal economy creates value for society through the building of *collective* goods, as well as the individual components of SWB (emotions sustained in face-to-face interactions). These collective goods are not 'owned' by individuals, but accessible to members of groups and communities, who in turn must sustain them through shared activities and communications. They are resources which both *restrain* certain actions (selfishness, greed, 'myopic choices', disloyalty, abuse and injustice), and *promote* others (collective action for solidarity, resistance, celebration, perseverance, social investment and so on).

We saw in that chapter that New Labour perceives community and social inclusion primarily in terms of a glue to keep society from fragmenting into conflictual groups. The language of *cohesion* is one in which a controlling influence is exercised by elders, religious leaders, voluntary agencies and traditional values, so that the individual liberty which is the dominant ethos of a market economy can be offset by responsibility towards others, at least not to do them harm. In this way, choice and mobility are supposed to co-exist with acceptable levels of mutuality.

We also saw that respect and the sense of belonging are two of the most important elements in a convivial society, conducive to well-being. But these are not collective goods which can be understood in terms of 'cohesion' – as glue to bond people together. They require the active interaction of members who attempt to understand their social world; and communicate about their interpretations, disputing and challenging as well as constructing and agreeing.

We noted that this idea of 'communicative action' is present in the rather abstract theories of Habermas (1989, 1998), as well as in accounts of the 'politics of recognition' (Fraser, 1992; Young, 1990) and 'deliberative democracy' (Dryzek, 1990, 2000).

In this chapter, and the next, I shall look at how community work and community social work contribute to these processes. I shall argue that the theory and practice of community work, directly derived from the work of Canon Barnett in the late nineteenth century, and of certain colonial development officers in the 1950s and

1960s, when African and Asian countries were being prepared for post-colonial independence (Batten, 1954), is highly consistent with the model of the interpersonal economy and communicative action outlined by these theorists.

Community work and community social work is also important for the promotion of well-being. In his best-selling textbook on the subject, Alan Twelvetrees defines community work as follows:

> ... the process of assisting people to improve their own communities by undertaking collective action ... The essence of community work is to ensure, first, that people, as residents of geographical communities or as members of high need groups (such as people with learning difficulties) get a better deal; and second, that they bring about this 'better deal' themselves, at least as far as possible, and develop more skills and confidence in the process. ... Citizen participation is also vital, in my view, as a means of holding politicians and policy-makers to account. Secondly, without assistance, many attempts of people to engage in collective action and other forms of participation fail, especially in 'excluded' communities.

(Twelvetrees, 2002: 1–2) (Emphasis in original)

To this definition, I would add that 'promote their quality of shared life', or 'enhance their collective well-being' are synonymous with 'improve their own communities', and that 'more skills and confidence' implies a richer *collective* culture, and more *shared* resources, as well as individual capacities.

In a similar way, the Barclay Report defined 'community social work' as an approach which:

> ... seeks to tap into, support, enable and underpin the local networks of formal and informal relationships which constitute our basic definition of community, and also the strengths of a client's communities of interest.

(Barclay, 1982: xvii)

The principal advocates of this approach to the organisation and methods of local authority social services add that its re-orientation of practice leads:

> ... away from individual situations and towards social analysis provides a context within which issues such as gender, race and political power can be recognised and understood, and more informed pressures for changes in policy and practice can develop.

(Hadley, et al., 1987: 23)

Unfortunately for the movement towards this approach (which flowered in the early 1980s, mainly in Labour-controlled local authorities which were resisting Thatcherism), the subsequent long period of neo-liberal domination of UK politics has been re-inforced by New Labour's policies. Community work (albeit under top-down, control-orientated policies) has flourished, but as part of the new initiatives, on social exclusion, urban regeneration and social cohesion, which have been developed quite separately from public sector social work. Instead of being able to bridge between community work and case work, this approach has been largely confined to practice in voluntary agencies.

In this chapter, I shall show that the analysis of practice in terms of relationships and the interpersonal economy can embrace community work and community social work as well as casework and groupwork. But this involves a closer consideration of how 'collective goods', 'conventions' and cultural resources are created, and how they are used by membership systems.

Under New Labour administrations in the UK, the attempt to foster inclusion, cohesion and respect has not involved any such analysis. The closest that government ideology has come to such an understanding is the concept of 'social capital' (Home Office, 2005b). As I shall show, this idea does have echoes of an economic theory of the value of collective resources for social action in communities, but it falls short of providing a systematic analysis which could demonstrate how such resources contribute to well-being. If community work can be based on such an analysis, it can strengthen its claims to be a central method of social policy interventions (rather than one which is confined to deprived and marginal districts), and also its links to social work practice.

Before entering on this theoretical exercise, I shall give three very diverse examples of interventions in social situations, against which my analysis will be tested. Only the first of these falls easily into the category of community work, but they allow me to show the communalities between actions which aim to change cultures and provide new resources for people to tackle their shared aspects of their well-being and quality of life.

Case Study 1

Blackbird Leys Estate, Oxford

The first example concerns an outer-city council estate, typical of those constructed from the late 1940s to the early 1970s all over Europe, from the northern suburbs of Paris to Petrzalka, on the opposite side of the Danube from Bratislava (Power, 1996).

The thinking behind these modernist monuments was that disadvantaged citizens and immigrants from run-down inner city districts could be given a new, clean environment, in which they could rebuild community links and establish a better life together.

Unfortunately this wave of construction coincided with the transformation of the economies of Europe, away from unskilled and semi-skilled employment in the industrial sector, in which men could earn a 'family wage' and towards more 'flexible' jobs in a mosaic of services, taken by women and part-time younger and older workers. This left these new estates inconveniently located for much of the new employment becoming available, and undermined the traditional, male-dominated working class cultures of the industrial era.

These social changes have provided a rich seam of tragi-comic TV dramas and films, such as *The Boys from the Black Stuff, Auf Wiedersehen Pet, Brassed Off, Common as Muck,* and *The Full Monty,* in which redundant male factory hands or council workers, who have lost the solidarities and companionships of their old working environments, re-create an improvised version of these in new 'flexible' activities (the informal economy or sub-contract culture) against a backdrop of a harsh post-industrial landscape.

Blackbird Leys in Oxford, is an older estate with a multi-ethnic population, which (under the policies of councils required to sell off their housing stock to tenants) has become a 'less desirable' district, with concentrations of poor people, sick people, lone parents and minority ethnic residents, and high unemployment. It briefly achieved national notoriety with an 'epidemic' of joyriding in stolen vehicles (Oxford is a very affluent city) and resistance against police interventions by gangs of local youths, which attracted substantial media attention. It was therefore an early target for New Labour's Social Exclusion Unit, which ran some projects on the estate.

Today, there have been changes in Blackbird Leys, which are recognised and acknowledged by residents (BBC Radio 4, 2006f). Central to these is a new community centre, mainly run by local volunteers, and providing facilities for a great range of community groups. However, not all residents feel represented by the organising committee of the centre, or involved in these activities. Interviewed for this radio report, two young black people said that there was nothing for them there.

A local politician from Oxford City Council commented that the government had put very few new resources into Blackbird Leys, and that the improvement in the culture and interactions of the residents could be attributed to their own efforts, and the support of the Council itself.

Case Study 2

Action to Tackle Honour Killings by Asian Community Leaders

In the late summer of 2006, a survey by the BBC revealed that 10 per cent of young Asian men from the Sikh, Muslim and Hindu communities in the UK thought that 'honour killings' were justified (BBC Radio 4, 2006g; BBC World Service, 2006b). Such killings involved the often brutal murder of family members, mostly women, who brought dishonour on the family by their behaviour. Such actions could vary from adultery to simply going out with a person of another faith, or even talking to such people on the way to school.

As commentators from these South Asian communities emphasised at the time, these practices are in no way derived from the articles of faith of these three religions. They reflect the norms and conventions of tribal communities in the Kashmir and Punjab, from which these families have migrated, and to which they still have links. In these cultures, honour is considered to reside in the purity, chastity and fidelity of women, and the reputation of the family is a very important economic asset. If a member of a family is seen to have violated these norms, bringing dishonour on all her kin, they all risk being shunned or expelled from their communities, with disastrous consequences for their material well-being.

What was more shocking for listeners to these radio reports was that such ideas and practices should persist, even among young men of the second and third generations living in UK cities. Like forced marriages and suicide bombings, these phenomena reminded mainstream, middle-class white citizens, who fancied themselves to be bearers of a liberal tradition of individual freedom and self-reflective tolerance, of the awesome power of collective identifications and cultural expectations. It also reminded them of the presence of 'others' among them, who rejected this same individualism and liberalism, in favour of a 'blood-and-guts code' of loyalty and solidarity.

On the same radio programme, leaders from the three faith groups surveyed by the BBC said that they were already acting together to tackle the phenomenon of honour killings. They unreservedly rejected these practices and disowned them as having no part of their religions. But they acknowledged that 'izat' (honour) was an integral part of the culture of South Asia, and much of the Middle East, and that it would take an enormous effort of cultural transformation and resocialisation to eliminate it altogether from the everyday thinking and practice of South Asian families living in Britain.

Case Study 3

Youth Offender Panels (YOPs) in Youth Justice

Under New Labour's policies for youth justice, the rationale of which is mainly to control delinquency by firm measures, and prevent re-offending, Referral Orders were introduced in 2002. As part of a radical overhaul under the Crime and Disorder Act, 1998, reforming the youth courts, these orders were intended to enable 'restorative justice' (Home Office, 2001a, Paragraph 9.21) defined in terms of 'responsibility' and 'reintegration'.

Their aim is to get young people (aged 10 to 17 years) to be responsible for their offending behaviour, consider the impact of their offences on their victims, and reintegrate into the law-abiding community.

'Restorative justice' is based on what are arguably very old principles, under which a community deals with wrongs done by one member to others, and restores both equilibrium and bonds of membership for all parties (Braithwaite, 1998). It therefore differs from state-led criminal justice, which imposes third-party enforcement of central government law on offenders, excluding both victims and the affected community from the process. New Labour turned to these new approaches in the face of costly youth justice policies which were punitive and ineffective (Smith, 2003, Pitts, 2005), following the development of Victim Support mediation schemes (Gavrielides, 2003) and experimental pilots in Scotland (Sawyer, 2000) which in turn were partly based on practice in New Zealand (Morris and Maxwell, 1998, Crawford and Newburn, 2003).

So far, the evaluations of the work of the Youth Offender Panels, which deal with Referral Orders, has been mixed. The Panel is made up of one worker from a Youth Offending Team (social worker, probation officer, police officer, education or health service staff) and at least two members of a Community Panel. The aim is to get the young person, who admits responsibility, for an offence, to make reparation to the victim, to undertake activity to avoid re-offending, and to re-integrate into the community (Home Office, 2002: 23).

But local evaluations, such as Jones and Roberts (2005) and Meades (2006), suggest that young people do not understand the purposes of the Panels, and expect punishment rather than restoration. Other evaluations felt insufficient attention was given to explaining the principles of restorative justice (Gavrielides, 2003) which resulted in limited participation by offenders in the process (Wilcox, 2003).

Although most young offenders accepted responsibility for their offences (Gray, 2005) the evidence of evaluations was that victims were in fact little involved, and offenders did not see the process in terms of their understanding and making some amends for the consequences.

Nor did they really discuss or recognise effects on the community. Finally, the Home Office's own evaluations of the pilots did not fully apply the standards of restorative justice, as their policy documents defined them, to the work of the YOPs, instead adopting a more pragmatic measure of their effectiveness. Although the YOPs were successful in several respects, they did not achieve the involvement and reintegration principles of the restorative justice model.

Discussion

The three case studies sketched here are very diverse, but their common theme is government interventions in policy areas which concern conflict and cohesion, and attempts to engage with community members' own ways of resolving contentious issues. None of them, with the partial exception of the first, can be seen as 'community work' in Twelvetrees' sense; but all are characteristic of the current UK administration.

New Labour's model of governance includes many such initiatives and reforms, but all co-opt and control the participants and engage them in negotiations around an agenda set by the government. Rather than airing differences and attempting discursive resolution, they draw various individuals and representatives of groups into 'invited spaces' (Gaventa, 2004) and allow them to negotiate within parameters defined by the state (Fraser, 1997: 88).

As critics have pointed out, attempts by government to create a cohesive and orderly civic culture through 'partnership' are undertaken partly to enable the state to withdraw from the provision of social services, and instead become the enabler of a 'mixed economy' of quasi-market providers of most of the social infrastructure (Shaw, 2003; Hodgson, 2004). This 'manufactures' a civil society in the image of New Labour's preferred order, through initiatives for 'regeneration' or 'cohesion' or 'renewal':

> The term manufactured is used, because these groups have not developed organically, but have been engineered, created or manufactured by the state . . . [which] can be said to be constructing a particular type of civil society built upon a government agenda, linked together by state policy and process and built upon a Third Way foundation; this despite the government's recent recognition that civil society operates best when groups 'develop organically'.
>
> (Hodgson, 2004: 145)

From research in South East Wales, Hodgson concludes that such 'manufactured' partnerships of statutory and voluntary organisations and coalitions of local groups, encouraged to merge through promises of external funding, included Sure Start programmes and local regeneration projects. A similar critique of partnerships in

Ireland has been made by Forde (2006); that excluded and marginal groups were consulted in a coerced rather than fully engaged way, that power rested with officials and firms, not local people, and that conflicts were not properly addressed and resolved. Hence ' . . . the basis for partnerships needs to be deeper than economic rationality or outside social engineering if these initiatives are to work' (Hodgson, 2004: 156).

Of the examples given, the Blackbird Leys community is much the least open to these criticisms. Partly because central government agencies were only peripherally involved in the response to the outbreak of local disorder, the community centre retains a strong element of local engagement and control. Although some residents claim that their groups (in this case, black youth) have no real stake in the centre, it does involve a substantial membership of the estate's community. Opportunities have been made to enable the activities of many elements among residents in a facility that allows them to interact informally, on their own terms.

The second example involves a feature of central concern to the government, as part of its growing anxiety about such phenomena as the threat to security from militant Muslim young men, the relationships between minority ethnic and white communities, and the problems of 'integration' and multiculturalism. After the suicide bombings in London on 7 July 2005, the government created a number of 'invited spaces' into which Muslim community and religious leaders were co-opted, to discuss strategies for better integration. Among the issues identified by these consultations were the gaps between the older generation of leaders and imams, and the younger generation; including those (such as the bombers) who were well-educated, and able to deploy critical intellectual analysis to political issues, such as foreign policy.

The problem of 'honour killings' in the Sikh and Hindu as well as the Muslim community, signals the limitations of the government's approach. A significant proportion of young men from all three South Asian minorities subscribed to the honour code, and justified such killings. This suggests a shared cultural commitment to certain values and practices which straddles the generations, and is not specific to any single faith. It also draws attention to the salience of gender relations for inter- and intra- community relations, as a potential source of conflict (Worley, 2005, 2006).

The various government initiatives on cohesion and integration have evidently done little to address these issues. The leaders of the three faith communities seem to have undertaken a very long-term task, in acting together to tackle the 'honour killings' issue and it is unclear how government agencies will assist them.

Finally, the YOPs are the clearest example of a New Labour 'manufactured' forum, with the various parties to an offence against a local resident brought together by a compulsory order against the offender. The goals of the YOPs are enlightened, but those who have studied them comment on the skill and time required to engage all the parties fully in a convincing version of restorative justice, which attempts 're-integration' in the community.

This again illustrates that the challenges for such projects are as much cultural as organisational. Within a highly individualistic culture, the practices which make up everyday life do not sustain repertoires and resources for such engagement. The point about the New Zealand experience of restorative justice was that it aimed to revive practices in Maori culture which were widespread in the informal life experience of the grandparents of young offenders. In the UK, they are not even part of folk memory, and refer to Anglo-Saxon history.

In other words, as in the case of 'honour killings', those who are trying to bring about change must try to create a new set of ideas, images and practices, within which the various parties can engage with each other. The YOPs, bringing together police and probation officers on the one hand, and offenders on the other, with occasional representation of victims, were too like the old juvenile courts to achieve this transformation process, and the professionals lacked the time and skills to bring about the necessary creative processes.

In the next section, I shall consider how these cultural factors might be addressed in practice, and how this relates to the analysis of value in the interpersonal economy. This will enable us to start to understand the contribution of the 'collective goods' of membership to well-being.

The value of social capital

The UK government sees 'social capital' – 'networks of reciprocity and trustworthiness' (Putnam, 2000: 19) – as central to community cohesion and responsible citizenship. It has commissioned extensive research on the current state of social capital in the country (Home Office, 2005b) and sees many of its new initiatives in civil society in terms of building social capital.

But although the concept of social capital clearly refers to the economic notion of an asset which is produced from other resources, that are invested for the sake of increased future production, this economic analogy is then undeveloped. Neither in his *Bowling Alone* (Putnam, 2000) nor in his contribution with Helliwell on the role of social capital in well-being (Helliwell and Putnam, 2005) does the leading theorist of this concept give a clear account of how the norms and bonds which make up 'networks of reciprocity and trustworthiness' create value and improve the quality of people's lives (Jordan, 2006b, chapter 2).

People interact to achieve their purposes – to clean up a neighbourhood, produce a play, form a sports club, organise a festival or rob a bank. Whether they are collecting money for a mosque, celebrating an anniversary, fighting a new motorway or supporting a football team, they act together because their interactions are producing something of value to them. Sometimes this value is pure pleasure of the moment, sometimes it is some future benefit or advantage, to which they are prepared to endure hard work and discomfort.

Whatever it is they are trying to do, they rely on communications among them to achieve their purposes. These communications may be simple rosters, lists of tasks and timetables, by which they coordinate practical activities (such as maintaining a sports field and club house, or running the bar of a social centre). Or they may be quite complex ideas and images, which express cultural aspirations and standards, as in mobilising people to perform a community play, planning a meeting to protest about a new development, or trying to start an environmental movement. In most associations and groups, however small and informal, they contain both of these elements, because the production of experiences which people value relies on getting practical things done (even if only making tea and finding somewhere to meet next time).

The idea of social capital suggests that bonds and connections of reliable reciprocity and trust are generated by these interactions, as a sort of by-product. People learn skills and build connections, they establish reputations and networks, and in this way they gain a kind of portfolio of competences and contacts, through which they are able to be more effective employees and citizens. This allows their interactions with others to be converted into assets which are 'owned' by individuals, and accessible to them in much the same way as their 'internal' capabilities. The social capital generated through shared activity ends up as something very similar to the 'human capital' we each accumulate through education, training and work experience – a kind of 'money in the bank' asset, that allows us to earn more and be more effective citizens.

My analysis of social capital is quite different from this. The kind of interactions I have described do indeed give us skills, competences, capacities and connections. But they also make us who we are, and embed us in a cultural milieu. In this sense, they as much create our identities and ways of seeing the world as we create them. In joining with others for common purposes, we have no alternative but to share in a set of cultural resources, through which members make sense of their common experiences. In describing what they do to each other, members both build up a vocabulary and categorisation of these experiences, and form themselves into a collective body, with a shared identity. As we have already seen in Chapter 6, these cultural commitments both restrain them from acting in certain ways, and enable them to act in others, within this collective identity (Bourdieu, 1990).

This is most obvious in those groups and organisations which demand strong loyalty from their members, such as religious faiths, militant political parties and football clubs. In these, the decision to be a member constitutes a commitment to a set of values and practices which determine the interpretation of important parts of the social world, and prescribe appropriate actions. Being a supporter of the BNP, Al Q'aida or Arsenal does not leave much room for debate about the nature of good and evil, right and wrong, in issues of ethnic purity, religious martyrdom and London football supremacy respectively. Even more casual forms of membership which commit an individual to joint undertakings with others affect identity and ways of thinking. They cannot be transferred to other clubs or associations without a process of disowning, purging and self-reinvention in some strong cases, such as changes in political and faith loyalty.

This is where the two sides of New Labour's social policy agenda are in such obvious tension with each other. The principles of individual independence, choice and mobility between options (see Chapter 2) suggest that switching and shifting is costless and painless, because the qualities one needs to be a participating, contributing member are transferable, and each will choose where they can get the most beneficial terms of membership. But the notions of community and citizenship imply loyalties and commitments which are not so easily broken, and practices which are meaningful for reasons which go well beyond material advantages.

In economic terms, the idea of costless shifting and switching is built into the model of the social services now being institutionalised in education, health and social care. Here, schools, hospitals and care facilities function like 'clubs' which can give members the best deal by specialising, or by delivering a certain quality at the lowest possible cost. But real-life clubs (for instance, sports clubs) are not like this at all.

In New Labour's preferred model for public finance, efficiencies are achieved in the provision of collective facilities by excluding non-members from those who share costs; and these in turn are maintained by competition between providers, so that members can move elsewhere for a better deal.

In real-life sports clubs, unlike Buchanan's (1965) swimming club, the facilities *must* remain open to non-members, to attract potential new blood, spectators, visitors from other clubs, and so on. They retain their members as much by sustaining loyalty, by providing opportunities for satisfying interactions – among non-participants as well as players – which reinforce loyalty, and as much by the shared histories and cultures of a tradition, as by their cost-effectiveness. It is the interactions themselves which constitute the culture of membership, and it is this that binds members together, and gives them the benefits of respect and belonging (Jordan, 2006b, Chapter 5).

Many clubs do not have any exclusive facilities. Rambling clubs, mountaineering clubs, angling clubs and surfing clubs, for example, use open natural facilities; darts clubs and quiz teams use pubs. Since the main point of membership is interaction with others, it makes little sense to join unless one is going to gain pleasure from this, to be loyal to whatever this interaction creates by way of a common culture. In football clubs, players may be recruited internationally, and transferred frequently, but the success of the club depends on a core of loyal, often life-long support.

So much of the value which is created by membership groups and associations consists in the cultural resources which are created through purposive and informal, incidental interactions between members. People join to achieve common purposes, use and create shared facilities; but they also participate in and develop common cultures, with shared loyalties and practices. These are accessible to members, and form part of their identities.

In less developed economies, community is a very important feature of economic activity. The collective infrastructure exists because of communal effort. To get fields irrigated, water drawn and waste disposed of requires communal work effort. Community is the way of getting collective tasks done, and collective goods and services provided.

In affluent societies, community is a residual category. It is what is left over when the state and commercial firms have provided all that they consider rational and profitable to supply. As we have seen in Chapter 6, this is now a very small space; there is not much for the interpersonal economy to *do*, because the state and commercial companies have taken over so much of the public sphere.

All this is pertinent to the examples given earlier. The 'invited spaces' for participation and engagement created by New Labour are established primarily to uphold or produce its version of the social order – 'responsibility', 'cohesion', 'security' and 'integration'. But this is not at all the same as the sense of loyalty and belonging, collective identity and commitment that springs from self-generated group activity for chosen ends.

The correlations discovered by social capital researchers between community, activism and well-being all relate to the latter type of membership. People feel better about their quality of life when they are fully engaged with others in building a shared social environment, and a shared set of cultural resources for interpreting it. Having an imposed order, and a readymade understanding of it, for the sake of 'cohesion' is not the same thing.

How then can community work and community social work practice in ways that promote well-being? How can they avoid the pitfalls of conflict and partisanship in complex and divided societies? These will be the topics of the next section.

The dilemma of community work

We are now at the crux of the dilemma of community work. On the one hand, as we have just seen, community groups and voluntary associations create value by tackling shared problems in collective ways, and producing cultural resources in that process. These resources are their ways of interpreting their social worlds, and keeping solidarity and loyalty in living together, or sharing aspects of their lives. They are what gives them common identities and the sense of belonging.

On the other hand, these same resources can be used to mobilise them against other districts, other groups or other associations. Where the memberships have a limited stock of cultural inputs (derived from specific ideologies, faiths, experiences and educations) they may indeed create loyalty and solidarity *in opposition* to other such groups, organisations, or mainstream agencies. This is not much of a problem if they are mobilising to compete with other football teams (though it is if their solidarity has ethnic or faith elements in it, as in the case of the old culture of Millwall or Glasgow Rangers). It is a big problem for community work in a divided, conflictual society, and an even bigger one where there is an undeclared civil war, as in Northern Ireland during the 'Troubles'.

In her research on *Informal Economic Activity in Belfast*, Madeleine Leonard (1993) found that one poor Catholic district, with very high rates of poverty and unemployment, also had very high rates of participation in undeclared cash work, bartering of skills and informal home production. These activities were based on gendered roles, the men doing construction, home repairs and car maintenance, and the women cooking, provisioning and care. They were strongly sanctioned by the IRA as the local paramilitary force, which regarded them as an expression of the solidarity of resistance against mainstream (UK) government agencies.

After the implementation of the Peace Process, under which the elected, Sinn Fein representatives agreed to begin a transition to power sharing, an attempt was made to bring districts like this into the mainstream, allowing outside firms to trade and government agencies to function.

As Leonard (2004) points out, this has had the effect of weakening the bonds of community, because commercial firms and state services have replaced the activities of informal organisations and groups. Some residents have increased their income by getting formal employment, but others have become *more* excluded than before, because they have lost access to informal contributions and support.

One aspect of these districts was the community work done by unqualified members, under the overall aegis of their paramilitary order. This work sustained solidarity, mobilised residents in the informal economy, and provided reliable support for groups (e.g. youth, recreation and culture). But this was vulnerable to professional-isation. As one community activist put it *before* the Peace Process began to influence this community:

> We're in control here, and we like to keep it that way. If we started to formalise, you might say that would be a good thing; it could lead to a few jobs being created. But who would those jobs go to? Certainly not any of us. We've no fancy qualifications. In fact, to be quite honest, we've no qualifications. So how would any of us have a chance? Who would employ us? The only way we can do community work is to do it voluntarily.
>
> (Leonard, 1999: 17)

The only way in which the theory of social capital can explain these paradoxes is in terms of the distinction between 'bonding' and 'bridging' versions of that concept (Putnam, 2000: 79). 'Bonding' social capital is the networks and norms which sustain people with similar social profiles and shared lives in districts such as these. It corresponds roughly to the norms and expectations of the 'blood-and-guts code' (Jordan with Jordan, 2000, chapter 2), and mobilises such communities against others.

'Bridging' social capital is that which is generated by more formal, organised links between groups who are unalike, in a complex civil society. But – as Leonard (2004) points out – this distinction masks some serious problems. If bridges can only be built by destroying some of the networks and practices of bonding communities, as in this case, then how are we to justify social capital as a single generic concept, or claim that it represents such a positive factor for well-being? In Belfast:

> Bonding social capital has had limited success while the rationale for bonding social capital continues to be dismantled. . . . In relation to economic linkages, the West

Belfast example demonstrates how bridging social capital benefited individuals rather than communities.

(Leonard, 2004: 940–1)

If community work is defined in Twelvetrees' (2002) terms, those who acted as informal community workers during the Troubles were closer to its essential features than the government officials who replaced them under the Peace Process. But the older partisan community workers helped sustain the Republican paramilitary order of these districts, with all its brutality, enforcement and traditional (e.g. gender-stereotypical) features.

We can begin to unravel those conundrums, when we recognise that all social groups generate cultural goods, for sustaining collective action, as described in the previous section. As members of such groups and organisations, individuals make themselves accountable for aspects of their behaviour to each other, in terms of this collective culture.

For example, where an action is proscribed as disloyal or deviant, they must point to some exceptional feature of their situation (coercion, confusion) to explain their behaviour, where this fails to observe that norm. This is the price of sharing in the benefits of solidarity, and being able to call in the support of other members.

Indeed, this notion of 'accountability' to cultural standards is the basis for qualitative research methods. We understand how groups and associations work for their members, and how norms and networks provide individuals with resources for identity and action, by seeing how they account for themselves to an interviewer (Cuff, 1980; Silverman, 2005). Not all the actions of residents of deprived districts are justified in terms of local loyalties and informal groups; some are legitimated by reference to mainstream standards, and even government rhetoric (Jordan et al., 1992; Jordan, 1993).

The 'discursive repertoires' (Wetherall and Potter, 1988) available to individuals may be drawn from a number of resources; they may account for their actions in several overlapping ways.

New Labour's initiatives, on community cohesion, respect and integration try to impose a top-down standard of 'Britishness', responsibility and 'order' on such communities, through participation in partnership arrangements such as the ones explained above. This means that workers in such projects are often required to justify themselves to their employers, or to umbrella agencies, in such terms. It imposes a structure of accountability from above, rather than engaging with the cultural resources of the members of groups and communities.

In addition to this, there is usually a strand of the economics of choice, and the managerialism of service delivery and cost-effectiveness, in these initiatives. Accountability in terms of quality, efficiency, outcomes and targets is often added to accountability for cohesion, respect and integration.

To criticise this is not to endorse an uncritical sharing of the standards and practices of deprived districts or resistance mobilisations. Community workers who are paid out of public funds *are* accountable in terms of the values of democracy, social justice, citizenship and the common good. They represent these values through their professional ethics, which transcend specific government initiatives.

But this should not tie them into a form of accountability which is imposed by the government or their agency, at the expense of acknowledging and supporting that of membership groups and communities. What is at stake is a form of accountability to residents and members, which accepts their commitments and loyalties to cultural practices, but also remains answerable to those professional standards, and the basis for democratic citizenship shared by all members of the society.

Community workers have, through training, professional support and their organisations, access to these wider cultural resources. Through dialogue with and between groups, they can help members generate new repertoires, based on fresh ideas, which challenge narrow preconceptions. They can broaden the possibilities for action, and help groups become more effective in pursuing their interests.

All this is more likely to be achieved if they make themselves *more* accountable to members, while making it clear that they retain a critical professional judgement (Doherty, 2002). But they must also address the harm and stigma caused by interactions between members in some groups and communities, and between communities in some societies. This will be the topic for the next chapter.

Conclusions

Starting from the definitions of community work and community social work given by Twelvetrees (2002) and Hadley et al. (1987) this chapter has analysed the kinds of collective action through which groups and communities improve their members' well-being, and the ways in which professional workers can support and enhance their efforts to achieve a better quality of life. The aim has been to clarify the processes by which the interpersonal economy of groups, associations and communities create value for members through interactions in both formal and informal contexts. The conclusions can be summarised as follows:

- Interactions between members of purposive groups and communities create value both by practices which increase the supply of 'collective goods', such as facilities for overcoming conflicts and problems, for mutual support and shared enjoyment, and by contributions and exchanges which create the sense of loyalty, solidarity, and belonging.

- These interactions in turn give rise to 'cultural resources', through communication of ideas, images and emotions, which create group identities and practices. These resources both restrain and enable individual actions and deeply influence how the social world is experienced, interpreted and acted upon by members.

- This means that members inevitably account to each other and to outsiders in terms of these cultural resources, and hence that any engagement with them **as members** of these groups and communities, must in some sense make professional workers accountable to these same ideas, images, norms, categories, etc.

- But professionals also represent and are accountable to the ideas and standards of democracy, equality, justice, liberty, human rights etc., derived from their professional ethics.
- The practice of community work and community social work involves a dialectic between these forms of accountability (which will be explored in the next chapter).

In this chapter, I have examined the way in which New Labour's initiatives on inclusion, regeneration, cohesion, respect and integration have created 'invited spaces' for action on these topics. Because these have been top-down interventions, with goals defined by the government in advance, and often managed in ways that make them accountable to Third Way models of cost-effectiveness, targets, outcomes, quality etc., these initiatives diverged from the understanding of community work as participatory collective action in the professional definition.

I have traced weaknesses in the UK government model to the economics of public finance, 'club theory' and individual choice on which its overall social policy is founded. This leaves little space for collective action, and there is no convincing analysis of purposive loyalty, solidarity and engagement, or the benefits of these for well-being.

But above all, the top-down nature of the government's engagement with groups and communities, and its advance prescription of the terms of participation and the desired outcomes, mean that those who join as 'partners' are accountable to the government's agenda, not their own. This limits the potential contribution to well-being of these initiatives.

To conclude this chapter, let me give an example of a very different kind of intervention, by a 'social entrepreneur' rather than the government. The celebrity chef, Jamie Oliver, decided to conduct a kind of crusade against the poor nutritional value of school dinners, which was broadcast as a TV series on Channel 4 (2005). The campaign to which this gave rise was subsequently carried through to government, and minimal nutritional standards, first introduced in 1944, abandoned in 1980, were re-established in August 2006.

In all this, Jamie Oliver was an ambiguous figure. He used his celebrity status and TV exposure to initiate a 'top-down' process, but one which had many features of a new social movement. Drawing on various cultural repertoires – his love of his own children, concern about health and obesity, a critique of 'choice' by children with little information about nutrition, implicit or explicit criticisms of the contracting out system in school meals, disdain for the practices of large firms of suppliers, critiques of the government for setting low budgetary requirements for meals, etc. – he set out to transform the debate about food and education in the public sector.

His methods were 'hands on' from the start. He worked alongside kitchen staff in a London secondary school to produce healthy meals within budget; these were then spurned by most children. He visited a primary school in County Durham (where most children were having free school meals) and managed to engage them in picking and preparing ingredients, to challenge the cultural assumptions and taboos under which they made their 'choices', and hence eventually, by very active processes, to transform their eating habits. He then returned to the London secondary school and, by much more interventionist methods, did manage to get more children to eat his meals. Finally, he set up training courses for school cooks, most of whom had little idea how to cook fresh ingredients.

Jamie Oliver is a professional chef, not a community worker. Acting as a social entrepreneur and TV celebrity, he was accountable to neither the education authorities nor the children and parents whose schools he visited. The social movement he started had no grass-roots membership organisation, and was mainly middle class. He used his celebrity status to gain access to government ministers, and to achieve major political change.

However, his work had some features to which I want to draw attention here:

- He challenged the cultures of the education authorities (including teaching staff) who had condoned the slide into appalling school nutrition; and of the children and parents who had followed 'choices' leading to obesity, constipation, risk of diabetes and poor concentration during classes.
- He successfully transformed aspects of these cultures, and used the media to widen the cultural resources available to those campaigning to challenge 'choice' and contracting in the public sector.
- He used group and community work methods with children and staff, to the extent that he mobilised their loyalties and informal interactions to change eating and cooking habits in a transformative way.

Jamie Oliver had many advantages – charisma, high TV profile, money, etc. – but this example challenges professional workers to examine the potential for transformation in their spheres of work. This will be another topic of the next chapter.

Chapter 8

Harm, Stigma and Exclusion in Communities

Introduction

In the previous chapter, I criticised the links made between social capital and well-being by theorists such as Putnam and Helliwell. I also criticised the UK government's initiatives for inclusion, cohesion, respect and integration, on the grounds that they promote forms of participation which limit possibilities for the improvement of citizens' quality of life.

But my analysis of the value created by the interpersonal economy of groups and communities has an obvious down side. On my account, such interactions produce stigma, harm and exclusion as well as respect, identity, self-esteem and the sense of belonging. So I must explain how the former can be minimised and the latter maximised through community work, youth work, and other professional interventions.

Social capital theory and New Labour policy are incoherent on this point. The claims made about the contribution of social capital to well-being insist that networks of reciprocity and trustworthiness are 'nearly always' conducive to higher rates of SWB (Helliwell and Putnam, 2005: 438).

But on closer examination this claim turns out to be misleading. Where community activism is most required to compensate for other adverse factors (as in strife-torn, impoverished, West Belfast, deserted by firms and markets, and excluding itself from state agencies and the mainstream culture), it turns out to reinforce these features, according to the theory. 'Bonding' social capital, of the kind produced by interactions between residents in Catholic ghettoes is an additional factor in exclusion, rejection of mainstream politics, condoning of violence and support for paramilitary activity. But 'bridging' social capital, when delivered by the Peace Process, turns out to bring with it deeper poverty for some residents, and isolation for others (Leonard, 2004).

This casts huge doubt on the UK government's agendas for inclusion, cohesion, respect and integration. They rely on a notion of 'responsible community' which is closely aligned with social capital theory. Introducing his 'Respect Action Plan' in January 2006, Tony Blair said:

> Poverty and exclusion from the material norms of a prosperous society provide fertile ground for crime. Anti-social behaviour is more common in poor areas.

Richard Sennett has written persuasively about the way the basic courtesies diminish with increasing material inequalities. The social capital literature also provides a large body of data to show that respect and trust are less evident in areas of high deprivation.

(Blair, 2006a)

This equates social capital with the positive virtues of mainstream society, and sees poor communities as demonstrating its absence. But – as we have seen from the Belfast example – high-density social networks, a very productive informal economy, and strong local solidarity are consistent with armed disaffection and extreme levels of violence.

Even on the measure of 'trust in neighbours', Northern Ireland comes out higher than England and Wales, for the simple reason that 'neighbours' refers to people of the same faith and income levels in this polarised 'ethnically cleansed' community (Lane, 2000: 124).

The obverse of this non-sequitur was shown by David Blunkett as Home Secretary, writing about 'Civil Renewal'. He argued that mutuality, solidarity, and activism were characteristic of 'strong communities' of all kinds, in a democratic society:

Solidarity is founded on the commitment to regard the well-being of others as an integral part of our own collective well-being. Mutuality stems from the readiness to embrace our interdependence as a positive motivation to cooperate in the search for solutions to our problems. And democratic self-determination holds that we are only truly free when we participate in the self-government of our communities. . . . It is relevant to everyone; the poor and vulnerable who need help to overcome their socio-economic exclusion and gain the confidence to participate in rebuilding their communities; the legal migrants our economy needs and our communities should welcome; the rich and powerful who need to be reminded why they should care for others in society rather than retreat into their own private 'gated communities', and citizens in general who need to realise that their personal interests are best safeguarded when they actively take part in the protection of the common good.

(Blunkett, 2003: 2, 5–6)

It is difficult to find fault with these sentiments as statements of the government's aspirations but – unlike Tony Blair's speech – they overlook several worrying features of our society. First, 'the poor and vulnerable' have made little progress towards socio-economic inclusion under New Labour. They are also the targets of special measures to deal with their failure to do so by compulsory means (benefits withdrawal for non-cooperation with the New Deals, parental orders, anti-social behaviour orders, and – most recently – targeting potential delinquents at or before birth).

Meanwhile, 'the rich and powerful' are under no such compulsion to care for others. Every measure of social policy reform facilitates their withdrawal from solidarity and mutuality, through tax cuts and the promotion of choice and mobility between options in the public sector. Even 'citizens in general' are enabled to use these services instrumentally, for their individual or family advantage, rather than encouraged to participate for the 'common good'.

Indeed, researchers on social capital have noted that there has been a polarisation of UK society in relation to the type of organisations to which citizens belong. As the 'new middle class' of service workers has grown, voluntary organisations have attracted new members from it. But this healthy state of civil society organisations has masked a rapid decline in the participation in mainstream associations of all kinds by the manual working class.

> . . . the more accurate image is of a nation divided between a well-connected group of citizens with prosperous lives and high levels of civic engagement and other groups whose networks, associational life, and involvement in politics are very limited. . . . The two groups who face marginalization from civil society are the working class and the young.

(Hall, 2002: 53)

Even more vividly, the evidence of surveys of three cohorts born since the war illustrates this polarisation. Among Class V men born in 1946 interviewed aged 36, 55 per cent belonged to organisations; for women it was 37 per cent. For Class V men born in 1970 interviewed aged 30, only 2 per cent were members of organisations, and among women 6 per cent. Whereas 48 per cent of the 1946 male Class V respondents belonged to trade unions, only 17 per cent of the 1970 cohort did so; and 46 per cent of males in the latter cohort had been arrested (Bynner and Parsons, 2003, Tables 10.1–9).

This last statistic, based on a very large sample, is the most alarming one. It illustrates the problem that has provoked New Labour's initiatives on inclusion, cohesion, respect and integration, as well as the attempts to impose order and the work ethic through measures of compulsion. This is the challenge for community work as well as the government. It illustrates that the informal and interpersonal economies of these communities create high levels of illegality, irregularity and deviance, as well as solidarity and mutuality, through informal collective action.

In this chapter, I shall analyse what is different about community work as a response to these challenges, and why it is difficult to theorise convincingly, yet exercises a powerful inspirational hold on the profession.

The first paradox of community work

The first of two paradoxes about the distinctiveness of community work is implicit in Twelvetrees' (2002: 1–2) definition which states that it is about disadvantaged people getting a 'better deal' and bringing this about for themselves, and that it aims to support their engagement in collective action, but to ensure that community groups are 'effective, inclusive, democratic and work for just ends' (p. 2).

Three features of this definition help distinguish community work from other human service activity. First, it puts a positive value on people acting for their own ends, rather than having things done for or to them. Second, it works through collective, rather than individual action. And third, it sees the ways that they should be enabled to act in moral and political, rather than technical or instrumental terms.

Autonomous action as a feature of community work

All these features of community work have important implications for its theory and methods. The first, the autonomy of people's activity, implies that it is they, rather than the professional worker, who choose the ends and the means; whatever happens is on their terms, and often on their territory, involving a 'natural setting', in which they have made the social (and sometimes the physical) environment through their own interactions. Operating in 'natural settings' is the paradigm of community work, and outreach youth work; but even when it is practised in settings such as community centres, it gives those who use such centres more scope to control the social environment, choose the activities, and set the terms of engagement with workers than in other professional settings.

This has important consequences for theory and practice. Progress in the analysis of professional skill and effectiveness, and the refinement and differentiation of interventions, in health and social care and in education have relied on taking individuals out of their everyday contexts, and putting them in hospitals, clinics, offices, assessment centres or classrooms, at least until some processes of diagnosis, testing, assessment or examination has taken place.

It has been the nature of this 'scientific' approach to human service professional activity that certain aspects of people's functioning as economic, social and physical beings should be abstracted from the general run of their lives, and that there should be a focus on these specifics, in which expertise is brought to bear on changing them for the better.

In social work, I have argued that the primacy of relationships and interaction does attenuate this feature of both theory and practice, but the fact remains that most activity takes place in offices or other specialist facilities, outside the stream of everyday life.

The fact that the paradigm of community work is the outreach or street worker, or one who meets with community groups in such facilities as halls and centres which are hired by numerous associations in their districts, has important consequences. It implies that the aim is not to abstract particular aspects of their interactions with the wider organisations of society and each other, and focus on these for the sake of change, but to engage with them in a far more total way. It suggests an approach to professional activity which deals in whole ways of life, in lived experiences, and in how the social world is interpreted, as the subject matter for interventions.

This is the antitheses of the 'service delivery' approach described in Chapter 2, in which 'packages' are consigned to individuals who have chosen them, as part of a series of discrete acts of consumption. Not only does it imply that expertise does not always consist in identifying and abstracting a specific aspect of malfunction or deviance; it also implies that relevant experiences are far more contextualised, and form much more of an interconnected whole, than such abstraction allows.

So the value of the intervention lies in its effects on how the social world is perceived and acted on by members of a community, not in isolating and altering specific patterns of behaviour or interaction.

Collective action as a feature of community work

The second feature, the collective nature of the action which is addressed, enabled and possibly challenged, is equally important. Although the understanding of people and their actions in collective terms, as reflecting interactions at a number of different levels, is central to social work as a whole, community work chooses to address this directly in its methods. It makes the collective features of the life of those with whom its works its explicit materials, and seeks to help them work more effectively together to achieve their goals, and improve their quality of life.

This has important implications, given what we have recognised – that deprived districts and marginal groups are far more likely to be identified as deviant, disaffected, criminal, disorderly, problematic, threatening or demoralised by the government, the media and mainstream population. Community work addresses those social problems which society feels most concern (or fear) about, but not in a way that identifies and singles out trouble makers, inadequates, criminals and mad people, and takes them out for special attention. Instead, it deals in the collective features of their social worlds, and the harms, stigmas and exclusions these generate.

This in turn implies that damage is done to individual well-being by the collective elements in their experiences – both by their interactions with fellow members of their communities, and by those communities' interactions with wider society. Community work chooses to deal in those aspects, and in how the cultural resources of communities are deployed to deal with individual behaviour, by sanctions, support or indifference. It tries to widen the repertoire of cultural resources, and make collective action more effective, both to reduce the costs to individuals in terms of well-being, and to increase the benefits of membership available to all those who are part of that community.

In other words, community work addresses the overall workings of the collective interpersonal economy, and its supply of 'collective goods', rather than the way individuals contribute to it or benefit from it.

The moral nature of community work

The third feature, the explicitly moral and political nature of community work, follows from the other two. Because it deals in natural settings and collective action, community work is necessarily concerned with how resources and power are distributed, both within communities themselves, and between them and wider society. It addresses issues of equality, justice, participation and change directly, through collective action which makes claims on mainstream society and the government, as well as in members' dealings with each other.

For these reasons, community work theory and methods are inseparable from these moral and political issues. There is, in effect, little in the way of 'technique' or 'expertise' which is not concerned with making such ideas available for debate, deliberation, negotiation and agreement, and mobilising community groups around them.

While many other activities – from the cultural to the recreational, and occasionally the economic – contribute to community work, its main thrust is moral and political. This leads to the dilemma outlined at the end of the last chapter. Because community work addresses such issues, and because its clientele is disadvantaged, it experiences continuous problems over accountability and professional ethics in a society of inequality.

And because power is constantly at stake in collective action, which must agree goals, rules, roles and responsibilities, and maintain solidarity, there are always potential conflicts to be resolved. Hence the theory of community work owes as much to politics as to psychology.

All this should make community work deeply suspect to New Labour, which attempts to create a mainstream consensus around a market order, property-ownership and personal responsibility, and abhors collective action by interest groups, especially poor people. But paradoxically the UK government has deployed a variation of community work in many of its new initiatives, using staff with titles like project worker, support worker and outreach worker to try to engage disadvantaged groups. Often these staff have been from minority ethnic or local disadvantaged backgrounds.

So the first paradox of community work in the present political configuration is that it appears to be favoured over social work in the expansion of services since 1997 (Jordan with Jordan, 2000). This seems very surprising, given that community work was seen as radical and threatening by the Thatcher administration, while social work, though devalued, was actually greatly expanded, because of the increased social problems spawned by her policies.

This paradox dissolves to a great extent when we recognise that the community work element in the new initiatives takes place within the 'invited spaces' (Gaventa, 2004) of urban regeneration, the New Deal for communities and the Social Exclusion Unit. The terms in which disadvantaged community groups engage with firms and state agencies in these initiatives are strictly defined, and follow the government's agenda.

They are also accountable according to detailed expectations of outcomes and targets. But it remains paradoxical that community work subscribes to these moral and political ideas, while participating in this kind of initiative on such restrictive terms. I shall return to this in the second half of this chapter.

The second paradox of community work

Because community work deals in the totality of social relations in a group or district, and in collective rather than 'therapeutic' methods, workers comment on and discuss plans for activities and campaigns, they suggest ways in which actions might more effectively achieve their goals, and they coach people in the roles and tasks they are undertaking. They mobilise, advocate for and represent groups and communities on various occasions, but always with their specific consent.

In all these respects, they use methods and skills which are familiar to service users and group members – ones which they deploy with each other, and with the other organisations and communities they encounter. They argue, cajole, encourage, support and egg on, just as members do to each other. There is nothing very esoteric about these methods; a community worker is someone who, through training and experience, has well-developed abilities of this kind, which members may use as models, if they trust and admire them.

Indeed, in my experience, uneducated and deprived people do learn to be very effective in groups and large meetings incredibly quickly, if they feel the support and encouragement of colleagues, and if the organisation is one that upholds the values they endorse, and represents the people with whom they identify (Jordan, 1973, 1997b).

When I was a member of a new social movement (the Claimants Unions) in the 1970s, my fellow members knew I was a probation officer, and several had been my clients. It was interesting to note which problems among members they perceived as requiring professional expertise to tackle. These did not include delinquency, alcoholism, child care or child protection, all of which members saw as moral or political issues, to be discussed, debated, negotiated and repaired or restored among the parties affected, including the statutory authorities. Indeed, only concerning two issues did they enlist my help, as a trained social worker (as probation officers were in those days). These were mental health problems and marital problems. The former were perceived as slightly scary, and requiring special sensitivity and knowledge. The latter were seen as too intimate and private to be aired in a larger group.

All this seems to imply that community work is different from casework and therapeutic groupwork, in that it uses skills which are available to lay people, albeit in disciplined, trained and well-considered ways. This appears to be consistent with the claim that community work is a more direct expression of the anti-oppressive, justice-orientated and inclusive values of social work than is casework. It is reflected in the findings that student and newly-trained community workers are most concerned with the ethical dilemmas of their accountability and political identity, with issues of personal loyalty and professionalisation of their role (Mayo, 2005) while social workers are more preoccupied with professional autonomy, judgement and the use of interpersonal skills in a bureaucratic setting (Dustin, 2004).

So it is striking that, although community work and community social work enjoy comparatively less status and career prospects (except in new government initiatives, under New Labour flagship programmes) than such 'expert' roles as child protection, court, foster care, care management and mental health social work, the great heroes of social work are community workers. The second paradox of community work is that the charisma required to be really effective in this role, and the dedication displayed by its leading practitioners, elevate them to a different level from the mere expertise of individual practice.

I am thinking here of two people in particular, Bob Holman, who has been working in deprived districts of England and Scotland since the early 1970s, and Camilla Batmanghelidjh, who sprang to prominence in the late 1990s for her work with delinquent and rootless young people in London. Both of these workers have a high public profile, and inspire enormous admiration, as much for their personal character-istics and the devotion they give to their work as for their interpersonal skills.

Bob Holman was a child care social worker, who went into social work teaching and became a professor. He suddenly found this unsatisfying, and gave it up to start a project for young people on a deprived estate in Bath. He started out from the idea that young people's careers through courts and care could be prevented, but not by traditional, office-based social work:

> . . . *Social workers tended not to live in the localities where they worked. Even their offices might be some miles from the people most in need of help. It followed that social workers could know closely neither the people nor the neighbourhoods where preventative work was needed. Prevention, I decided, would be more effectively pursued by someone who could concentrate on it and who lived in or near the locality where they worked. . . . The growing desire to move out of the university was reinforced by a long-felt nagging inner voice telling me to practise again as a social worker. The voice, no doubt, stemmed from certain political and Christian beliefs which for some years, I had tried to relate to my everyday life.*
>
> (Holman, 1981, p. 2).

Twenty years later, after working for that period on a similar project in Easterhouse, Glasgow, Bob Holman evaluated the impact of the initiative, which still continued. His interviews with 51 participants indicated that they valued most highly a leadership style which was friendly, approachable, trusted and supplied good organisation (youth clubs, activities and support). The project fostered community spirit, and kept many youngsters, if not out of trouble, then at least out of detention centre, prison or care. As he summarised it:

> *The 51 former members, now adults, are agreed that it provided them with leisure activities which they would otherwise have missed, with friendships, with individual relationships with adults they trusted. Some are convinced it steered them away from crime and other anti-social behaviour. Some believe that its influence, values and practices stayed with them into adulthood.*
>
> (Holman, 2000: 103)

Camilla Batmanghelidjh was the daughter of a privileged member of the Iranian elite under the Shah when (in 1979) his regime fell to the revolution of Ayatollah Khomeini and his allies. She was attending a boarding school in England when she found herself as a refugee, without resources, in this country. After training as a psychologist she began an enterprise, *Kids' Company*, which took children in trouble off the streets of London, and gave them activities and training which engaged their energies and commitment.

She describes these children as 'urban warriors' – 'feral children', with experience of carrying weapons and using drugs, violent and often malnourished. She says they are 'like terrorists' who have already given up their lives, and have nothing to lose. Threats do not work with them, because they have already experienced abuse and violence. She and her staff offer them love and 'emotional contracts' in the environment of her centres – what she describes as 'robust compassion' (BBC Radio 4, 2006i).

She identifies the turning point of her professional career as being the recognition that the Children and Adolescents Mental Health Services assumed the existence of a reliable adult to bring a troubled child to an appointment at a clinic. Her centres allowed children to self-refer, and they now deal with some 10,000 children.

Her style and charisma are very different from Bob Holman's, yet there are similarities also. She too is able to communicate her faith in the children she engages with, her willingness to listen to and take full account of their views, and her courage to challenge them, once she has won their trust. She is also very gifted as a media contributor, and very good at getting her message across to politicians and the public.

As a result, she has been able to show that children and young people demonised in many news stories and press releases have great potential for development and change.

The point about these leading figures is that they are models of commitment to the groups and communities they serve. Without claiming specific technical expertise, they achieve great things by sheer courage, persistence and unconditional effort on behalf of disadvantaged people. They therefore overthrow the general rule that specialists and those who can command esoteric competences are valued more highly than outreach, street and support workers. Their exemplification of the core values of practice is what makes them influential, admired and courted by politicians and the media.

The second paradox of community work is that these leaders transcend the dominance of economics, managerialism and accountancy to offer a very different model to practitioners. The fact that they are treated with near-reverence shows that, even as practitioners struggle to legitimate their work according to the canons of New Labour orthodoxy, they still yearn for a very different ethic of care and commitment, and a culture of collective solidarity with disadvantaged members of our society.

Analysing the value of community work

For all these reasons, community work is both a very important factor in the potential of practice to improve well-being, and a very difficult one to analyse in terms of economic models. It is concerned with collective life and the cultural resources which sustain it, but – as in the case of neighbourhood projects and youth work – it seeks to influence these elements in people's interactions directly, as well as through the individuals who participate as members.

This is why books and articles about community work do not usually set out theoretical analyses, which are then illustrated with detailed examples of how change occurred, and outcomes were achieved. They tend instead to work from case studies, each of which is a rich description of the context in which members lived, and the nature of their collective life. They then go on to describe various changes which were achieved, both in the context and the culture, which influenced the well-being of members in positive ways.

Textbooks on community work, like Twelvetrees (2002), present various classifications of interventions and activities, often in the form of a series of examples and case studies. Case studies are a respectable method of social research, but do not command the same status as, say, randomised controlled trials (RCTs). Textbooks on community work seldom spell out 'methods' in the way that books on casework do, or try to show how a strategic plan was implemented to produce certain outcomes. Indeed, this would violate the commitment to supporting groups and communities in finding a 'better deal', as defined by themselves.

Many of the texts focus on the role of the community worker in facilitating communication and establishing an effective division of labour. For example, Shulman writes:

> . . . the worker is assigned the special responsibility of paying attention to the way in which the group works on these important structural tasks, monitoring the process to pick up cues signalling as they emerge and helping the group members pay attention to these problems.
>
> (Shulman, 1998: 769)

He adds that failure to focus on these ' . . . results in a loss of group *cohesion*, the property of the group that describes the mutual attraction that makes each other feel' (ibid).

Yet it is important to identify the ways in which changes at the level of collective life and cultural resources do improve well-being, because these are exactly the dimensions which are missing form the UK government's initiatives. Simply paying attention to communication and structure says little about how organisations and movements recruit or exclude memberships, and on what terms.

It does not help identify the goals and purposes which are legitimate, or the limits on tactics and strategies which may be deployed. Above all, it does not deal directly with the fact that communities do harm and scapegoat members, and may even injure or kill them, if they come to be seen as disloyal, treacherous and deviant. They also can mobilise against other groups and communities, with similar consequences.

One very obvious way in which community work can address these issues is when a group or movement is formed in order to try to overcome divisions and mutual damaged done by residents to each other, or to members of other communities. When this is the explicit aim of a group or movement, a worker can identify with this goal, and help hold members to this task. The worker can then help participants to identify ways in which divisions and scapegoating, exclusions and threats, weaken the collective life of the community, and make its quality of life lower.

There have been many examples of groups and movements of this nature, formed as a result of tragedies and crises in communities. Northern Ireland spawned many such organisations, the most famous of which was the Peace Women, recognised by the award of the Nobel Prize. Similarly, there have been groups and movements formed in response to gangland gun violence in black communities, often by relatives of those killed by rival gangs, or caught in the crossfire between them.

Here the focus of the group allows any support worker to overcome moral, political and methodological problems, by constantly helping a group to identify ways in which conflict, exclusion or revenge damage not only the direct victims, but also the well-being of the whole community.

In these examples, what is made explicit is the ways in which mutual respect, and the valuing of difference, strengthen the ability of communities to overcome shared problems, as well as allowing them to live together more convivially. This implies that members constantly look for ways of including those who are isolated, as well as reasoning with and trying to change those who use bullying, violence and threats to achieve their ends.

It means that members come together to share an understanding of common problems, to identify why harmful and destructive features of a culture have developed, and to look for collective ways to overcome these problems.

The value of community work in these instances therefore lies in the workers' capacities to help members identify the nature and causes of the harms being done to individuals and groups, how these weaken the collective capacities of the community as well as its quality of life, and how to move forward in addressing these issues.

The fact that a group or movement has already mobilised to try to combat the harmful effects of mutual damage by members (or sometimes the pernicious influence of outsiders, such as racist political groups, or extremists in faith groups, who wish to foment conflicts and divisions) enables workers to give unequivocal support to the overall purpose of the group, and the collective efforts of the members.

But not all activities and organisations are of this nature. For example, much community work addresses the more amorphous, informal life of districts, where much of the petty, everyday harm is done, to the shared physical environment (malicious damage, vandalism, litter), to the culture of respect and mutual concern (rowdiness, rudeness, lack of consideration for others) and to specific individuals who are scapegoated for being different. This is far more difficult, both because it is too insidious and commonplace to be identified by residents as a focus for common action; and because any attempt to mobilise such action could be seen as breaking solidarity and loyalty, and siding with such disliked outsiders as the police, teachers, or even statutory social workers in child protection teams.

This is where leaders like Bob Holman and Camilla Batmanghelidjh have set such an outstanding example. They have shown that it is possible, simply by providing shared facilities, activities and opportunities, to address these very engrained and long-term features of communities, and reach agreement among residents and members about how to overcome them. The value of this kind of practice is that it allows the taken-for-granted, repetitive, and tacitly condoned harmful features of a local culture to be recognised and challenged. This is achieved by giving members the chance to find new ways of doing things together, which do not involve the ingrained nastinesses they have come to see as inevitable features of their shared lives.

This is not at all easy to achieve because only someone who earns the trust and admiration of members can attain the moral standing to bring about such a transformation. If a community worker tries to take the high ground in challenging everyday practices of mutual oppression and abuse, they risk being rejected as an outsider who doesn't belong and doesn't understand. Only by supplying residents and members with something they really value, which includes the acceptance of *their* value and potential contribution, *their* strength, endurance and resistance to external *power*, and their capacity to survive and endure, will a worker gain the moral credit to make such challenges.

It is only then that these will be seen, not as criticisms and rejections, but as promptings for transformation and improvement, by someone who believes in their potential, and values their strengths.

Finally, these are ways of addressing these issues which arise in the course of other kinds of community work, which are not specifically designed to tackle the harms done by members to each other. These come about because, once members of an organisation or group come to trust each other in pursuit of any joint activity or goal, they are likely to recognise these issues through discomforts in their interactions, or in their contacts with members of the wider community.

For example, when I was involved with a Claimants' Union in the 1970s, it was quickly apparent that success in achieving our goals – to mobilise all those claiming social security benefits on behalf of common interests in changing the system to a more generous, less conditional one – was likely to be limited by divisions among members. These reflected longstanding political discourses on claiming benefits, and especially distinctions between 'deserving' claimants (who had paid social insurance contributions, and were 'legitimately outside the labour market through retirement, sickness, disability or unavoidable unemployment), and 'undeserving ones', such as lone parents and long-term unemployed people.

There was a real danger that the movement would be weakened by the fact that the core membership consisted of the latter groups of claimants, and were ready targets for media stigmatisation as 'scroungers' or worse.

We were determined to show that we represented **all** claimants, including pensioners and widows, disabled and sick people, and that we rejected the divisive ideas and images propagated about some of our most committed, able and active members (Jordan, 1973). But we also had to tackle these same members' stereotypes of other claimants who joined the movement – people from 'up-country', young college 'drop-outs' and 'hippies', and even certain well-known individuals from our own midst. The solution was to adopt a constitution which stated unequivocally that we would support the claims and interests of all on benefits, regardless of their gender, skin colour, political affiliation, sexual orientation or culture.

Whenever the core membership began to get a bit frustrated with a particular member, or were let down by someone who had promised help, someone would quickly remind them of 'Article Two' of the constitution, and – usually amid wry laughter – we would return to our task of demonstrating solidarity and support. This, along with the unswerving support of certain key members of the mainstream local community – clergy, politicians, decent and upright citizens – made sure that we could not be easily scapegoated or divided.

As a result, we were able to be very effective in representing members in disputes with the benefits authorities, but we achieved far more than this. The movement generated mutual support across a whole range of issues, as well as material benefits such as a collective garden (giving free vegetables to members), a cooperative shop, and many recreational activities and outings. It created a very strong morale and spirit among a group of people who – at a time of growing unemployment and political instability – might otherwise have suffered exclusion, stigma and blame.

Above all, it gained for members the (often grudging) respect of people who were not natural supporters of our cause. By our success in attracting publicity, holding meetings and protests, and actually changing policy, we maintained a high profile, nationally as well as locally.

All this demonstrated that long-term claimants could take a leading role in civic affairs, could speak convincingly about political issues, and could contribute to action which improved their own well-being in very valuable ways.

Of course, a major gain from all this was in the confidence and self-esteem of active members, many of whom had suffered from unjust treatment from the authorities and employers in the past. Self-respect, as well as the respect of other citizens, the sense of belonging and support, were all part of this process. Many leading members went on to take jobs in which they used these skills.

Conclusions

In this chapter, I have tried to tackle the paradoxes and dilemmas of community work in the disadvantaged districts and groups of UK and other affluent societies. Because public policies have facilitated the 'exit' of more resourceful citizens from such communities, by offering opportunities like the right to buy council houses in more desirable districts, and the chance to choose schools, health and social care facilities, these groups have been left in concentrations of poverty, ill health and cultural deprivation (Jordan, 1996).

They have in turn suffered from approaches to these problems which further stigmatised and disadvantaged them – cuts in resources to local amenities, withdrawal of services to more distant offices, and enforcement practices which were at times summary and draconian. Statutory social work, and especially child protection work, was not exempt from these developments. Hence residents and members identified themselves in opposition to the authorities, and were mistrustful and resistant to official interventions of all kinds.

They also developed 'resistance practices' and cultures which were deviant, and often damaged themselves and their collective lives as much as they imposed costs on societies. These have been well captured in the literature of poor people's responses to their situations (Scott, 1985, 1990). Seldom organising in any formal way, they relied instead on informal networks to undertake covert activities – working for cash while claiming, petty crime, hustling, drug dealing, begging, prostitution and so on (Jordan et al., 1991; Jordan and Travers, 1998).

As we saw from the Belfast example, the strength of such bonds between members could also generate open resistance, in the form of organised, violent action, and coerced solidarity among members.

But there have also been examples of resistance cultures which were so destructive of members as to be fatal for many of them. For instance, in September, 2006, a black 15-year-old, Jesse James, was found killed by gun shots in a park in Moss Side, Manchester. Although there was no indication that he, a popular, sociable schoolboy, was involved in any gang activities, the district (like others in the city) had a reputation for drug-related gangs and gang conflict, involving guns. Out of 150 recorded shootings in the previous three years, only one had led to a witness coming forward to give evidence. This level of violence and intimidation had become part of the taken-for-granted everyday culture, and local solidarity seen as more important than saving life.

In the radio reports and interviews with residents at the time (BBC Radio 4, 2006h) it was emphasised that this was a 'strong community' with close-knit relationships and bonds. As we have seen, this was no contradiction; it is perfectly possible to have strong loyalty, solidarity and the sense of belonging while also sustaining a culture of violence and death. One reporter commented on a large piece of graffiti in a nearby district, commemorating the 'fallen soldiers' of other gang gunfights, and pledging to uphold their traditions.

This chapter has argued that community work cannot evade these uncomfortable aspects of deprived groups and neighbourhoods. But it does not have to tackle them in the prescriptive, formulaic and top-down ways that New Labour has adopted. To be fair, Tony Blair's government has devoted considerable resources and efforts to tackling issues of inclusion, cohesion, respect and integration; his predecessors did little or nothing. But New Labour has done so in ways that were closely aligned both to enforcement measures against 'deviants', and to 'partnerships' with commercial firms, with no real roots in these communities.

To be true to the values of community work, and to be effective in addressing issues of harm, stigma and scapegoating, workers need to take full account of the following features of their interpersonal economies:

- Relationships that are often based on mistrust of outsiders and authorities, and on a blood-and-guts code which puts loyalty above all other virtues.
- Residents' practices reflect the need to undertake unorthodox, informal economic activities, for the sake of material survival and self-esteem, and to be active members of a resistance culture. These include petty crime and drug dealing in many districts, and violent conflict in a few.
- Any worker who wishes to give effective support to the strengths of such communities must win their trust, and offer something that they need (a facility, a skill, a link to some other resources) as part of winning their trust.
- But this trust will not fully realise its potential contribution to the improvement of well-being unless it is also used to challenge stereotypes, prejudices, hatreds, blame and grudges held by members, and to create the recognition of the harms these do to all.
- This can be most effectively achieved in collective facilities and through methods which mobilise and activate members in their common interests.
- The goal should be nothing short of the transformation of cultures of conflict, violence and scapegoating, and the adoption of inclusive, fair and open practices as the norms of membership and participation.
- Respect and belonging can be achieved without violence and bullying, and can include all members; the aim should be to make this part of everyday experience, rather than empty rhetoric.

I have tried to illustrate all these points in this chapter. In the next, I shall show how they relate to structural, economic and geo-political issues in today's society and world.

Chapter 9

Conclusions: Social Reproduction in a Service Economy

During my working lifetime, the UK economy has been transformed from a declining industrial producer, with frayed institutions inherited from the age of empire and world manufacturing leadership, to a market-orientated financial headquarters, with aspirations to lead the integration of the world economy. It has also been transformed from a collectivist welfare state, holding anxiously on to the loyalty of its working class, to a competitive individualist society in which each takes responsibility for their own adaptation to new challenges.

These transformations have had costs and benefits, winners and losers, but overall the consequences for the average well-being of citizens have been neutral. We are no happier (overall) with our lives than we were in the 1960s and 1970s, when I first started work as a social worker. Enormous efforts of adaptation have been made, by governments, institutions, groups and individuals, and all that this has achieved – in terms of well-being – is the *status quo*.

In this book, I have argued that this has been because the gains we made in the post-war period, through collective measures for social protection and social services, have been sacrificed for the goals of more flexible market-orientated systems and people. What has been gained in adaptability to the demands of global capitalism and consumerism has been compensated by losses in mutual respect, civility, consideration and acceptance.

We live in a more stressful, competitive and demanding culture, in which we expect far more of ourselves and each other; and then we soothe and comfort ourselves for our disappointments by eating and drinking, buying fashion items, taking expensive holidays, and undergoing expensive therapies.

We move around more, change partners more often, swap from one supplier or organisation to another, in a restless search for satisfaction, which is never quite accomplished. (I spent 12 years travelling around Europe as a visiting professor, so I know.)

There is a growing realisation among social scientists, and – more surprisingly – this includes economists), that there is something wrong with these processes, which are ultimately self-defeating. The cult of the self, and the culture of change, of adaptation to the demands of markets, does not give us the best possible quality of life, given our technological and organisational capabilities. There is something in economics itself (or, as a Marxist might say, in the logic of capitalism) which limits the possibilities for improving our happiness. Well-being has stalled.

When economists themselves are blaming the narrowness of their assumptions and models for their impasse, the rest of us should recognise an opportunity. For the past 25 years, we have been ruled in the name of faster economic growth, higher consumption and greater personal responsibility. We have been hectored and harangued about how competitiveness, cost-efficiency and self-development are the necessary pre-requisites for success in a globalised environment. We have been through the chaos and disruption of the fragmentation of our public services, and seen the wreckage of the careers of valued colleagues, and the waste of important cultures and traditions. All this has been done in the name of our economics of choice, mobility and individual autonomy. Now at last this model has come under question, by its high priests themselves.

Throughout this book, I have argued that social work has undersold itself during this period. I do not blame my colleagues in education and social practice for this, because I have experienced many of the pressures and constraints that have brought it about. We have all been under intense demands to justify ourselves according to alien criteria, and to make claims about our effectiveness by the narrowest of measures and standards. Although it has always been possible to hang on to our best traditions and practices, justifying them in public has sounded defensive and backward-looking.

A few years ago, I was very politely and charmingly challenged, by a social worker from South America, as to why I and others like me (such as Bob Holman) did not go on a 'crusade' for social work, redistribution and a decent ethos for the public services. I found this question very difficult to answer, and felt ashamed of the inadequacy of my response. The fact was, I felt it took all my energy to hold on to what I knew and believed, to adapt it to a changing world, and to be ready for the tide to turn. I think most practitioners feel the same.

In March 2006 a social work lecturer at Nottingham Trent University, Jim Wild, organised a conference on 'Affirming Our Values' for social workers. It was attended by 2,000 people, and the atmosphere was electric. I felt that Jim had been able to achieve what I was challenged to attempt, partly because he is a brilliant impresario, but also because the tide *has* turned in our favour.

I have argued that there is a strong, coherent case to be made for the contribution of social work to well-being, and that this is a particularly opportune moment to make it. There is nothing specially original or path-breaking in the analysis I have set out; in Chapter 3 I showed that it is derived directly from the ideas and practices of the founders of the profession. All that is needed is a clear re-statement of these principles and methods, in unpretentious language that can be understood by anyone, even an economist.

Social work is of value because it deals in relationships, which are the main components of well-being, and of its destruction. This simple fact cannot be stated too often. It also links our profession to those of teaching, nursing, public health and many others that are practised in the state services and which have undergone similar fragmentations and disjunctions during that period. The goal should not be to claim special distinction, but to affirm that our work has the same kind of value as theirs.

All this implies that the present UK government is in trouble, because it has nailed its colours to the mast erected by Margaret Thatcher. It must therefore rise to the challenges posed by the 'well-being turn' in the social sciences, in popular consciousness, but also in (of all places) the Conservative Party.

David Cameron has, as I have indicated got under the guard of Tony Blair with some very shrewd blows, landing exactly on New Labour's soft underbelly of sloppy thinking. His words resonated with many public sector workers who have suffered under Third Way ideological assaults. I cannot count the number of conversations I have had in which friends and colleagues acknowledged, with some wry embarrassment, that they had quietly cheered when they read Cameron's words. Even if he cannot deliver on them, he has shifted the argument onto more promising ground.

Undoubtedly this is because Cameron has done his homework. For at least a decade, he took the straight path of Thatcherism, writing Michael Howard's election manifesto in 2005. If he has changed, it is because the focus groups told him to – public awareness has shifted, as people count the costs of their lifestyles and think about the consequences for their children, and for the rest of the world.

Tony Blair has spent his final year in office arguing that the key issues for British politics are security, immigration and integration. This suggests an external threat to a society which has achieved a viable order, based on individualism, markets, choice and property – the threat of destructive, anti-democratic, archaic, holy war. In this chapter, I shall argue that there is a much more important challenge to this order, and that it stems from its own contradictions and incoherences.

A highly mobile, individualistic culture is unbalanced, because people are encouraged to rely on exit strategies to solve all their issues and problems. This does not only mean moving to better jobs and districts, changing schools and health authorities. It implies moving further from kin and friends, shifting to new organisations and informal groups. It sets no store on participation to make things better, or on the value of solidarity and loyalty. As David Cameron put it, 'There comes a time when you have to stop choosing, and commit'.

It even means that people see leaving a partner as the best way to improve their well-being, or fear having children because they know it implies a lifelong commitment to them. A culture which relies on individual self-development, without a balance of respect for and belonging with other members, is in danger of not being able to reproduce itself. It is not so much vulnerable to terrorism as it is to self-destruction.

In this final chapter, I shall develop these themes, focusing on the different visions for children's socialisation as citizens projected by the government and the human service professions. I shall argue that there is a growing consensus that the public services, and the workers who staff them, have something of enormous value to offer to our future citizens, and that current ideology and organisations who run these services are denying the opportunity to express this, or impact it to children.

A service economy offers opportunities for a high quality of life, which are not being realised.

Preparing children for their roles in society

The way we bring up our children is a very reliable indicator of how we see our society, and ourselves in it. Since the UK has lost its imperial mission to the world (except as a canine companion to the USA on its excursions into pre-emptive war) and has also ceased to be a major industrial producer, its identity is fluid. Margaret Thatcher projected an image of robust strength and independence of spirit, but was essentially a Cold Warrior, now an out-of-date concept. What does our society stand for in the twenty-first century, and how can children be brought up to play their part in achieving it, adapting it, carrying it forward to the next generation and beyond (i.e. social reproduction)?

These are questions about our collective culture and cultural adaptation. Margaret Thatcher tore down the institutions of the post-war settlement, in the name of the property-owning democracy. Her vision took little account of the one third or more of households without savings or home ownership. It assumed that inward migration would remain at the historically very low levels which prevailed in the 1970s and 1980s, and would be more balanced by emigration. It relied on state power to keep down the poor, and (American style) the aspiration to mainstream status and a browbeaten mentality among the dispossessed to enable materialism to supply the essentials of the social order.

In the USA, this oppression of the poor has gone further than in the UK. Tax credits, essentially subsidies to low-paying employers, are complemented by tough enforcement of menial service work in irregular and unprotected conditions. Enforcement measures, such as benefit cuts, are taken against 50 per cent of claimants of social assistance programmes in some Florida jurisdictions (Fording et al., 2006). In this way the poor, whose well-being would be enhanced by receiving more money, are made to serve the rich for a pittance.

The Third Way thinking of Bill Clinton and Tony Blair went beyond this model, trying to conceive of a new social order, both globally and at home, after the collapse of Soviet state socialism. In this model, rich countries could reciprocate with poor ones in an integrated world economy, by supplying the finance and technology for development, and by trade. In rather the same way, at home the financial sector could fund the regeneration and inclusion of the blighted districts and ruined lives of the post-industrial rustbelts.

The role of the public sector professions was to help drive through these processes of adaptation, under which the poor would become flexible (but oppressed) service workers, with prison as the only alternative to compliance. Higher immigration would provide the competition to keep them on their toes, and also fill the gaps where indigenous workers just refused to be *that* exploited and degraded.

Now this model is in trouble, both because its culture is too brittle and conflictual to sustain respect, solidarity and the sense of a common good, and because government ideologies and official agencies have been unable to sell it to our most disadvantaged citizens. In the USA, the flooding of New Orleans confirmed what many minority ethnic and poor citizens had suspected – that they were expendable commodities under this order. In the UK, resistance has been stubborn, covert and enduring; there is a minority that has adapted to new conditions in ways which are sharply at odds with the government's expectations.

This includes many disadvantaged indigenous citizens. It has little to do with current rates of immigration, mainly from Central Europe, of smart, advantaged workers, willing to do the dirty work for a short time, to save for a better life back home.

The growth of a consensus of criticism of this new order was reflected in a letter to *The Daily Telegraph* (hardly an Old Labour mouthpiece) by more than 100 education-alists, child health experts and cultural leaders, which I quote in full, because of its eloquent summary of these points.

Modern life leads to more depression among children

SIR – As professionals and academics from a range of backgrounds, we are deeply concerned at the escalating incidence of childhood depression and children's behavioural and developmental conditions. We believe that this is largely due to a lack of understanding, on the part of both politicians and the public, of the realities and subtleties of child development.

Since children's brains are still developing, they cannot adjust, as full-grown adults can, to the effects of ever more rapid technological and cultural change. They still need what developing human beings have always needed, including real food (as opposed to processed 'junk food') real play (as opposed to sedentary, screen-based entertainment) first-hand experience of the world they live in, and regular interactions with real-life, significant adults in their lives.

They also need time. In a fast-moving, hyper-competitive culture, today's children are expected to cope with an even earlier start to formal schoolwork and an overly academic test-driven primary curriculum. They are pushed by market forces to act and dress like mini-adults and exposed via the electronic media to material that would have been considered unsuitable for children even in the very recent past.

Our society rightly takes great pains to protect children from physical harm, but seems to have lost sight of their emotional and social needs. However, it's now clear that the mental health of an unacceptable number of children is being unnecessarily compromised, and that this is almost certainly a key factor in the rise of substance abuse and self-harm among our young people.

This is a complex socio-cultural problem to which there is no simple solution, but a sensible first step would be to encourage parents and policy-makers to start talking about ways of improving children's well-being. We therefore propose as a matter of urgency that public debate be initiated on child-rearing in the 21st century.

This issue should be central to public policy-making in the coming decades.

(The Daily Telegraph, 2006)

The letter was signed by Baroness Susan Greenfield (Director of the Royal Institution) Sir Jonathan Porritt (Environmental campaigner) Dr Penelope Leach (Author on childcare issues) Sir Richard Bowlby (President, Centre for Child Mental Health) Professor Tim Brighouse (Commissioner for London Schools) Mick Brookes (General Secretary, Association of Headteachers) Dr John Dunford (General Secretary, Association of School and College Lecturers) Dr Dorothy Rowe (Psychologist and writer) Philip Pulman (Novelist) Jacqueline Wilson (Novelist) and 100 others.

I would want to draw attention to the following features of the letter:

- It attributes the rise in depression, self-harm and behaviour problems among children to factors affecting the child population *as a whole*, and not simply those experiencing adverse economic and social circumstances.
- It analyses these factors in terms of *mainstream* culture, and the influences which drive it, and not the minority or deviant cultures of disadvantaged communities and groups.
- Its analysis deals in such diverse factors as eating habits, play, the school curriculum, the testing and league table culture, parenting practices and the commercialisation of childhood. It suggests that these are linked and mutually reinforcing features of a *collective* culture, and reflect a transformation of our cultural resources and collective institutions.
- It implies that policy-makers and political leaders have led these changes, and that major shifts across a whole range of policy domains are required, if trends in child mental health are to be reversed.
- It implicitly rejects the narrow interpretation of the 'well-being agenda' in terms of increased individual 'personal education' for children in secondary schools, as failing to address these pervasive cultural and collective influences.

All this may be contrasted with the explanation of new measures to 'deter bad behaviour and invest in good behaviour', offered by the Prime Minister in January 2006 (Blair, 2006a), and of those to 'identify children at birth as at risk of offending in later life', announced by him in September, 2006 (Blair, 2006b).

In the first speech, he described the 'Respect Action Plan' as one to target the 'eradication of anti-social behaviour'. He, too, encouraged an intellectual debate, but launched it in a very different way. He also traced the issues to the decay of a traditional culture:

The old civic and family bonds have been loosened. . . . Since the self-reinforcing bonds of traditional community life do not exist in the same way, we need a radical new approach if we are to restore the liberty of the law-abiding citizen. My view is very clear; their freedom to be safe from fear has to come first. . . . All of this, in the end, however, comes down to how we view our obligations to each other in the society we live in. Respect is a way of describing the very possibility of life in a community. . . . More grandly, it is the answer to the most fundamental question of all in politics which is: how do we live together? . . . Of course, the overwhelming majority of people understand this intuitively and have no trouble living side by side with their neighbour. . . . We will make it easier to address anti-social behaviour, sometimes without needing to go to court. The Respect Action Plan does seek to ensure that wrong-doing is punished . . . and . . . [that we] invest in good behaviour. This is what makes the case for action against anti-social behaviour a progressive cause.

(Blair, 2006a: 1–3)

The features which distinguish this speech from the letter in *The Daily Telegraph* seem to me to be:

- The insistence that the 'overwhelming majority' already show each other respect, and that it is their liberty which must be protected.
- The implied claim that a competitive, individualistic, market economy with widespread property ownership supplies a viable social order, and that only a deviant minority are unable to accept their responsibilities under this order.
- The rejection of the notion that there is anything in mainstream culture or collective life which generates anti-social behaviour.
- The belief that control and enforcement will be the best way to deal with anti-social behaviour.

The second speech took these perspectives on offending, and specifically children's delinquency, even further. In addressing the Joseph Rowntree Foundation in York, Tony Blair stated that action at or before birth was needed to counter exclusion and risk among problem families. Announcing measures quickly dubbed 'FASBOs' by one of the tabloid newspapers (short for Foetal Anti-Social Behaviour Orders) he argued:

I am saying that where it is clear – as it very often is – at a young age, that children are at risk of being brought up in a dysfunctional home where there are multiple problems, say of drug abuse or offending, then instead of waiting until the child goes off the rails we should act early enough with the right help and support and discipline framework, for the family to prevent it. . . . It may be the only way to save them and the community.

(Blair, 2006b)

Here, in addition to the elements identified above, there were two additional assumptions:

1. That children who would offend in costly and harmful ways belong to a small minority which can be identified from the characteristics of their parents' behaviour (e.g. taking drugs or committing crimes).

2. That very early surveillance and risk-management interventions could reduce the risks of these costs and harms arising.

Some such interventions had indeed been attempted in the USA in the 1950s, with counterproductive results. But what was more indicative of the New Labour approach to issues of children's well-being was the notion that problems attributable to *exclusion* (i.e. the outcomes of actions by the mainstream, in moving away from contact with, or blocking access for, these families) could be countered by programmes directed at individuals, on the basis of future trouble they would cause. This implies that the choices of mainstream citizens, in isolating and rejecting these families, should be reinforced by special measures to deal with individual deviances by the children of those so isolated and rejected.

The authors of the letter in *The Daily Telegraph* subscribed to a model of society as a system of interdependence, in which each member's actions affect all others. If mainstream parents compete to get their children the best schools and recreational facilities, then those with fewest resources for such competition, based on mobility, will get the worst. If mainstream families strive to give their children lavish consumer lifestyles, fashion accessories and electronic toys, then poor families will strive to do the same, either failing and losing self-esteem, or resorting to dishonest means.

If government sets tests, and grades pupils by performance, but finds no ways to value the least academic in their populations, these will in turn reject mainstream measures of their worth, and subscribe to other cultures, which bestow value in other ways, rewarding loyalty to violent or reckless codes.

These examples show that we are now in the midst of a debate about well-being which goes to the heart of social policy in the past 25 years. It is about the basis for the social order, and the nature of a good society. Tony Blair was right when he said it concerned the fundamental question about how we can live *well* together. Social work has an important contribution to make to this debate, and to reaching a progressive way forward from the current impasse on well-being, and the poor quality of life for *all* children in the UK.

The basis for the social order

Since the advent of Margaret Thatcher, the UK has been ruled by governments which believe that the best basis for the social order is self-responsible individual citizens, who are competent market actors, who compete, work and save, in pursuit of their own interests. These citizens have their needs satisfied by firms and government agencies, producing goods and services, which they in turn can choose, by shifting between a range of options.

This model has a perfectly respectable intellectual and political pedigree. It has been upheld by enlightened and literal philosophers, such as John Locke, Adam Smith, David Hume and John Stuart Mill, since the end of the seventeenth century (Hirschman, 1977). It was introduced as a response to two centuries of religious wars (including the English civil war) and dynastic conflicts in Europe. The peaceful pursuit of material prosperity, it argued, was far superior as a basis for human well-being than the fervent search for religious purity, or the glorious quest for military honour, which brought nothing but death, destruction and ruin (Jordan, 2004).

By the time New Labour came to power in 1997, the British electorate had recognised that this model was incomplete and incoherent in several ways. Tony Blair's government, taking its cue from Bill Clinton's USA, offered to buttress the individualism and materialism of the Thatcher legacy with a new attention to community and inclusion, a modest amount of 'targeted' redistribution (through tax credits), and a set of initiatives to regenerate deprived districts. The regime of 'tough love' (Jordan with Jordan, 2000) has now had nearly ten years to demonstrate its effectiveness, and the letter to *The Daily Telegraph* records the list of its failings.

The situation of children and young people is a fair test for the revised model's viability, as a basis for the social order. Their well-being should be the cornerstone of any society, seeking a sound foundation for its own self-reproduction. The education and socialisation of children expresses the efforts of one generation to equip the *next* for a better quality of life than they themselves have enjoyed.

It also expresses the attempt to equip the new generation with the personal and cultural resources to adapt to the changes in the wider world which are anticipated. In this case, it means to allow our society to flourish in an integrated global economy, with high rates of movement of people, as well as money, goods and technology, across borders. This will be a world economy in which manufacturing is done primarily in newly-industrialising countries like China, India, Brazil and the East European states, including Russia.

As we have seen in Chapter 2, the UK fares very badly, in comparison with other EU countries, by measures of child well-being. This is above all because children's relationships with parents, peers, neighbours and the wider community are among the least positive and most damaging in Europe. This is why the letter in *The Daily Telegraph* should strike a chord, not only with social workers, but with all human service professionals.

It confirms the arguments that I have presented in this book – that well-being can only be served in public policy and individual decisions by taking proper account of the value of relationships for intimacy, respect and belonging, as key elements of well-being. As the founders of social work argued (Chapter 3) a purely materialistic basis for the social order will not supply a sustainable system for improving well-being. Eventually, it will not even supply a social order which can reproduce itself.

As our industrial sector continues to shrink, and our national income relies increasingly on the financial sector, on science and technology, and on services, for foreign earnings, it is time to re-examine these fundamental questions. Our current social order is patterned by our government's belief that commercial services could supply the basis – in employment, as well as in provision for our needs – for a prosperous economy, which would in turn give us social stability and a good quality of life together.

Under regimes headed by both major parties, commercial services have indeed extended their reach, in terms of the numbers they employed, as well as the material value of what they produced. This process has been facilitated by the expansion of the tax credit system, which has subsidised low-paid, part-time and irregular employment in such services as retailing, hospitality, tourism, cleaning and personal care. This has allowed lower unemployment and faster growth than in Continental European countries such as Germany, France and Italy, where minimum wages are higher, regulation is more extensive, and social insurance contributions more costly (Jordan, 2006a).

The time has now come to question whether either of the two rival models for affluent post-industrial societies – the Anglo-American and the European – provides a convincing basis for the social order in the twenty-first century. The phenomenon of stalled well-being indicates that none of them, not even the Scandinavian countries, which enjoy the highest levels of SWB among their citizens, has found the answer.

I have argued in this book that social work has much to contribute to the debate, and to the eventual solution.

The role of human services in service economy

Because the prevailing government orthodoxy sees services as like goods, except that they are consumed in the instant they are produced, it regards their production in much the same light as the production of material commodities. It aims to promote a service economy which runs on competition, allowing efficient use of resources to be rewarded by profit, and hence a return to shareholders. As the customers of service producers and shareholders of service firms, citizens are the beneficiaries of this efficiency, the choice it offers, and the dividends it distributes.

As the international trade in service expands, promoted by the World Trade Organisation's General Agreement on Trade in Services, UK companies will thrive on exports of services like health care, education and social care, since they will have had experience of public finance initiatives and public-private partnerships in these sectors. In this way, services will replace manufacturing, extractive and construction industries as the main generators of foreign currency, as well as the main sources of domestic employment (Jordan, 2006b, chapters 4–6).

I have argued that this model overlooks or discounts the following features of human services:

- That they are provided through relationships, and often deal in relationships (both parts specially true of social work).
- That they also contribute to the collective cultures and contexts which frame our social life, because they involve communicating, negotiating and sharing in ideas and images, and developing the practices of everyday living.
- That they often involve long-term independencies, and sustain the social systems which allow children, people with illnesses and disabilities and frail older people to become or remain active members of society.

- That they involve or promote collective action to improve the quality of life of certain groups and communities; and to improve their access to cultural resources.
- That they therefore contribute directly to individual well-being in these many ways, and that these are systematically concealed or ignored by the forms of economic analysis which inform public policy.

Once these features of human services are recognised, it becomes clear that they are part of the answer to the sort of questions which should be emerging from the debate about well-being. Once we recognise that services are not like manufacturing (because they involve relationships), that they are not consumed like material commodities (because they affect the emotions, the identities, the relationships and the systems of meaning and communication of those who use them), and that they concern cultural resources and collective potentials of services users, then their role in public policy is radically altered.

If the goal of post-industrial governance is to sustain and enable adaptable social reproduction, rather than to maximise economic growth, then the contribution of the human services to well-being becomes central. They do not compete with their counterparts in the newly industrialising or developing countries in direct ways, and should not be allowed to. Above all, there is no demand on these services to perform like such commercial organisations as banks, supermarkets or package holiday companies, as is the explicit requirement of New Labour ministers. Instead they can justify themselves in accordance with the measure of their contribution to a high and sustainable quality of life for all citizens.

This has important implications for the organisation of human services, which are not immediately obvious. It implies that public services should supply an appropriate overall context for interactions between free and equal citizens, in which they are enabled to show each other respect, and not encouraged to be selfish, rivalrous and careless. It also demands that these services themselves, through the practices of their staff, should set an example of how such interactions should be conducted. Both of these were explicit aims of the post-war welfare state, built into the structures of the NHS, and the education and personal social services.

However, this does not directly address the deeper needs of citizens for intimacy (close, supportive, reliable, loving relationships) and belonging (bonds of mutuality, identity and solidarity). The experience of both welfare states and state socialism lead us to question whether these elements in well-being are appropriately supplied by public bodies, or state officials.

The former (loving relationships) seem always to have relied on partnerships, families and friendships networks, deriving from shared experiences and emotions, and leading to shared lives. But the ability of such social interactions to satisfy the needs which are central for well-being is enormously influenced by the wider culture and social environment, which in turn is responsive to government and the public infrastructure.

For example, the research on three cohorts of people born in post-war Britain, referred to on p. 119, compared their satisfactions with their partners of several thousand married people in their early thirties, born respectively in 1946 and 1970. Of those born in 1946, only 2 per cent of men, and 4 per cent of women, said they were dissatisfied with their spouse. Among those born in 1970, 22 per cent of men, and 26 per cent of women, were dissatisfied (Ferri and Smith, 2003: 110, Table 4.1). The disparities were similar for unmarried couples.

This shows that a culture of individualism, based on autonomy, choice and self-development, and involving more frequent changes of partners both before and after marriage, is associated with higher expectations of relationships, and hence greater disappointments. In terms of well-being, it may lead to a 'hedonic treadmill', where expectations and demands constantly rise, so that actual improvements are taken for granted, rather than appreciated.

This is the basis for Offer's (2006) claim that affluence has led to a culture of intimacy in which women and children are especially vulnerable, because men are advantaged in a society based on markets, property and mobility.

Social work has always been closely associated with an ethic of care – interdependence rather than autonomy, equality of value irrespective of economic contribution, and compassion with empathy rather than rights and duties (Tronto, 1993; Sevenhuijsen, 2002; Williams, 2005; Meagher and Parton, 2004). This represents a genuine alternative to the individualism and self-realisation which underpin the current social order.

It is this alternative view of close relationships which is social work's potential *cultural* contribution to a new approach to well-being, as much as its expertise in relationships. Until this cultural shift has begun, and the economic value of caring is advantaged, social work's full potential cannot be realised.

The second element, belonging, seems to be derived from civil society associations and informal groups, movements and communities, more than it is from national or official institutions. In the UK, the government has promoted the transfer of public service responsibilities to voluntary agencies, usually under contract. Such arrangements have often stipulated quality standards, levels of service, outcome measures and unit costs. It is a highly prescriptive, top-down and market-driven approach, which does little to foster the advantages that voluntary organisations have in creating the sense of belonging. Rather the reverse; it makes them like firms or official agencies.

As we have seen in Chapters 7 and 8, the government has also encouraged local groups and associations to join initiatives on inclusion, cohesion, respect and integration, but on terms which limited their scope for engaging their members. These 'invited spaces' have addressed issues on the government's agenda, not that of local people. They have promoted the goals of their respective programmes, not the sense of belonging, collective identity, or engagement in improving a shared quality of life.

For all the reasons given in Chapters 7 and 8, I have argued that community workers should enable groups and movements to act in pursuit of their interests, and improve their own well-being, wherever possible. This implies that the organisation of these activities should, as far as practicable, be under the control of these people themselves, and not of government or professionals.

I have suggested ways in which local cultural practices might be challenged and transformed within this framework. But one of the main advantages of this form of social organisation is that it allows disadvantaged people to participate, and be active in shaping the collective circumstances of their lives.

One of the factors limiting the scope for this form of self-organisation is the current tax-benefit system. As it stands, it is deliberately constructed to reward low-paid, part-time and irregular formal employment (such as stacking shelves in supermarkets, or serving in hamburger bars) through tax credits. Conversely, it penalises voluntary, community, cultural and political work, by requiring those claiming benefits to be actively seeking paid employment. It is also systematically ungenerous to carers.

For many years, I have argued for a reform of the tax-benefit system which would treat such unpaid activities (including child care by parents) the same as paid work (Jordan, 1973, 1996, 2006a and b). This would consist of a guaranteed sum of money (the equivalent of a tax allowance, tax credit or benefit) for each citizen, irrespective of their work or household status. This would allow couples to negotiate paid and unpaid work as equals, and members of disadvantaged communities to engage in community work without falling foul of these authorities.

The evidence of stalled well-being seems to me to strengthen the case for this reform. An ethic of care and a citizenship of active engagement would be far easier to promote if all paid work and unpaid work received the same treatment from the tax and benefit authorities. Indeed, a policy for increasing well-being, rather than income and employment, would be impossible without this measure.

The evidence presented in this book of the economic value of interpersonal transactions answers the common objections to the reform – that it gives everyone something for nothing. If the only measure of value is formal work, material consumption and paid service, this appears to be so. But, once we recognise the value of care, of empathy, of interactions themselves, of culture, engagement and social life, most of them dissolve.

This Basic Income principle (as it is called) would simply give everyone an allowance, as a valued member of society, as recognition of their contribution to our interdependent well-being.

The organisation of services – public, associational and informal – could then take place according to the requirements of SWB rather than GNP. Each human service could be structured in the ways that best promoted intimacy, respect and belonging, not income, cost-effectiveness, productivity and export revenue.

There are plenty of branches of the economy which would still have to meet those traditional economic requirements. But human services should not be one of them.

A coming struggle

It would be naïve to suppose that the debate on well-being will be conducted in terms of philosophy and social science. There are very powerful interests at stake, and very large sums of money. The coming struggle over the direction to be taken by our society will occur both inside and between the main political parties.

There are Conservative interests with a strong stake in the existing order, because it serves the purposes of (for example) major commercial suppliers of health, education and social services, major construction, retailing and leisure companies, and a swathe of financial interests. There is also the New Labour establishment, which will not easily be converted to the new agenda, because it has spent 15 years constructing a political coalition and an ideological consensus around the current order.

It is ironic that David Cameron (partly because of the 'honeymoon effect') seems to be finding it easier to convert the party of Margaret Thatcher to a politics of environmental conservation, compassion, public service and quality of life than the Labour rebels are finding it to overthrow Tony Blair.

But this should not be surprising. Ten years of opposition have taught the Tories some hard lessons; ten years of government have made New Labour defensive of the status quo.

The immediate problem is that it is now the New Labour leadership, not the Tories, who want to shift political debate onto the divisive ground of immigration, integration, security, order and crime. As we have seen in Chapters 7 and 8, the government wants to blame disorder, deviance, childhood depression, terrorism and intercommunal conflict onto a disaffected, irresponsible or subversive minority. In the name of cohesion and integration, it seeks to limit immigration to those who can prove their economic value, in terms of productivity and the skills gap among the home workforce.

For the sake of security, it wants to promote 'Britishness' – a national version of the culture of individual autonomy, choice and property-ownership, which has nothing to do with belonging, loyalty or patriotism, and everything to do with the market-driven logic of its incoherent social order.

Social work values embrace openness to others, and deplore barriers to inclusion and communication. I have argued that Muslim extremism and violence are a response to successful integration into critical Western thinking and political action, together with despair about the partisan and imperialistic features of UK foreign policy.

This is not to justify terrorism and cruelty. It is to contend that, as in community work, a real dialogue about the acceptable limits of protest and collective action can only start where there is trust, and the willingness to listen to criticisms of one's own actions and attitudes. The UK government has a good way to go before it can achieve this kind of dialogue with British Muslim youth.

As long as the debate about well-being takes place on the terrain of immigration, integration, cohesion and security, it will be difficult for social work to make its full potential contributions. This is why social workers should have common cause with the other human services professions, to take part in debates such as those raised by the authors of the letter to *The Daily Telegraph*. It should also be open to discussions with members of all political parties and groups, rather than restricting itself to debates with old allies within local government and the trade unions.

The coming struggle is as much about global issues as domestic ones. As has been shown in meetings of the G8, and in negotiations over the Doha Round of the WTO's trade liberalisation programme, as well as in the rejection of the EU constitution and the fears about further enlargement of the Union, the phenomenon of stalled well-being reflects a wider problem of world development.

Because the affluent countries have lost their dominance of industrial structures and institutions for their social order, questions about social reproduction have come to the fore in every country. They have become defensive and inward-looking.

The real issue for the future is how there can be reciprocity between those who supply the capital for the expansion of material production (the rich states) and those who make the goods (the newly-industrialising giants of the Far East, South America and Eastern Europe). At present, the affluent countries are too insecure about their societies' capacities to sustain their quality of life to trade fairly with the industrialising and less developed ones, or to open their infrastructures up to penetration by their services and workforces.

At the same time, there is a pressing need for international agreements on the environment, and for a shift towards sustainable lifestyles. Here again the rich world is anxious and insecure, and unable to lead, for fear of jeopardising its own fragile balance of interests.

Instead, under the lead of the USA and UK, it pursues an aggressive strategy for forced absorption of all regimes into the integrated global marketplace, hoping that economic forces will offer a world order that it lacks the moral authority to propose.

Social work can seem parochial and humble in the face of these massive challenges. It might be doubted what it can offer to resolve the titanic clash of interests that will occur on a global scale, before these issues are resolved.

But this is too fatalistic. Every profession and interest group can play a part, and social work's is highly relevant. It represents the value of relationships of all kinds as the key to well-being, and the inclusion of all members in the common good. This will be the crucial factor in any resolution of the problem of stalled well-being.

Conclusions: signs of change

I want to conclude this book on a more positive note, relating to practice. I have castigated the UK government in this chapter for its adherence to an incoherent version of the social order, which jeopardises the very fabric of social reproduction. I have illustrated this incoherence in relation to the socialisation of children, about the lives set out by the authors of the letter to *The Daily Telegraph*. I have also argued that social workers should make common cause with other professionals, to modify this model of society in radical ways.

But something of this is already happening, from the bottom rather than the top. The idea of well-being has been introduced into the public discourse on children, young people and adults with social needs. This provides an opportunity for practitioners to reshape our human services by what they *do*, in partnership with other professionals.

For example, since the publication of *Every Child Matters* (DfES, 2004) there has been an 'Outcomes Framework', published with the guidance document *Every Child Matters: Change for Children*, 1 December 2004 (DfES). This – in true New Labour style – identifies 26 PSA targets and a total of 13 other key indicators, as well as criteria for inspection of facilities. They contain the usual lists of harms to be avoided and needs to be provided for, and this list especially applies to children looked after by the local authority. Councils can respond with strategies, plans and priorities of their own. I have seen one of these, in which a new ethos is apparent.

Under the heading 'Make a Positive Contribution' are listed the following headings for the Ofsted inspectors, who will inspect the various joint facilities provided by the new joint education and child care authorities:

1. Children and young people are helped to develop socially and emotionally.
2. Children and young people are helped to manage changes and respond to challenges in their lives.
3. Children and young people are encouraged to participate in decision making and to support in the community.
4. Action is taken to reduce anti-social behaviour.
5. Children and young people who are looked after are helped to make a positive contribution.
6. Children and young people with learning difficulties and disabilities are helped to make a positive contribution.
7. Children and young people are supported at key transition points in their lives.
8. Children and young people are encouraged to participate in the planning and management of services and activities.
9. Action is taken to challenge and reduce bullying and discrimination by children and young people.

This list provides plenty of scope for social workers to join with educational staff in promoting a better quality of life and culture in these facilities. They also can gain some purchase on the well-being agenda by the requirements that children and young people should *enjoy*, as well as achieve – for instance, that they should 'enjoy recreation', and have 'a range of accessible recreational provision' (no more selling school playing fields, please).

The development of early learning facilities and extended schools should gradually increase the opportunities to build on these expectations, within a climate of public opinion that is growing more favourable to such professional activities. The very word 'well-being' has now entered the official vocabulary and public consciousness in a way that enables these links to be made.

Indeed, UK educational and child care staff can increasingly draw on international expertise and research to justify approaches which only a few years ago would have been seen as subverting the serious business of achievement, targets and league tables.

Early Years guidance for the DfES now refers extensively to a literature on personal, social and emotional development, and encourages reflective practice that promotes these, through training materials prepared by the Sure Start Unit and the King's Fund (Sure Start, 2005).

There are many educational journals, newsletters and groups promoting an approach to education which is broadly in line with the goals of *The Daily Telegraph* signatories, and concerned with well-being. For instance, the journal *Early Education*, published by the British Association for Early Childhood Education, contains articles which are consistent with this view. The *Refocus Journal*, an international publication, brings together educators who are:

> . . . quietly, but firmly, challenging old ways of thinking, provoking new ideas and strengthening our resolve and commitment to 'researchful practice' that starts with the child – [containing] a wide range of informed perspectives, philosophical and practical, international and home grown . . . that will inspire and energise us on our journey through the changing early years landscape.
>
> (Jaeckle, 2006: 2)

This journal uses much of the same vocabulary (of creative, meaningful relationships, contexts for meaning-making and citizenship) which are deployed in this book. It shows that teachers have much in common with social workers, once a well-being perspective is adopted.

But perhaps the most important evidence of a shift is in the way that the new inspection criteria are being interpreted.

They show clear signs of a shift towards the perspectives derived from the well-being agenda. For example, inspectors' reports on day nurseries dwell on such factors as whether they 'demonstrate a sense of belonging', 'playing well together cooperatively and negotiating well during their play'.

Staff are observed to 'interact well with children and respond to their needs', 'offer new experiences', and inspectors comment on how they behave towards others in the group, and whether they 'treat one another with respect'.

The word 'well-being' is now part of the requirements for the Educational Improvement Professionals. It is usually appended to 'outcomes' or linked with 'quality'. All this provides further openings for cooperative development with colleagues in education.

For all these reasons, well-being is part of the explicit agenda of social work practice in the UK – as much in social care for adults (Chapter 5) as the care of children. So the first steps have already been taken along the road to re-establishing the true basis for social work practice in this country, and perhaps even a better basis for the whole social order, with social work in its proper role in that order.

None of this can be a smooth progress, for the reasons identified in this chapter. The agendas on anti-social behaviour, security and immigration and integration cut straight across these policies and practices, and could undermine them fatally. Every gain will have to be negotiated and fought.

Above all, the *frames* for progress will have to change before well-being and social justice can become the main goals of social reproduction in a service economy (Fraser, 2005). We need new institutions which enable a better work-life balance, more mutually supportive family relationships, and communal solutions to shared social issues.

These require government action, but social workers can play a part, with many other occupational groups, in demanding these changes, and making them work for the advantage of all.

References

Adams, R. (2003) *Social Work and Empowerment*, London: Macmillan.

Adams, R., Dominelli, L. and Payne, M. (Eds.) (2005) *Social Work Futures: Crossing Boundaries, Transforming Practice*, Basingstoke: Palgrave.

Ainslie, G. (1992) *Picoeconomics: The Interaction of Successive Motivational States within the Person*, Cambridge: Cambridge University Press.

Argyle, M. (1999) Causes and Correlates of Happiness, in Kahneman, D. (Ed.) *Well-being: The Foundations of Hedonic Psychology*, New York: Russell Sage Foundation.

Atkinson, A.B. (1995) *Public Economics in Action: The Basic Income/Flat Tax Proposal*, Oxford: Oxford University Press.

Bailey, R. and Brake, M. (Eds.) (1976) *Radical Social Work*, London: Edward Arnold.

Barclay Report (1982) *Social Workers; Their Roles and Tasks*, London: NISW/Bedford Square Press.

Barnados (2001) *Better Education, Better Futures, Research, Practice and the Views of Young People in Public Care*, London: Barnados.

Batten, T.R. (1954) *Communities and Their Development: An Introductory Study, with Special Reference to the Tropics*, Oxford: Oxford University Press.

BBC Radio 4 (2006a) *News*, 9 January.

BBC Radio 4 (2006b) *Today* and *News*, 4 August.

BBC Radio 4 (2006c) *Today*, 12 August.

BBC Radio 4 (2006d) *Today*, 23 August.

BBC Radio 4 (2006e) *Face the Facts*, 25 August.

BBC Radio 4 (2006f) *Today*, 5 September.

BBC Radio 4 (2006g) *News Briefing* and *Today*, 5 September.

BBC Radio 4 (2006h) *Today*, 11 September.

BBC Radio 4 (2006i) *Desert Island Discs* (Camilla Bakmanghelidjh). 3 November.

BBC World Service (2006a) *News*, 26 August.

BBC World Service (2006b) *The World Today*, 5 September.

BBC2 TV (2005) *Making Slough Happy*, 24 November, 1 and 8 December.

Becker, G.S. (1976) *The Economic Approach to Human Behaviour*, Chicago: Chicago University Press.

Becker, G.S. (1991) *A Treatise on the Family*, Cambridge MA: Harvard University Press.

Begg, F., Fischer, S. and Dornbusch, R. (1997) *Economics*, 5th edn., London: McGraw Hill.

Berg, I.K. (1994) *Family-Based Services: A Solution-Focused Approach*, New York: Norton.

Berg, I.K. and Miles, S.D. (1992) *Working with the Problem Drinker: A Solution-Focused Approach*, New York: Norton.

Berg, I.K. and Miller, S.D. (1995) *The Miracle Method: A Radical Approach to Problem Drink*, New York: Norton.

Bertolino, B. and O Hanlon, B. (1999) *Invitation to Possibilityland: An Intensive Teaching Seminar with Bill O Hanlon*, Philadelphia; Brunner/Hazel.

Beveridge, Sir W. (1942) *Social Insurance and Allied Services*, Cmnd 404, London: HMSO.

Blair, T. (1996) Speech to Labour Party Conference.

Blair, T. (2000) Values and the Power of Community, speech to Global Ethics Foundation, Tübingen, 30 June.

Blair, T. (2005) Preface to DoH, *Independence, Well-being and Choice*, Cm 6499, London: Stationery Office.

Blair, T. (2006a) Speech on Respect and Respect Action Plan, 10 January.

Blair, T. (2006b) Speech on Anti-Social Behaviour, 5 September.

Blunkett, D. (2003) *Active Citizens, Strong Communities; Progressing Civil Renewal*, Scarman Lecture to the Citizens Convention, 11 December.

Blunkett, D. (2004) *New Challenges to Race Equality and Community Cohesion in the Twenty-First Century*, speech to the IPPR, 20 June.

Bourdieu, P. (1990) *The Logic of Practice*, Stanford: Stanford University Press.

Bradshaw, J., Hoelscher, P. and Richardson, D. (2006) An Index of Child Well-being in the European Union , *Journal of Social Indicators*, forthcoming.

Braithwaite, J. and Strang, H. (Eds.) (2001) *Restorative Justice and Civil Society*, Cambridge: Cambridge University Press.

Brindle, D. (2005) Opinion: Long Neglected, Mental Health Might Yet Become the Governments Highest Priority, *Guardian Society*, 11 May.

British Association of Social Workers (2003) *Code of Ethics for Social Workers*, Birmingham: BASW.

Brown, P. (2005) *Life in Dispersal: Narratives of Asylum, Identity and Community*, PhD Thesis, University of Huddersfield, School of Human and Health Sciences.

Bruni, L. and Porta, P.L. (Eds.) (2005) *Economics and Happiness: Framing the Analysis*, Oxford: Oxford University Press.

Buchanan, J.M. (1965) An Economic Theory of Clubs , *Economica*, 32, 1–14.

Bynner, J. and Parsons, S. (2003) Social Participation, Values and Crime, in Ferri, E., Bynner, J. and Wadsworth, M. (Eds.) *Changing Britain, Changing Lives: Three Generations at the Turn of the Century*, London: Institute of Education.

Cameron, G. (2006) Speech in Hertfordshire, 22 May.

Capisarow, R. and Barbour, A. (2005) *Informal Economic Activity in London*, London: Community Links.

Carter, M. (2003) *T.H. Green and the Development of Ethical Socialism*, Exeter: Imprint Academic.

Castells, M. (1997) *The Power of Identity*, Oxford: Blackwell.

Channel 4 TV, (2005) *Jamie's School Dinners*, 24 February, 2 and 9 March.

Clark, C.L. (2000) *Social Work Ethics; Politics, Principles and Practice*, Basingstoke: Macmillan.

Clarke, J., Cochrane, A. and McLaughlin, E. (1994) *Managing Social Policy*, London: Sage.

Cohen, J.L. and Arato, A. (1992) *Civil Society and Political Theory*, Boston, MA: MIT Press.

Cole, G.D.H. (1920) *Social Theory*, London: Methuen.

Cole, G.D.H. (1945) A Retrospect of the History of Voluntary Social Service , in Bourdillon, A.F.C. (Ed.) *Voluntary Social Services*, London: Methuen, 3–26.

Coleman, J.S. (1990) *The Foundations of Social Theory*, Cambridge: Cambridge University Press.

Cormack, U. (1945) Developments in Social Casework, in Bourdillon, A.F.C. (Ed.) *Voluntary Social Services*, London: Methuen.

Cornes, R. and Sandler, T. (1986) *The Theory of Externalities, Public Goods and Club Goods,* Cambridge: Cambridge University Press.

Corrigan, P. and Leonard, P. (1978) *Social Work Practice Under Capitalism,* London: Macmillan.

Council of the European Union (2000) *Charter of Fundamental Rights of the European Union: Explanations Relating to the Complete Text of the Charter,* Luxemburg: European Commission.

Crawford, A. and Newburn, T. (2003) *Youth Offending and Restorative Justice: Implementing Reform in Youth Justice,* Cullompton: Willan House.

Cuff, E.C. (1980) *Some Issues in Studying the Problem of Versions in Everyday Situations,* Department of Sociology, Manchester University, Occasional Paper 3.

Curtis, Dame M. (1946) *Report of the Care of Children Committee,* Cmnd 6922, London: HMSO.

Daily Telegraph (2006) *Letters to the Editor,* 12 September.

Davidson, R.J. (2005) Well-being and Affective Style: Neural Substrates and Bio-Behavioural Correlates, in Huppert, F.A. et al. (Eds.) *The Science of Well-being,* Oxford: Oxford University Press.

Davies, H. (1992) *Fighting Leviathan: Building Social Markets that Work,* London: Social Market Foundation.

Davies, M. (1994) *The Essential Social Worker,* Aldershot: Arena.

de Shazer, S. (1991) *Putting Difference to Work,* New York: Norton.

de Shazer, S. (1994) *Words Were Originally Magic,* New York: Norton.

Dean, H. (Ed.) (2004) *The Ethics of Welfare: Human Rights, Dependency and Responsibility,* Bristol: Policy Press.

Department for Education and Skills (2004) *Every Child Matters,* London: Stationery Office.

Department of Health (1998) *Modernising Social Services: Promoting Independence, Improving Protection, Raising Standards,* Cm 4169, London: HMSO.

Department of Health (2000) *Valuing People: A New Strategy for Learning Disability in the 21st Century,* London: DoH.

Department of Health (2005) *Independence, Well-being and Choice: Our Vision of the Future of Social Care for Adults in England,* Cm 6499, London: Stationery Office.

Department of Social Security (1998) *A New Contract for Welfare,* Cm 3805, London: HMSO.

Dickens, C. (1852) *Bleak House,* London: Chapman and Hall, 1961.

Diener, E. and Suh, E.M. (1999) National Differences, Subjective Well-being, in Kahneman, D. et al. (Eds.) *Well-being: The Foundations of Hedonic Psychology,* New York: Russell Sage Foundation.

Doherty, P.K. (2004) *Managing Participation in an Age of Diversity,* PhD Thesis, Cork: University College Cork, Department of Applied Social Sciences.

Dominelli, L. (1988) *Anti-Racist Social Work,* London: Macmillan.

Dominelli, L. (1998) Anti-Oppressive Practice in Context, in Adams, R., Dominelli, L. and Payne, M. (Eds.) *Social Work: Themes, Issues and Critical Debates,* Basingstoke: Macmillan, pp 1–22.

Dominelli, L. and McLeod, E. (1989) *Feminist Social Work,* London: Macmillan.

Dorling, D. and Thomas, B. (2003) *People and Places: A 2001 Census Atlas of the UK,* Bristol: Policy Press.

Douglas, C.H. (1920a) *Economic Democracy,* London: S. Nott.

Douglas, C.H. (1920b) *Credit Power and Democracy,* London: C. Palmer.

Douglas, M. (1987) *How Institutions Think,* London: Routledge and Kegan Paul.

Drakeford, M. (2002) Poverty and the Social Services, in Bytheway, B. et al. (Eds.) *Understanding Care, Welfare and Community,* London: Routledge.

Driver, S. and Martel, L. (1997) New Labour's Communitarianisms, *Critical Social Policy*, 17: 52, 27–56.

Dryzek, J. (1990) *Discursive Democracy: Politics, Policy and Political Science*, Cambridge: Cambridge University Press.

Dryzek, J. (2000) *Deliberative Democracy and Beyond*, Oxford: Oxford University Press.

Durrant, M. (1993) *Residential Treatment: A Co-operative Competency Approach to Therapy and Programme Design*, New York: Norton.

Dustin, D. (2004) *Care Management and Community Care*, PhD thesis, London Metropolitan University, Department of Social Work.

Easterlin, R.A. (1974) Does Economic Growth Improve the Human Lot? in David, P. and Reder, M. (Eds.) *Nations and Households in Economic Growth: Essay in Honor of Moses Abramovits*, New York: Academic Press.

Easterlin, R.A. (2005) Building a Better Theory of Well-being, in Bruni, L. and Porta, P.L. (Eds.) *Economics and Happiness: Framing the Analysis*, Oxford: Oxford University Press.

Ellis, K. (2004) Dependency, Justice and the Ethic of Care, in Dean, H. (Ed.) *The Ethics of Welfare: Human Rights, Dependency and Responsibility*, Bristol: Policy Press.

Ellis, K. and Rogers, R. (2004) Fostering a Human Rights Discourse in the Provision of Social Care for Adults, in Dean, H. (Ed.) *The Ethics of Welfare*, Bristol: Policy Press.

Elshtain, J.B. (1981) *Public Man, Private Woman: Women in Social and Political Thought*, Oxford: Martin Robertson.

Elshtain, J.B. (1998) Antigone's Daughters, in Phillips, A. (Ed.) *Feminism and Politics*, Oxford: Oxford University Press.

Esping-Andersen, G. (1999) *Social Foundations of Post-industrial Economies*, Oxford: Oxford University Press.

Elster, J. (1985) *Making Sense of Marx*, Cambridge: Cambridge University Press.

England, H. (1986) *Social Work as Art*, London: Allen and Unwin.

Ester, J. (1985) *Making Sense of Marx*, Cambridge: Cambridge University Press.

Etzioni, A. (1993) *The Spirit of Community: The Reinvention of American Society*, New York: Touchstone.

Feinstein, C.H. (1976) *Statistical Tables of National Income, Expenditure and Output of the UK, 1855–1965*, Cambridge: Cambridge University Press.

Ferri, E. and Smith, K. (2003) Partnership and Parenthood, in Ferri, E., Bynner, J. and Wadsworth, M. (Eds.) *Changing Britain, Changing Lives: Three Generations at the Turn of the Century*, London: Institute of Education.

Fletcher, K. (1998) *Best Value Social Services*, Caerphilly: SSSP Publications.

Foldvary, F. (1994) *Public Goods and Private Communities: The Market Provision of Social Services*, Aldershot: Edward Elgar.

Forde, C. (2006) *Invited Spaces for Participation: A Critical Analysis of Local Social Partnership in Ireland*, PhD Thesis, Department for Applied Social Studies, University College, Cork.

Fording, R., Schram, S. and Soss, J. (2006) *Devolution, Discretion and Local Variation in TANF Sanctions*, Lexington: University of Kentucky Centre on Poverty Research, Discussion Paper 2006–04.

Fothergill, S. (2006) *A Million Off Incapacity Benefit?* paper presented at a seminar on Poverty and Place, Cambridge/MIT Institute, 29 September.

Fraser, N. (1992) Rethinking the Public Sphere: A Contribution to the Critique of Actually Existing Democracy, in Calhoun, C. (Ed.) *Habermas and the Public Sphere*, Cambridge, MA: MIT Press.

Fraser, N. (1997) *Justice Interruptus*, New York: Routledge.

Fraser, N. (2005) Reframing Justice in a Globalizing World, *New Left Review*, 36, 69–88.

Frey, B. and Stutzer, A. (2002) *Happiness and Economics: How the Economy and Institutions Affect Human Well-being*, Princeton NJ: Princeton University Press.

Gaventa, J. (2004) Towards Participatory Governance: Assessing the Transformation Possibilities, in Hickey, S. and Mohan, G. (Eds.) *Participation: From Tyranny to Transformation?* London: Zed Books.

Gavrielides, T. (2003) Restorative Justice: Are We There Yet?, *Criminal Law Forum*, 14, 385–419.

Gergen, K.J. (1999) *An Invitation to Social Construction*, London: Sage.

Gibbs, A. (2000) New Managerialism, in Davies, M. (Ed.) *The Blackwell Encyclopaedia of Social Work*, Oxford: Blackwell.

Giddens, A. (1991) *Modernity and Self-Identity: Self and Society in the Late Modern Age*, Cambridge: Polity.

Gilroy, P. and Ouseley, H. (2005) Race and Faith Post 7/7 *Guardian*, 30 July.

Goodhart, D. (2005) It s Paranoia, not Islamophobia, *Guardian*, 15 July.

Goodley, D., Armstrong, D. et al. (2003) Self Advocacy: Learning Difficulties and the Model of Social Disability, *Mental Retardation*, 41, 149–60.

Gorman, K., Gregory, M., Hayles, M. and Parton, N. (2006) *Constructive Work with Offenders*, London: Jessica Kingsley Publications.

Gore, C. (c1900) *Christianity and Socialism*, London: CSU.

Gore, C. (1922) Introduction, in Group of Churchmen, *The Return to Christendom*, London: CSU.

Gray, P. (2005) The Politics of Risk and Young Offenders' Experiences of Social Exclusion and Restorative Justice, *British Journal of Criminology*, 45, 938–57.

Guardian (2006a) Cameron Looks Left and Right on Crime, 12 July.

Guardian (2006b) Is it Any Surprise that the People who Live Here are the Happiest in the World? 12 September, p.23.

Guardian (2006c) Kelly Vows that New Debate on Immigration Will Engage Critically with Multiculturalism, 25 August.

Guardian (2006d) Action at Birth Needed to Save Problem Children, Says Blair, 6 September.

Habermas, J. (1989a) *The Theory of Communicative Action: Lifeworld and System*, Cambridge: Polity.

Habermas, J. (1989b) *The Structural Transformation of the Public Sphere*, Cambridge: Polity.

Hadley, R., Cooper, M., Pale, P. and Stacey, G. (1987) *A Community Social Worker's Handbook*, London: Tavistock.

Hall, P.A. (2002) Great Britain: The Role of Government and the Distribution of Social Capital, in Putnam, R.D. (Ed.) *Democracies in Flow*, Oxford: Oxford University Press, 21–58.

Harris, K. (2006) *Respect in the Neighbourhood: Why Neighbourliness Matters*, Lyme Regis: Russell House Publishing.

Hayek, F.A. Von (1960) *The Constitution of Liberty*, London: Routledge and Kegan Paul.

Hayek, F.A. Von (1978) *New Studies in Philosophy, Politics and Economics*, London, Routledge and Kegan Paul.

Helgoy, I., Revensburg, B. and Solvang, P. (2003) Service Provision for an Independent Life, *Disability and Society*, 18, 481–7.

Helliwell, J.F. (2003) How's Life? Combining Individual and National Variables to Explain Subjective Well-being, *Economic Modelling*, 20, 331–60.

Helliwell, J.F. and Putnam, R.D. (2005) The Social Context of Well-being, in Huppert, F.A. et al. (Eds.) *The Science of Well-being*, Oxford: Oxford University Press.

Hill, O. (1891) Our Dealings with the Poor, *Nineteenth Century*, XXX, 61–70.

Hirschman, A.O. (1970) *Exit, Voice and Loyalty: Responses to Decline in Firms, Organizations and States*, Cambridge, MA: Harvard University Press.

Hirschman, A.O. (1977) *The Passions and the Interests: Political Arguments for Capitalism Before its Triumph*, Princeton, NJ: Princeton University Press.

Hodgson, L. (2004) Manufactured Civil Society: Counting the Cost, *Critical Social Policy*, 24: 2, 139–64.

Holland, H.S. (1900) Sacerdotalism and Socialism, *Commonwealth*, V: 2, 21–40.

Holman, B. (1981) *Kids at the Door: A Preventive Project on a Council Estate*, Oxford: Blackwell.

Holman, B. (2000) *Kids at the Door Revisited: A Follow-up into Adulthood*, Lyme Regis: Russell House Publishing.

Home Office (1997) *No More Excuses: A New Approach to Tackling Youth Crime in England and Wales*, London: Home Office.

Home Office (2001) *Community Cohesion: Report of the Independent Review Team Chaired by Ted Cantle*, London: Home Office.

Home Office (2001b) *The Introduction of Referral Orders into the Youth Justice System: First Interim Report*, London: Research, Development and Statistics Directorate.

Home Office (2001c) *The Introduction of Referral Orders into the Youth Justice System: Second Interim Report*, London: Research, Development and Statistics Directorate.

Home Office (2002) *Referral Orders and Young Offender Panels: Guidance for Courts*, London: Home Office/Lord Chancellor's Department/Youth Justice Board.

Home Office (2003) *Building a Picture of Community Cohesion*, London: Home Office.

Home Office (2004) *Strength in Diversity: Towards a Community Cohesion and Race Equality Strategy*, London: HMSO.

Home Office (2004a) *The End of Parallel Lives: Report of the Community Cohesion Panel*, London: Home Office.

Home Office (2004b) *Integration Matters: A National Strategy for Refugee Integration*, London: Home Office.

Home Office (2005a) *Improving Opportunity, Strengthening Society*, www.homeoffice.gov.uk.

Home Office (2005b) *Social Capital: A Report on Research*, London: HMSO.

Horner, N. (2003) *What Is Social Work? Context and Perspectives*, Exeter: Learning Matters.

Howe, D. (1993) *On Being a Client: Understanding the Process of Counselling and Psychotherapy*, London: Sage.

Huppert, F.A., Baylis, N. and Keverne, B. (Eds.) (2005) *The Science of Well-being*, Oxford: Oxford University Press.

International Federation of Social Workers/ International Association of Schools of Social Work (2001) *Code of Ethics*, New York: IFSW/IASSW.

Iversen, T. and Wren, A. (1998) Equality, Employment and Budgetary Restraint: The Trilemma of the Service Economy, *World Politics*, 50: 4, 507–46.

Jaeckle, S. (2006) At the Beginning of the Beginning, *ReFocus Journal*, 3, Summer.

Jones, S. and Roberts, C. (2005) *Examining the Involvement in Community Involvement: A Case Study of Referral Order Volunteers in One Youth Offending Team*, Oxford: University of Oxford.

Jordan, B. (1973) *Paupers: The Making of the New Claiming Class*, London: Routledge and Kegan Paul.

Jordan, B. (1984) *Invitation to Social Work*, Oxford: Martin Robertson.

Jordan, B. (1990) *Social Work in an Unjust Society*, Hemel Hempstead: Harvester.

Jordan, B. (1993) Framing Claims and the Weapons of the Weak, in Drover, G. and Kerans, P. (Eds.) *New Approaches to Welfare Theory*, Aldershot: Edward Elgar.

Jordan, B. (1996) *A Theory of Poverty and Social Exclusion*, Cambridge: Polity.

Jordan, B. (1997a) Social Work and Society, in Davies, M. (Ed.) *The Blackwell Companion to Social Work*, Oxford: Blackwell.

Jordan, B. (1997b) Partnership with Service Users in Child Protection and Family Support, in Parton, N. (Ed.) *Child Protection and Family Support: Contradictions and Possibilities*, London: Routledge.

Jordan, B. (2004) *Sex, Money and Power: The Transformation of Collective Life*, Cambridge: Polity.

Jordan, B. (2006a) *Social Policy for the Twenty-First Century: New Perspectives, Big Issues*, Cambridge, Polity.

Jordan, B. (2006b) *Rewarding Company, Enriching Life: The Economics of Relationships and Well-being*, http://www.billjordan.co.uk.

Jordan, B. (2006c) Public Services and the Service Economy: Individualism and the Choice Agenda, *Journal of Social Policy*, 32: 1, 143–62.

Jordan, B. and Travers, A. (1998) The Informal Economy: A Case Study in Unrestrained Competition, *Social Policy and Administration*, 32: 3, 292–306.

Jordan, B. with Jordan, C. (2000) *Social Work and the Third Way: Tough Love as Social Policy*, London: Sage.

Jordan, B., James, S., Kay, H. and Redley, M. (1992) *Trapped in Poverty? Labour Market Decisions in Low-Income Households*, London: Routledge.

Joseph Rowntree Foundation (1999) *The Costs of Independent Living*, www.jrf.org.uk.

Kahneman, D. (1999) Objective Happiness, in Kahneman, D. et al. (Eds.) *Well-being: The Foundations of Hedonic Psychology*, New York: Russell Sage Foundation.

Kahneman, D., Diener, E. and Schwartz, N. (Eds.) (1999) *Well-being: The Foundations of Hedonic Psychology*, New York: Russell Sage Foundation.

Keith-Lucas, A. (1972) *Giving and Taking Help*, Chapel Hill, NC: University of North Carolina Press.

Kelsey, J. (1995) *Economic Fundamentalism: The New Zealand Experiment – A World Model for Structural Argument*, London: Pluto.

Kettle, M. (2006) Cameron Has the Edge, *Guardian*, 23 May.

Knack, S. and Keefer, P. (1997) Does Social Capital Have an Economic Payoff? A Country Investigation, *Quarterly Journal of Economics*, 112, 1251–88.

Koehn, D. (1994) *The Ground of Professional Ethics*, London: Routledge.

Kureishi, H. (2005) The Carnival of Culture, *Guardian*, 4 August.

Lane, R.E. (2000) *The Loss of Happiness in Market Democracies*, New Haven CT: Yale University Press.

Laslett, P. (Ed.) (1967) *Two Treaties of Government (John Locke, 1690)*, Cambridge: Cambridge University Press.

Layard, R. (2005) *Happiness: Lessons from a New Science*, London: Allen Lane.

Leonard, M. (1993) *Informal Economic Activity in Belfast*, Aldershot: Avebury.

Leonard, M. (1999) Informal Economic Activity: Strategies of Households and Communities, paper given at 4th ESA Conference, Will Europe Work? Amsterdam, 18–21 August.

Leonard, M. (2004) Bonding and Bridging Social Capital: Evidence from Belfast, *Sociology*, 38: 5, 927–44.

Lishman, J. (1998) Personal and Professional Development, in Adams, R. et al. (Eds.) *Social Work*, Basingstoke, Macmillan.

Lister, R. (1997) *Citizenship, Feminist Perspectives*, Basingstoke: Macmillan.

Loch, C.S. (1884) *How to Help Cases of Distress*, London: Charity Organisation Society.

Loch, C.S. (1895) Manufacturing a New Pauperism , *The Nineteenth Century, XXXVII:* 218, 698–9.

Macadam, E. (1945) *The Social Servant in the Making*, London: Allen and Unwin.

Macdonald, G. (1998) Promoting Evidence-Based Practice in Child Protection, *Clinical Child Psychology and Psychiatry*, 3: 1, 71–85.

Macdonald, G. (1999) Evidence-based Social Care: Wheels off the Runway? *Public Policy and Management*, 29: 4,25–32.

Marquis, R. and Jackson, R. (2000) Quality of Life and Quality of Service Relationships; Experience of People with Disabilities, *Disability and Society*, 15, 411–25.

Mayo, M. (2005) Ethical Dilemmas of Frontline Regeneration Staff, paper presented at a Conference on Communities and Care: Research, Policy and Practice, Brighton University, 23 August.

McVicar, D. (2006) Spatial Differences in Disability Benefit Rolls, paper presented at a seminar on Poverty and Place, Cambridge University, 29 September.

Meades, J. (2006) *How Was It for You? Young People's Views of Young Offender Panels*, Plymouth: University of Plymouth.

Meagher, G. and Parton, N. (2004) Modernising Social Work and the Ethics of Care, *Social Work and Society*, 2: 1, 10–25.

Milburn, A. (2002) Reforming Social Services, speech to Annual Social Services Conference, Cardiff, www.doh.gov.uk/speeches

Miles, A. P. (1954) *American Social Work Theory*, New York: Norton.

Mises, L. Von (1966) *Human Action*, 3rd Edn. Chicago: Contemporary Books.

Monckton, Sir W. (1945) *Report by Sir W. Monckton on the Circumstances Leading to the Boarding out of Dennis and Terence O'Neill at Bank Farm, Minsterley, and the Steps Taken to Supervise their Welfare*, Cmnd 6636, London: HMSO.

Morris, A. and Maxwell, G. (1998) Restorative Justice in New Zealand: Family Group Conferences as a Case Study, *Western Criminological Review*, 1, 1.

Myers, D.G. (1999) Close Relationships and Quality of Life, in Kahneman, D. et al. (Eds.) *Well-being: The Foundations of Hedonic Psychology*, New York: Russell Sage Foundation.

NDPG (2006) *A Quick and Small Scale Service Evaluation Looking at Some Aspects of Service Modernisation*, 15 February.

National Disability Authority (2003) *Exploring Advocacy*, Dublin: NDA.

National Evaluation of Sure Start (2004) *The Impact of Sure Start Local programmes on Child Development and Family Functioning*, Preliminary Report, Guildford: Surrey University, Department of Sociology.

Newman, A.L. (2002) When Opportunity Knocks: Economic Liberalisation and Stealth Welfare in the United States, *Journal of Social Policy*, 32: 2, 179–98.

Nicolson, R. (2006) *Asking the People Who Count: Service Users Perceptions of Community Reablement Versus the Agency's Aims and Objectives*, Plymouth: University of Plymouth.

North, D.C. (1990) *Institutions, Institutional Change and Economic Performance*, Cambridge: Cambridge University Press.

Nussbaum, M. (2005) Mill between Aristotle and Bentham, in Bruni, L. and Porta, P.L. (Eds.) *Economics and Happiness*, Oxford: Oxford University Press.

OECD (2001) *Social Indicators*, Paris: OECD.

O'Hanlon, B. (1993) Possibility Theory, in Gilligan, S. and Price, R. (Eds.) *Therapeutic Conversations*, Organisation for Economic Co-operation and Development (2001) New York: Norton.

Observer (2006) Layard to be New Happiness Czar, 25 July.

Offer, A. (2006) *The Challenge of Affluence: Self-Control and Well-being in Britain and the United States since 1950*, Oxford: Oxford University Press.

Oliver, M. (1990) *The Politics of Disability*, London: Macmillan.

Oliver, M. (1992) A Case of Disabling Welfare, in Harding, T. (Ed.) *Who Owns Welfare?* London: NISW.

Oliver, M. and Sapey, B. (2006) *Social Work with Disabled People*, London: BASW.

Olson, M. (1965) *The Logic of Collective Action: Public Goods and the Theory of Groups*, Cambridge, Mass: Harvard University Press.

Olson, M. (1983) *The Rise and Decline of Nations: Economic Growth, Stagflation and Social Rigidities*, New Itaca, CT: Yale University Press.

Orage, A.R. (1935) Selected Essays and Critical Writings. *The New Age*.

Pavilion/SACCS/Journal of Children's Services (2006) *Squeezed to the Margins*, Conference on Therapeutic Services for Children, ORT House, London, 5 July.

Parker, R. (1966) *Decision in Child Care*, Allen and Unwin.

Parton, N. (1985) *The Politics of Child Abuse*, London: Macmillan.

Parton, N. and O'Bryne, P. (2000) *Constructive Social Work: Towards a New Practice*, Basingstoke: Macmillan.

Phillips, T. (2005) Speech on Multiculturalism, 4 May.

Pigou, A.C. (1920) *The Economics of Welfare*, London: Macmillan.

Pitts, J. (2005) The Recent History of Youth Justice in England and Wales, in Bateman, T. and Pitts, J. (Eds.) *The RHP Companion to Youth Justice*, Lyme Regis: Russell House Publishing.

Polanyi, K. (1944) *The Great Transformation: The Economic and Political Origins of Our Times*, Boston: Beacon Press.

Power, A. (1996) *Estates on the Edge: The Social Consequences of Mass Housing in Europe Since 1850*, London: Routledge.

Pusey, M. (2003) *The Experience of Middle Australia: The Dark Side of Economic Reform*, Cambridge University Press.

Putnam, R.D. (1993) *Making Democracy Work: Civic Traditions in Modern Italy*, Princeton, NJ: Princeton University Press.

Putnam, R.D. (2000) *Bowling Alone: The Decline and Revival of American Community*, New York: Simon and Schuster.

Ragg, N. (1977) *People Not Cases*, London: Routledge and Kegan Paul.

Ramadan, T. (2005) Living Together Takes Effort, *Guardian*, 9 July.

Redley, M. and Weinberg, D. (2006) *Learning Disability and the Limits of Liberal Citizenship: Interactional Impediments to Political Empowerment*, Cambridge: Cambridge University, Department of Sociology.

Reid, W.J. and Epstein, L. (1977) *Task-Centred Practice*, New York: Columbia University Press.

Reinders, H.S. (2000) *The Future of the Disabled in Liberal Society: An Ethical Analysis*, Notre Dame, Indiana: University of Notre Dame Press.

Robbins, L. (1931) *The Nature and Significance of Economic Science*, London: Allen and Unwin.

Rose, N. (1996) *Inventing Ourselves: Psychology, Power and Personhood*, Cambridge: Cambridge University Press.

Russell, B. (1918) *Roads to Freedom*, London: Allen and Unwin.

Rutter, M. and Smith, D. (1995) *Psychological Disorders in Young People*, Chichester: Wiley.

Sahlins, M. (1974) *Stone Age Economics*, London: Tavistock.

Sampson, R.J., Rondenbusch, S. and Earls, F. (1997) Neighbours and Violent Crime: A Multi-Level Study of Collective Efficacy, *Science*, 277, 9184–9.

Sawyer, B. (2000) *An Evaluation of the SACRO (Fife) Young Offender Mediation Project*, Edinburgh: Scottish Executive.

Schwartz, N. (1961) The Social Worker in the Group, in *New Perspectives on Services to Groups: Theory, Organization and Practice*, New York: NASW.

Schumpeter, J. (1934) *The Theory of Economic Development: An Enquiry into Profits, Capital, Interest and the Business Cycle*, Oxford: Oxford University Press (1961).

Schwartzmantel, J. (1998) *The Age of Ideology: Political ideologies from the American Revolution to Postmodern Times*, Basingstoke: Macmillan.

Scott, J.C. (1976) *The Moral Economy of the Peasant*, New Haven, CT: Yale University Press.

Scott, J.C. (1985) *Weapons of the Weak: Everyday Forms of Peasant Resistance*, New Haven, CT: Yale University Press.

Scott, J.C. (1990) *Domination and the Arts of Resistance: Hidden Transcripts*, New Haven, CT: Yale University Press.

Seebohm Report (1968) *Report of the Committee on Local Authority and Allied Personal Social Services*, Cmd 3703, London: HMSO.

Seligman, M.E.P. (1995) The Effectiveness of Psychotherapy: the Consumer Reports Study, *American Psychologist*, 50, 965–74.

Sen, A. (1985) *Commodities and Capabilities*, Oxford: Elsevier Science.

Sennett, R. (2003) *Respect: The Formation of Character in an Age of Inequality*, London: Penguin.

Sevenhuijsen, S. (2002) A Third Way? Moralities, Ethics and Families: An Approach through the Ethic of Care, in Carling, A., Duncan, S. and Edwards, R. (Eds.) *Analysing Families*, London: Routledge.

Shaw, M. (2003) Gilding the Ghetto (1977) CDP Inter-Project Editorial Team, London: In and Against the State (1979) London–Edinburgh Weekend Return Group, Pluto Press, London, *Community Development Journal*, 35(4) .401–413.

Sheldon, B. (1998) Evidence-Based Social Services, *Research Policy and Planning*, 16: 2, 16–8.

Sheldon, B. (2001) The Validity of Evidence-Based Practice in Social Work, *British Journal of Social Work*, 31, 8019.

Sheppard, M. (2006) *Social Exclusion and Social Work: The Idea of Practice*, Aldershot: Ashgate.

Shulman, L. (1999) *The Skills of Helping Individuals, Families, Groups and Communities*, 4th edn. Ithaca, Il: F.E. Peacock.

Silverman, D. (2005) *Doing Qualitative Research*, London: Sage.

Smith, A. (1776) *An Enquiry Concerning the Wealth of Nations*, (Eds. Campbell, R.H. and Skinner, A.S. 1976) Oxford: Clarendon Press.

Smith, D. (2003) New Labour and Youth Justice, *Children and Society*, 19, 226–35.

Smith, J. (2002) Speech to Community Care Live Conference, London.

Smith, S.R. (2001) Fraternal Learning and Interdependency: Celebrating Differences within Reciprocal Commitments, *Policy and Politics* 30: 1, 47–59.

Spector, M. and Kitsuse, J. (1987) *Constructing Social Problems*, Hawthorne, NY: Aldine de Gruyter.

Statham, D. (1978) *Radicals in Social Work*, London: Routledge and Keegan Paul.

Sugden, R. (2005) Correspondence of Sentiments: An Explanation of Pleasure in Social Interaction, in Bruni, L. and Porta, P.L. (Eds.) *Economics and Happiness*, Oxford: Oxford University Press.

Sure Start (2005) *Early Years Foundation Stage*, www.surestart.gov.uk.

Tawney, R.H. (1922) *The Acquisitive Society*, London: Bell.

Tawney, R.H. (1926) *Religion and the Rise of Capitalism*, London: Bell.

Tawney, R.H. (1900–49) *R.H. Tawney's Commonplace Book*, (Winter, J.M. and Joslin, D.M. Eds. 1972) Cambridge: Cambridge University Press.

Thompson, N. (1993) *Anti-Oppressive Practice*, London: Macmillan.

Thompson, N. (2002) *Building the Future: Social Work with Children, Young People and their Families*, Lyme Regis: Russell House Publishing.

Tiebout, C. (1956) A Pure Theory of Local Expenditures, *Journal of Political Economy*, 42, 416–24.

Tronto, J. (1993) *Moral Boundaries: A Political Argument for an Ethic of Care*, London: Routledge.

Tronto, J. (1994) *Moral Boundaries: A Political Argument for an Ethic of Care*, London: Routledge.

Turnell, A. and Edwards, S. (1999) *Signs of Safety: A Solution and Safety-Oriented Approach to Child Protection Casework*, New York: Norton.

Twelvetrees, A. (2002) *Community Work* 3rd edn. Basingstoke: Palgrave/BASW.

Vernon, A. and Qureshi, H. (2000) Community Care and Independence: Self-Sufficiency or Employment? *Critical Social Policy*, 20, 255–76.

Voet, R. (1998) *Feminism and Citizenship*, London: Sage.

Walter, I., Nutley, S., Percy-Smith, J., McNeish, D. and Frost, S. (2004) *Improving the Use of Research in Social Care Practice*, London: Social Care Institute for Excellence, Knowledge Review 7.

Wetherall, M. and Potter, J. (1988) Discourse Analysis and the Identification of Interpretative Repertoires, in Antaki, C. (Ed.) *Analysing Everyday Explanations*, London: Sage.

White, M. and Epston, D. (1990) *Narrative Means to Therapeutic Ends*, New York: Norton.

Wilcox, A. (2003) Evidence-Based Youth Justice? Some Valuable Lessons from an Evaluation of the Youth Justice Board, *Youth Justice*, 3: 1, 20–33.

Williams, F. (2001) In and Beyond New Labour: Towards a New Political Ethics of Care, *Critical Social Policy*, 21: 4, 467–93.

Williams, F. (2005) Practical and Political Ethics of Care and Implications for Child Welfare, paper presented at the Centre for Supplied Childhood Studies, University of Huddersfield, 27 February.

Woodroofe, K. (1962) *From Charity to Social Work in England and the United States*, London: Routledge and Kegan Paul.

Worley, C. (2005) 'It's Not About Race, It's About the Community': New Labour and Community Cohesion, *Critical Social Policy*, 25: 4, 483–96.

Worley, C. (2006) *Identity, Community and Community Cohesion: Policy Discourses and the Everyday*, PhD Theses, University of Huddersfield, Department of Social Work.

Young, I.M. (1990) *Justice and the Politics of Difference*, Princeton, NJ: Princeton University Press.

Younghusband, K. (1981) *The Newest Profession: A Short History of Social Work*, London: Community Care/IPC Business Press.

Name Index

Subject Index